Almost Every Answer for Practically Any Teacher!

Walk Thru the Bible Ministries, Inc., exists to contribute to the spiritual growth of Christians worldwide through Bible teaching, tools, and training.

Almost Every Answer for Practically Any Teacher! is a resource produced as part of Walk Thru the Bible's *Applied Principles of Learning Curriculum*. This video training series consists of *The 7 Laws of the Teacher* by Dr. Howard G. Hendricks and *The 7 Laws of the Learner* by Dr. Bruce H. Wilkinson, with other video training series in production. Information on the complete teacher training packages available in the *Applied Principles of Learning Curriculum* may be obtained by calling 1-800-868-9300.

Information on other Walk Thru the Bible products, including Walk Thru the Old Testament and New Testament Seminars as well as devotional and Bible study magazines, may be obtained by calling or writing:

Walk Thru the Bible Ministries, Inc.
61 Perimeter Park N.E.
P.O. Box 80587
Atlanta, Georgia 30366
U.S.A.
Telephone (404) 458-9300
Product information 1-800-868-9300

EDITED BY

Dr. Bruce Wilkinson

Almost Every Answer for Practically Any Teacher!

A Resource Guide
for all who desire to teach . . .
for lifechange!

MULTNOMAH

Portland, Oregon
in cooperation with
Walk Thru the Bible Ministries, Inc.
Atlanta, Georgia

Cover design by Randy Drake

ALMOST ANY ANSWER FOR PRACTICALLY ANY TEACHER!
© 1992 by Bruce H. Wilkinson
Published by Multnomah Press
10209 SE Division Street
Portland, OR 97266
in conjunction with Walk Thru the Bible Ministries, Inc.,
61 Perimeter Park NE, Atlanta, GA 30341

Multnomah Press is a ministry of Multnomah School of the Bible
8435 NE Glisan Street, Portland, OR 97220

Printed in the United States of America.

Library of Congress Cataloging-in-Publication Data

Almost every answer for practically any teacher! : the 7 laws of
   the learner / edited by Bruce H. Wilkinson.
      p.   cm.
   Includes bibliographical references and index.
   ISBN 0-88070-473-X
   1. Christian education- -Teaching methods. 2. Teaching- -
Religious aspects- -Christianity. 3. Classroom management. I.
Wilkinson, Bruce.
   BV1534.A62   1991
   268'.6--dc20
                                             91-32034
                                               CIP

92 93 94 95 96 97 98 99 - 10 9 8 7 6 5 4 3 2

Contents

Chapter 1: Law of the Learner

Chapter 2: Law of Expectation

Chapter 3: Law of Application

Chapter 4: Law of Retention

Chapter 5: Law of Need

Chapter 6: Law of Equipping

Chapter 7: Law of Revival

Dedication

This "Resource Guide," *Almost Every Answer for Practically Any Teacher!*, is affectionately dedicated to a person who has been a "resource guide" both to me and Walk Thru the Bible for many years, Mr. Pat MacMillan. Pat is the person to whom such a volume of resources should be dedicated, for a "resource" is what he has been to us! Throughout the conception, birthing, and launching of the Applied Principles of Learning Curriculum, of which *The 7 Laws of the Learner* and this volume are parts, it was his creative resources which many times kept us going. Pat is recognized across America and around the world as an expert in his field—conceptualizing, creating, communicating, and consulting—and it has been my unique privilege to enjoy his personal wisdom and friendship in my own life, and to see our ministry blossom in areas where he has applied his nurturing and cultivating touch.

Pat, my brother, friend, and faithful co-laborer, thank you for all you mean to me and the Walk Thru family. May God continue to refresh and expand your wonderful ministry in the years to come.

> Bruce H. Wilkinson
> Founder and President,
> Walk Thru the Bible Ministries, Inc.

Acknowledgements

Heartfelt thanks are due those members of Walk Thru the Bible's Research and Development team who have labored faithfully to bring *The 7 Laws of the Learner* video series, and related resources such as this volume, to completion: Gordon Wilkinson, Vice-President of R&D; Randy Drake, art director; Mary Lee Griffith, project manager; William Kruidenier, editorial director; Rob Lassetter, artist; and Kevin Johnson, video producer. This creative group of people can transform an embryonic idea into a mature product in jaw-dropping fashion. My worst nightmare is that I come to work and they're gone!

Managing editor Al Janssen and copy editor Robin Georgeoff of Multnomah Press provided patient and cheerful support for our Walk Thru staff during the production of this volume. Additionally, Rae Pamplin and Carolyn Bush labored diligently on permissions, proofing, and copy editing. Many sincere thanks to these good friends as well.

Introduction

The American cultural and political pollster, George Gallup, made a startling observation this year. It shocked me, and may shock you as well. He observed, "Fewer than ten percent of Americans are deeply committed Christians." A key reason for this sad state of affairs is that, in his opinion, "Overall, the Sunday school and religious-education system in this country is not working."

Though without the statistical research data of a Gallup poll to prove my intuitive observations, I have felt the same thing for years. Having travelled the globe, and specifically traversed the terrain of American Christianity, I am deeply concerned at the lack of lasting lifechange I see taking place. Among those who profess Christ as their personal Lord and Savior, too little actual difference is observable. The lack of Christlikeness in the church is, in my opinion, one of the principle deterents to effective evangelism and societal change. In Christ's day, sinners were attracted to His totally different lifestyle, purity, and message. In Him they found power, strength, forgiveness—a hope for their future. Too often, though, the world today does not find the same thing in the church.

I have reflected on this situation for years, asking God how my life and ministry could be used to help reverse the lamentable lack of lifechange among the saints. Again and again I have been impressed by God that lifechange takes place through the faithful communication of the truths of His Word—the Bible—by teachers who are empowered and called by the Spirit of God to teach the church the truth. Not just *tell* the truth, but *teach* the truth!

The delicate link between the Bible and the believer is the person for whom this volume has been prepared: the teacher of the truths of God. If that teacher is equipped and prepared to teach the Word for lifechange, lives will be changed. If that teacher is only telling what the Bible says, minds will be filled with facts while lives remain transfixed instead of transformed.

It was to contribute to the equipping of Christian teachers around the world that God led Walk Thru the Bible Ministries to establish the *Applied Principles of Learning™ Curriculum.* So far, two video teaching series have been produced in this curriculum, with a third under production.

First, one of the greatest teachers in the American church, Dr. Howard Hendricks, taught *The 7 Laws of the Teacher.* This video training series, which addresses the characteristics of the effective teacher, is being used in many thousands of churches and schools around the world, along with a course textbook, student workbook, and seminar leader's guide.

Next came my own video training series, *The 7 Laws of the Learner,* addressing the critical issue of how and why true teaching produces lifechange—and demonstrating that if lives aren't changing, teachers aren't truly teaching.

Our third series, *Teaching With Style* (currently in production) will demonstrate how the variety and style with which God communicates to us can be employed by the Christian teacher to banish forever the number one hinderance to lifechanging teaching: BOREDOM! Neither God, nor His Word, are boring! Yet this is the chief complaint among students about their teachers. In the church and out, too many teachers succeed in boring their students. But bored students don't change.

With that backdrop in place, let me define the piece of the pedagogical puzzle you are holding in your hands right now. *Almost Every Answer for Practically Any Teacher!* is exactly what its subtitle indicates: a Resource Guide for the Christian who teaches (including professional and lay teachers, parents, employers, group leaders, and pastors and church education teachers and leaders, all of whom are seeking to effect lifechange from the perspective of God's Word).

This volume is a corollary resource to Walk Thru the Bible's video training series *The 7 Laws of the Learner.* That series, consisting of seven video tapes (fourteen sessions), a textbook, course workbook, and seminar leader's guide, presents seven laws which, if implemented by teachers, will produce lifechange in students. This book follows the outline of the seven-part video series, covering the laws of the Learner, Expectation, Application, Retention, Need, Equipping, and Revival.

Recognizing that often the Christian teacher needs real answers to practical questions faced in a teaching ministry—answers beyond the scope of the video series—we purposed to gather one hundred of the very best resources we could find to provide those answers. Our research staff poured over literally hundreds and hundreds of articles and chapters from books trying to find the most helpful and straight-to-the-point resources we could find to expand on the seven laws of learning presented in the video series.

I believe we have succeeded! The one hundred articles contained in this Resource Guide are written by teachers, for teachers. This book is long on practice and short on theory and debate. It is produced to be used, not admired. If it remains neat and clean rather than scuffed up and dog-eared, you will have purchased it amiss. If it finds a home in a bookcase rather than a briefcase, you will have made it an orphan. This book is designed for one purpose, and one purpose only: *to help the Christian called to communicate God's truth do so in a way that meets real needs and produces Christlikeness in the lives of those who listen.* If you will treat this book for what it is—a gold mine with nuggets waiting to be collected and spent—your teaching will never be the same.

And so I send this volume to you, faithful teacher, parent, pastor, employer. I know you want those whom you teach to become like Christ. I want that for you—*I want you to be a great communicator of God's truth!* And I believe this volume will help you become just that.

All of us at Walk Thru the Bible want the best for you in your life and ministry and pray God's richest blessing upon you and your teaching as we all work together for lifechange in the church. I trust that the next time George Gallup surveys the church, he will see something different, and that it will be because you and I are causing our students to learn, and become like Christ!

Bruce H. Wilkinson, Editor
Founder and President,
Walk Thru the Bible Ministries

Learner

LAW ONE

TOPICAL SURVEY

How to Build a Successful Teaching Staff

Jo Berry

What does "teacher recruitment" mean in the average church?
Unfortunately, not what it should. A veteran educational consultant and
teacher outlines what successful teacher recruiting should look like.

The truth is that most churches have a problem procuring Sunday school staff. Why? I have asked many teachers, pastors, and Sunday school administrators as well as laymen who have refused a class. The basic reason, I discovered, is that most people will not teach because they are afraid they can't handle such a lofty task.

Men and women of God are not too selfish to give of their time and they do want to trust the Lord, to let his perfect love cast out fear. They know something of their gifts, too. But Christian educators, whether pastors or laymen in positions of responsibility, are not preparing people; and God's people have enough common sense to refuse to get into something for which they are not qualified.

If we want well-staffed, competent Sunday schools, therefore, we need to rethink our basic approach to providing staff. We must look at our philosophy of recruiting and training teachers. To introduce this, let's look at some dangerous misconceptions about what a Sunday school teacher is supposed to be.

COMMON MISCONCEPTIONS

1. One misconception is to think all Sunday school teachers will automatically know how to teach, present material, and set up a classroom, as if they were superhuman saints.

2. We also make a mistake when we act as if all a teacher has to do is teach Sunday school. Intellectually, we may agree that there are minor incidentals in their lives, such as homes, families, and jobs; yet we act as if Christian teachers always have time to study devotedly for hours and attend endless, and sometimes meaningless, meetings.

3. Also, we erroneously envision each teacher as a haloed saint whose entire life is devoted to being a Sunday school teacher, one who never has the urge to miss church on a sunny Sunday. And of course this devoted educator, no matter how severely or unfairly he is criticized, never gets upset or snappy!

4. Due to a final misconception, we consider a teacher someone who never makes a mistake—especially in front of his class!—and who will know the answer to every question that is asked.

No wonder the average layperson is afraid to teach and is fearful about meeting the requirements of our unrealistic stereotype! He knows he has many weaknesses, he is torn between various commitments, and he has difficulty maintaining his priorities. He is afraid if he adds another, especially one as demanding as teaching, it will be the proverbial straw that breaks the camel's back.

CAREFUL RECRUITING

1. First and foremost, recruiting should be done continually, not annually, semiannually, quarterly, or when things reach panic proportion.

2. Bulletin announcements should be made frequently, so the needs of the Sunday school are presented to the congregation on an ongoing basis.

3. Leaders must provide opportunities for prospective teachers and workers to go into classrooms to see what a position would involve.

4. Pulpit announcements should be made as often as necessary. If the pastor regularly stresses the value and importance of the Sunday school, the congregation will be more responsive.

Some recruiting amounts to looking for a live body to fill a space. In a way it is coercion, trapping someone who doesn't know how to say "no" to a person in authority and shoving that person into a task he or she cannot do. This approach cannot be justified in light of Paul's admonition to Timothy that we should not place a novice in a position of authority.

COMPETENT TRAINING

Those responsible for building a teaching staff must be willing to function on the premise that competent educators don't just happen: they are trained and developed.

The secular world recognizes this. So must the church. Even if someone has been gifted by the Holy Spirit, he must be trained to use his gifts properly, within the framework of his own local church. Christ shepherded the Twelve: he called them, then devoted himself to teaching and nurturing them so they would be effective when they were sent to serve.

No matter how large or small your church, if you want good teachers, and enough of them, you must offer to train them for the job. You must set standards, lay down requirements for service, and be selective about who is to be allowed to hold the influential position of teacher.

But how can you challenge people to attend training sessions? Most important, it should be a stringent requirement that anyone who is going to teach must complete the church's training course. Too often we are willing to compromise important standards just to get volunteers. I have observed that churches with the fewest staffing problems have the most demanding training courses: classes of eight to twelve sessions that include written homework assignments and classroom observation and allow absences only for illness.

Also, leaders would be wise to choose a time for the course that will encourage attendance. Since most volunteers are regular churchgoers, they will be more apt to attend if training sessions are on Sunday mornings or Wednesday evenings as part of the regular schedule.

Several small churches have ongoing programs where the pastor disciples individual members who are going to teach. Sometimes the Sunday school superintendent spends several weeks in a one-on-one basis with trainees before they go into classrooms. In some cases, teachers train their own replacements before leaving. It should be a hard and fast rule never to put people into classrooms until they are properly trained.

CONSISTENT SUPPORT

We commit a second error if we offer no secondary support systems to teachers. Once they have started to teach we ignore them. But the basic training they have received is not sufficient; they need additional classes to help them develop expertise and to stimulate their creativity.

Periodically churches should offer courses on a variety of topics, as needs are noted. Teachers need practical suggestions on how to improve constructing bulletin boards, preparing lessons, developing lecturing and questioning techniques, disciplining the unruly child, and preparing interest centers. Also "how to" courses are needed: how to teach a song, make interesting arts and crafts, conduct group discussions, or use the overhead projector. A good in-service program will eliminate the weaknesses and undergird the strengths of the teaching staff.

CONSISTENT FEEDING

Another mistake we make is to shut teachers off from the chance to be students themselves in a Bible class. In most churches all classes occur at the same time, so this seems impossible. But we might, for example, offer an adult class on a week night for Sunday school teachers only. Or we might find ways to give each teacher a tape of the class of his choice. Nursery workers and children's church workers who must miss the worship service could receive a copy of the pastor's sermon.

But even beyond this, a teacher needs to be refueled; he or she should have a time for rest and recuperation. The easiest way to assure that teachers get some relief is to establish a quarterly rotation system whereby a person can take off one quarter out of every four. This means he will teach nine months and then take a "mini-sabbatical" for three. This is accomplished by developing a full staff, regardless of the size of the church.

COMPLETE CATEGORIES

Use of supplemental teaching positions will allow for flexibility, and several staff categories might be established.

1. The first is the full-time teacher, who will teach for three quarters and then take off one quarter (not necessarily the summer). The timing will depend on the needs of the Sunday school and the teacher's schedule.

2. The second category is part-time teacher. This person will teach only one or two quarters a year, filling in for full-time teachers.

3. Category three is the back-up teacher. He is being discipled by the regular teacher, and sits in the class of his chosen grade level as often as possible. He may be called on by the full-time teacher to substitute or to do team teaching. He should always be prepared with the week's lesson, even if he is not planning to attend the class. Every grade level should have one back-up teacher.

4. The fourth category is substitute. Such a person will teach on an "on call" basis and serves when the back-up teacher is not available to fill in. Those in junior high through career-age brackets make good substitute teachers.

5. The last category is aide, who does not teach or prepare lessons, but assists with the physical manipulations in the room. People with special talents—such as pianists and secretaries—are in this category. Aides can supervise nonteaching children's activities, such as storytelling and arts and crafts. Many young persons who start in this capacity end up as full-time teachers.

If a teacher knows he will have a back-up/support system, he will more readily accept a position. He needs the freedom to miss a Sunday or to go out of town without feeling guilty or thinking he is deserting the cause of Christ.

COMMON SENSE SERVICE

Most churches discourage prospective teachers because they overwork the ones they have. Word gets around—once a teacher, always a teacher. Leaders and educators have to be more empathic about the service they expect and more selective about whom they allow to teach. If they truly want a quality Sunday school they must be more concerned with proper placement than merely with having "teachers" in the classrooms.

Hudson Taylor said, "God's work done in God's way never lacks God's supply." To put the wrong person in the wrong position just because he's there at a time of a vacancy can cripple the working of the whole body.

Pastors, Christian education directors, and administrators must rely on the leading of the Spirit in the hearts of people rather than on their own begging or coercion. They must commit themselves to the premise that they would rather not have a teacher in a class than to have someone with an unwilling spirit.

CORRECTING TRADITIONS

Another erroneous concept is that women, not men, should teach children. Have you ever noticed how we feminize the children's division in the church? In most churches a huge majority of teachers in grades six and below are women. In some congregations all are. Why? Certainly not because of any biblical injunction. Probably not because it is written or required policy. I am afraid it is for that old excuse, "We've always done it this way."

If we accept this premise and exclude the possibility of having the men in the congregation teach children, we cut our resources for recruiting almost in half. This "women teach the kids" policy is a loss to the entire body. Children, even very young ones, need a father figure. Many little ones in our churches come from broken homes and desperately need a masculine touch—a representative of God the Father. A man in the classroom can help control behavior, improving the overall quality of instruction. By including men we also open the possibility of having husband-wife teams.

ENCOURAGING THE SHEEP

Along with reevaluating educational philosophy and the approach to recruiting and training staff, Christian educators also need to encourage teachers by:
1. being available to them.
2. being supportive of them.
3. providing the services and materials needed to make their jobs easier.
4. providing both initial and ongoing training.
5. offering opportunities for study.
6. covering expenses to send teachers to appropriate training events.
7. seeing that supplies and materials are be easy to obtain. Teachers should not have to grovel to get the tools of their trade, whether crayons, workbooks, duplicated outlines, or slide projectors. Even small churches should see that teaching materials are a high priority in the budget. Both children and adults are accustomed to sophisticated methods and materials—the world goes all out to attract us—and unless the church strives for quality, we will lose the interest of our students.
8. making it convenient, even easy, for teachers to shift or resign their positions.

A Sunday school whose leaders are not willing to revamp their philosophical approach and training methods will always have staff problems.

■ Excerpted and reprinted by permission from *Christianity Today* 24, no. 4 (February 22, 1980), pp. 18-22.

Our Most Precious Possession

J. Oswald Sanders

What teacher ever feels he or she has too much time? Though we can't manage time—it marches on oblivious to our desires—we can plug leaks, prioritize, and plan. A venerable leader shares his insights.

Here are three constructive suggestions which may be of help to those who are seriously seeking to fill their lives with the greatest possible usefulness to God.

1. Stop leaks. Let us not consider our day only in terms of hours but in smaller areas of time. If we look after the minutes, the hours will look after themselves. For example, it is amazing how much reading can be squeezed into fragments of time redeemed from the trash pile. It is vain to wait until we get time to read seriously—we will never get it. We must make time to read by seizing the minutes we have. From the suggested analysis of our week, we should seek to detect unsuspected leakages of time, and with purpose of heart, plug the leak.

2. Study priorities. Much time which is not actually wasted is spent on things of only secondary importance. A fool has been described as a man who has missed the proportion of things. Some of us have the unfortunate tendency to be so engrossed in the secondary that we have no time left for the primary. We give such undue attention to petty details that matters of major importance are squeezed out. Especially is this so where spiritual things are concerned. Check on your analysis to see whether the spiritual is receiving adequate time or whether it is relegated to a secondary place by that which is good. Are we doing the most important things or do we, because of the demands they make, procrastinate where they are concerned? Weigh carefully the respective values of the opportunities and responsibilities which claim attention. Omit altogether, or give a very minor place to things of little importance. We should from time to time review the analysis of our week to see if we have our priorities right.

3. Start planning. Without a proper plan we all tend to drift. In the attitude of prayer ask, "How can I best plan today?" Divide it into parts. There are certain obvious obligations and duties, both spiritual and temporal, which naturally demand a place and adequate time should be allowed for these. Then there are secondary things which should be carefully pruned to a minimum and fitted in. When two duties pull in different directions, choose that which, after prayer and thought, seems more important. If a secular claim crowds a spiritual, do not concede the point unless you have good reasons for doing so. In most lives, there are every day short gaps left in the program which seem too short to fill with anything important, but these gaps must be filled. Why not write a letter? Don't wait until you get time to write—do it at once! Waiting until a more convenient time is the death knell of letter writing. Allow sufficient time to insure punctuality, but not too much. Buy up the spare minutes as eagerly as a miser hoards his money. Start planning your days.

■ From *Spiritual Leadership* (© 1967, 1980 by The Moody Bible Institute of Chicago), and *A Spiritual Clinic* (© 1958 by The Moody Bible Institute of Chicago), both by J. Oswald Sanders. Reprinted by permission of Moody Press.

Has Anyone Seen My Time?

Gordon MacDonald

Though many teachers may feel they are not disorganized, some telltale signs will reveal the truth. A productive pastor/leader gives clues that evidence when he—and probably others—are slipping into disorganization.

The world is full of disorganized people who have lost control of their time. A man or woman may be multitalented, possess enormous intelligence and remarkable communicative gifts, and yet end up squandering it all because of an inability to seize control of time. None of us, I am sure, wants to come to the end of our lives and look back with regrets on things that could have been accomplished but were not. But to prevent that from happening, it is necessary to understand how we can command the time God has given to us.

The first step we may have to take is that of ruthless self-appraisal about our habits of time use. Let us consider the traits of a disorganized life.

My desk. My desk takes on a cluttered appearance when I'm slipping into disorganization. The same thing happens to the top of my bedroom dresser. In fact, almost every horizontal surface in the path of my daily travel becomes littered with papers, memos to which I have not responded, and pieces of tasks that are unfinished.

My car. The symptoms of disorganization tend to show themselves in the condition of my car. It becomes dirty inside and out. I lose track of its maintenance schedule and I find that I am pressing deadlines for things like changing snow tires and getting the annual safety sticker.

Appointments/messages/deadlines. I know I'm disorganized when there are a series of forgotten appointments, telephone messages to which I have failed to respond, and deadlines which I have begun to miss. The day becomes filled with broken commitments and lame excuses. (I must be careful to say, incidentally, that I am not thinking of times when events beyond my control have conspired to derail even the best of intentions. All of us have those kinds of days, even the most organized of us.)

Unproductive tasks. If I am disorganized, I tend to invest my energies in unproductive tasks. I actually find myself doing small and boring things just to get something accomplished. There is a tendency toward daydreaming, an avoidance of decisions that have to be made, and procrastination.

Intimacy with God. Disorganized Christians rarely enjoy intimacy with God. They certainly have intentions of pursuing that camaraderie, but it never quite gets established. No one has to tell them that time must be set aside for the purpose of Bible study and reflection, for intercession, for worship. They know all of that. They simply are not doing it. They excuse themselves, saying there is no time, but they know it is more a matter of organization and personal will than anything else.

Personal relationships. If I am in a state of disorganization, the quality of my personal relationships usually reveals it. The days pass without a significant conversation with my son or daughter. My wife and I will be in contact, but our conversations may be shallow. I may become irritable, resenting any attempt on her part to call attention to things I have left undone or people I appear to have let down.

Self-esteem. The fact of the matter is that when we are disorganized in our

17

control of time, we just don't like ourselves, our jobs, or much else about our worlds. And it is difficult to break the destructive pattern that settles in. This terrible habit pattern of disorganization must be broken, or our private worlds will fall quickly into total disorder.

BUDGETING TIME

The central principle of all personal organization of time is simple: *Time must be budgeted!* Most of us learned this about money a long time ago. When we discovered that we rarely had enough money to do all the things we wanted to do with it, we found it prudent to sit down and think through our financial priorities.

With money, the priorities were obvious. Since my wife and I are committed to God's plan of stewardship, our first financial priority has always been our tithe and offerings. Then the fixed expenditures, food, house, utilities, and so on have been set aside in amounts that we have learned to anticipate.

When money is limited, one budgets. And when time is in limited supply, the same principle holds. The disorganized person must have a budgeting perspective. And that means determining the difference between the fixed—what one must do—and the discretionary—what one would like to do.

THE LORD OF TIME

It is worth taking time to ask how our Lord's command of time is demonstrated. What caused Him to be such an organized person?

The first thing that impresses me is that *He clearly understood His mission.* This is quite apparent during His final walk toward Jerusalem, where He would be crucified. Approaching Jericho, Luke writes (chapter 18), His ears picked up the shrill voice of a blind man and He stopped, much to the consternation of both His friends and critics. They were irritated that Jesus did not appreciate that Jerusalem was still six or seven hours away, and that they would like to get there to achieve their purpose, the celebration of Passover. From where they were standing, it appeared that Jesus was misusing His time. From where Jesus was standing, however, the time was well spent, for *it fit the criteria of His mission.*

A second insight into Jesus' personal organization of time is that *He understood His own limits.* Strange as it may seem, He knew what we conveniently forget: *that time must be properly budgeted for the gathering of inner strength and resolve in order to compensate for one's weaknesses when spiritual warfare begins.* Knowing His limits, such private moments were a fixed item on Jesus' time budget. And it was very hard even for those closest to Him to fully appreciate this.

I think Jesus included a third important element in his philosophy of time budgeting, for He set time aside for the *training of the twelve.* With a world of millions to reach, it is instructive that Jesus budgeted the majority of His time to be with just a few simple men. Prime time was invested in taking them through the Scriptures and sharing His heavenly insight. We might have been tempted to ask why Jesus was spending so much valuable time with a group of simple-minded men when He could have taught men who could have intellectually appreciated His theological expertise. But Jesus was aware of where true importance lies, where the priorities are. And where your priorities are, there your time will be.

■ Excerpted from *Ordering Your Private World* (Nashville: Thomas Nelson Publishers, © 1984, 1985 by Gordon MacDonald). Used by permission.

It's About Time!

Charles R. Swindoll

Let's face it. Most teachers haven't had the luxury of a "time management" or personal organization seminar. Not to worry. Here is the simplest tool ever devised for being productive and successful!

In a book I read, *The Time Trap*, I came upon a list of the most popular time wasters. It helped pinpoint some specific areas of inefficiency I must watch.

- Attempting too much at once.
- Unrealistic time estimates.
- Procrastinating.
- Lack of specific priorities.
- Failure to listen well.
- Absence of self-appointed deadlines.
- Inability to say no.
- Perfectionism—sidetracked by details.
- Lack of organization.
- Failure to write it down.
- Reluctance to get started.
- Doing it myself—failure to delegate.
- Not doing first things first.

Who hasn't heard the true story of Charles Schwab and Ivy Lee? Schwab was president of Bethlehem Steel. Lee, a consultant, was given the usual challenge: "Show me a way to get more things done with my time." Schwab agreed to pay him "anything within reason" if Lee's suggestion worked. Lee later handed the executive a sheet of paper with the plan:

> Write down the most important tasks you have to do tomorrow. Number them in order of importance. When you arrive in the morning, begin at once on No. 1 and stay on it until it is completed. Recheck your priorities, then begin with No. 2, then No. 3. Make this a habit every working day. Pass it on to those under you. Try it as long as you like, then send me your check for what you think it's worth.

That one idea turned Bethlehem Steel Corporation into the biggest independent steel producer in the world within five years. How much did Schwab pay his consultant? Several weeks after receiving the note, he sent Lee a check for $25,000, admitting it was the most profitable lesson he had ever learned.

Try it for yourself. If it works, great. But don't send me any money for the idea. I'd just blow it on another time-management book . . . which I don't have time to read.

■ Excerpted from *Make Up Your Mind. . . About the Issues of Life* by Charles R. Swindoll, © 1981 by Multnomah Press. Published by Multnomah Press, Portland, Oregon 97226. Used by permission.

"A+" Parent-Teacher Conferences

Kenneth Meyers and George Pawlas

Is any event more dreaded by teacher and parent alike (not to mention the student!) than a conference? Probably not! The authors give tips for making this meeting positive, productive, and enjoyable.

The parent-teacher conference is still the best way for you and parents to jointly explore students' education. And if you take the right steps, it should always be a positive experience. For a successful conference, you must address three main steps: preconference homework, conference communication, and follow-up.

STEP 1: PRECONFERENCE HOMEWORK

•**Establish a climate for communication.** To help yourself relax before a conference, remember that most parents react against situations and are not usually angry at the teacher. If you are poised and relaxed, parents usually relax, too. This is the best communication climate.

•**Know the child's history.** Review all background information: folders, former teachers' notes, social history, referrals for testing, past standardized test results, report cards, and discipline records. Dated samples of students' work show improvement or decline. These provide direction for the discussion. You should also know the student's social background including recent changes in family structure such as divorce, death, etc.

•**Determine the area or areas for discussion.** Successful conferences usually deal with only one or two issues. There are two reasons for this. Multiconcern conferences can overwhelm parents (especially if solutions require their support at home). Also, time does not permit thorough discussion of more than two areas. Be prepared to discuss only those predetermined issues.

•**Prepare a conference form for record keeping.** Commercial forms have space for conference topics and highlights. Or you can make your own. This tool helps focus the discussion and aids future conferences.

•**Decide whether it's beneficial to include the principal.** Give the parent the same opportunity. If you invite the principal, do so well in advance.

STEP 2: THE CONFERENCE

•**Set the climate.** Prepare a comfortable seating area around a table rather than your desk. (The desk can be a communication barrier.) On the table, arrange work samples, documents, etc. Introduce yourself with a friendly voice and smile. Informal conversation helps everyone relax. But keep opening comments brief to allow more discussion time.

If parents requested the conference, you can focus the discussion by saying, "Mrs. Jones, I understand you requested this conference to discuss Susan's grade in math. Before I show you some information on that, perhaps you could share with me exactly what you feel the problem is." Don't hesitate to include the student in the conference. After all, isn't he or she the reason for the conference? Sometimes major solutions result from the student's input.

•**Maintain momentum and focus.** To keep the discussion from straying, gently refocus the talk on the identified topic or two. If the parent shows interest in a separate concern, simply say, "That's a good question. Could we hold that until we finish discussing the topic?"

•**Write the separate concern on the conference sheet as a reminder.** Bring it up at the end of the conference, and, if needed, schedule another conference on that topic. The conference is not a one-person show. Allow parents to participate and facilitate their involvement. Ask questions, listen closely, take notes, and paraphrase them to the parents. Being an all-knowing "expert" doesn't work; it can hinder parent participation. One study shows that teachers tend to monopolize parent-teacher conferences by talking 75 to 98 percent of the allotted time. Your goal is to keep the parents involved.

What if you disagree with the parents' reason for the child's behavior? Acknowledge it; then suggest other possible causes, ones you feel should be considered.

•**Use the conference form.** As you go from concerns to conclusions, make thorough notes. Before making notes, ask yourself these questions: "Is this statement necessary?" and, "Will this be helpful to the pupil and future teachers?"

Tell parents the notes provide a record of the meeting for both parties, and that you will give them a copy. Include a record of agreed-upon solutions involving teacher action at school and parent action at home.

In your initial conference, develop goals for the year. List them and include dates for them to be completed. This shows you are serious about helping the student and keeping the parents involved.

•**Conclude the meeting.** To complete the conference successfully, briefly review the purpose of the conference, highlights, conclusions, and agreed-upon actions for you and the parents.

Parents should read and sign the conference form (now with notes, goals, etc.). Provide them a copy before they leave.

If needed, set a date for another conference. And finally, thank the parents and walk them to the door. Parents should leave with a clear understanding of what was discussed and the actions to be taken.

STEP 3: THE FOLLOW-UP

•**Send a note home with the child the next day.** Be sure to thank the parents for their time and interest.

•**Evaluate the conference.** For future reference, add notes to your conference form about discussion specifics.

•**After a week or so, send a progress report to parents.** Or better yet, make a phone call. You can request another conference, or, if appropriate, report progress and offer your congratulations.

•**Keep your principal informed.** A personal report and copy of the conference log will suffice; it may be needed in subsequent conferences when you are not present.

A well-planned approach to parent-teacher conferences aids your chances of success. And more important, it greatly increases the student's chances of success by assuring communication between home and school.

■From *Instructor* 69, no. 2 (September 1989). Reprinted by permission of Scholastic, Inc.

Overcome Burnout Before It Overcomes You!

Larry E. Neagle

Every teacher develops "the Elijah syndrome" at some point. When extended work and peak experiences leave one deflated, what can be done? Here is practical help for a prevalent condition among teachers.

Remember the story of Moses and the burning bush? God set that shrub aflame in the wilderness to talk to his servant. The bush blazed, yet was not consumed. Regrettably today some Sunday school teachers who were once burning bushes are now scattered soot. Burned out. Consumed. Charred and empty. You know the type: loyal workers for years, active in many areas. Then suddenly they vanish from church altogether, impervious to the love of those trying to pull them back in. They have become classic examples of spiritual burnout.

CAUSES OF BURNOUT

What is burnout? Why does it happen?

A simple definition for burnout is *stress gone haywire.* We all have stress. Some of it is beneficial, some not. Burnout occurs when we have a stress overload. Herbert J. Freudenberger, a psychoanalyst, says burnout is "someone in a state of fatigue or frustration brought about by devotion to a cause, way of life, or relationship that failed to produce the expected reward."[1]

Christians, especially Sunday school teachers, are highly susceptible to burnout. Why? Because as one researcher observes, burnout is only possible if you have a fire. Sunday school teachers commonly have an intense desire to make a difference for Christ in the lives of those they teach. We want to help them grow spiritually. We labor to see tangible spiritual betterment in their lives. We have a vision and struggle to fulfill it. Yet when our vision fails to mesh with God's reality, when the results we desire don't come, when we commit ourselves beyond what we're able to perform, we become prime candidates for burnout. The result is what one writer calls "the Elijah syndrome."

THE ELIJAH SYNDROME

Burnout typically follows one of two events: extended, but unsuccessful, efforts toward a goal; or an intense peak experience. For Elijah, it was, very literally, the last. He drank victory deeply in his mountaintop confrontation with the prophets of Baal. Supercharged by that event he even outran Ahab's chariot. Then abruptly he was as burned out as the sacrifice he left behind on Mt. Carmel.

Elijah showed all the classic symptoms. He grew depressed, sad, and felt separated. He journeyed alone into the wilderness, leaving behind not only Jezebel's threats, but also his servant. Elijah longed just to be alone. Getting away from everyone didn't help though. He soon gave in to emptiness and despair. He flopped down under a juniper tree and asked to die. An angel ministered to him there, and aroused him enough to shoo him on to Mt. Horeb. Yet the change of location didn't remedy Elijah's condition. In his encounter with God there, he vocalized his feelings of bitterness, of aloneness, of being mistreated and persecuted.

HOW TO AVOID BURNOUT

The good news for Elijah was that God ultimately renewed him. The better news for us is that the condition can be avoided altogether. How?

•**Pray about how you feel.** Elijah did. He was honest and open with God; God was honest and open with him. And the end was better than the beginning.

•**Realign your priorities.** A significant part of burnout is overcommitment. Too many irons in the fire means none of the irons receive adequate attention. And it usually means your family does without one of its most precious parts—you. Learn how and when to say no. Your family will appreciate it even if some committee chairman does not.

•**Practice the art of thanksgiving and praise.** Freudenberger says that one of the best ways to avoid burnout is to "get into the habit of noticing—and nurturing—the unspectacular good things that happen to us."[2] There is something about giving thanks and praise that chases off burnout like the sun does an early morning fog.

•**Learn the art of physical relaxation.** According to psychologist Jerry R. Day, it is impossible to worry when you're relaxed. Try this simple activity. Take ten to twenty minutes at the end of the day to sit in a comfortable chair and enjoy a good stretch. Coax your body and mind to relax. If it helps, you might imagine yourself basking on a warm South Seas beach or strolling through a country meadow.

•**Exercise.** Almost all researchers agree that one of the best antibiotics for burnout is exercise. So run, play tennis, garden, golf, or whatever. But if such activity isn't enjoyable, don't force yourself into it and into a new set of tensions.

•**Develop your own relief devices.** Revive an old interest or hobby. Or start a new one. Recreate. Take a walk. Smell a flower. Read a good book. Try a little creative loafing. As James Thurber observed, "It's better to have loafed and lost than never to have loafed at all."[3]

•**Find someone to share with.** Don't try to go it alone. Shutting yourself off increases the problem rather than solves it. Find someone you trust to talk with.

•**Do the best you can for each day.** Take it a day at a time. Obviously burnout can't be overcome overnight. But, equally obvious, you <u>can</u> survive. Ultimately this too will pass. So relax. Stop "awfulizing"—complaining to yourself about how miserable things are—and do the best you can. You will overcome.

Notes
1. Herbert J. Freudenberger, *Burn-out: The High Cost of High Achievement* (Doubleday, 1980).
2. Ibid.
3. James Thurber, *Reader's Digest*, "Quotable Quotes," March 1976, 137.

How to Evaluate Your Teaching

Kenneth O. Gangel

"The effectiveness of learning depends largely on the effectiveness of teaching." But how effective are we? A master educator gives teachers five sources from which evaluation may be sought and received.

In church education we frequently talk about evaluating learning but rarely about evaluating teaching. Yet, we surely admit that the effectiveness of learning depends largely on the effectiveness of teaching. We need to get serious about analyzing what we are doing, how well we are doing it, and whether or not we are accomplishing stated goals. This is not to minimize the evaluation of learning. But somehow in my own mind, I have never been able to separate the two. It seems that when we evaluate our students and what they have learned under our teaching, we are thereby evaluating ourselves and how well we have been communicating information, ideas, and attitudes.

EVALUATION BY STUDENT

Just as an effective teacher must frequently conduct an evaluation of students, he must also be willing to be evaluated by students. The teacher's evaluation of students is, in effect, an evaluation by students. Let me be specific.

Let's say that Jim Shelton gives a written test after one quarter of study in the Book of Acts with his junior high boys' class. Let's also imagine that out of a possible twenty questions, no one in the class scores higher than eight, and most of the boys answer fewer than five questions correctly. What do we conclude? Does Jim have a class of stupid boys? Is the Book of Acts too difficult? Did the boys fail to study?

Though all of these possible conclusions must be considered, I would suggest two other possibilities: Jim's failure to teach the content effectively so that the boys internalized and retained the information, and his ineffectiveness in testing.

Of course, a teacher's evaluation by his students is not limited to the tests which he prepares for them. He may also use some type of instrument to specifically secure information about his effectiveness. This is done frequently on college campuses and is mandatory is some colleges. Of course, such evaluation by students is most effective with junior high, senior high, and adult classes, but a more informal verbal exchange can be profitable for a teacher even in the children's division. In other words, let the people who eat the food you cook tell you how it tastes.

EVALUATION BY STAFF

Peer evaluation is important in effective teaching. Teachers in church education should not feel competitive among themselves but rather supportive. If I can learn something from you, some technique or idea you are using in your class which would work in my class, by all means share it. Or if I can give you some helpful hints to help you become a better teacher, I hope you will be willing to hear them. This kind of mutual exhortation is not only pedagogically sound; it is biblical.

But it will work only if teachers welcome the evaluation of their peers. If you invite me to come in because you are particularly concerned about self-improvement, then we have a basis for cooperation, and perhaps I will invite you to visit my class. Then our time of sharing and mutual prayer can help make both of us better teachers.

EVALUATION BY STANDARDS

Many evangelical denominations now prepare and provide standard evaluation forms for the total church education program and also for individual teachers. Publishers of Sunday school curriculum materials also have standardized guidelines which can be applied throughout an entire Sunday School and measure an individual teacher in comparison with his peers.

When this is done on a denominational basis, it gives us an even better understanding of how we compare with others who are doing the same thing we are attempting to do in our church ministries. Apart from materials produced by denominational and independent curriculum publishing houses, such forms are available in books on church education.

EVALUATION BY SUPERVISORS

Every teacher is a man or woman under authority. That immediate authority may be the departmental superintendent, the general superintendent of the Sunday school, the director of some other church education program, or the Board of Christian Education. Whoever is directly responsible for the quality of teaching in a given class should also take the responsibility for evaluating that teaching. Observation is the most effective method of evaluating teaching. A departmental superintendent should spend time in the classes of his teachers, checking on the effectiveness of their teaching.

Several things are implied here. First of all, it should be assumed that a superintendent or supervisor is an effective teacher himself and therefore has the qualifications to measure the work of other teachers. Second, the supervisor or observer must know what he is looking for when he makes the evaluation. Subjectivism can run rampant in supervisory evaluation if there is no clearly defined set of criteria.

A third important guideline for supervisory evaluation is that those criteria for effectiveness mentioned above should be well known by the teachers who are being evaluated. If, for example, a certain teacher does not know that his supervisor is most concerned about the use of visual aids, he may make little effort to utilize visuals in his teaching and therefore be in for a negative report when the observer does his work.

EVALUATION BY SELF

In the final analysis, only that teacher will improve who deliberately and designedly wants to improve. A teacher who really is concerned about quality in his teaching will seek out forms of evaluation, utilize the information he gathers, and constantly strive to be a better teacher. Self-evaluation should be going on constantly. If a teacher is properly using his lesson plan, he probably will have evaluative remarks written down after each teaching session. If he is spiritually minded, he probably will be constantly praying that the Spirit of God will show him weaknesses in his teaching.

Finally, self-evaluation can be done by designing a simple form which no one need see but the teacher himself. In that way it is different from the evaluation by standards which I have described. Any Sunday school teacher can develop or adapt a form for self-evaluation which will help him to constantly improve as a teacher of truth.

■ Reprinted from *Christian Educator's Handbook* by Kenneth O. Gangel, published by Victor Books (1985), Scripture Press Publications, Inc., Wheaton, Illinois 60187. Used by permission.

Teaching Behavior Inventory

Harry Murray

Do students ever talk about their teachers? Do they ever not!? Unfortunately, the teachers rarely get to hear this feedback. Here's a tool for discovering what your students think—but were too afraid to say!

I n this inventory students are asked to assess their teacher's specific classroom behaviors. This instrument is not copyrighted and may be reproduced for any valid research or instructional development purpose.

Student Instructions: For each specific teaching behavior, please indicate your judgment as to whether your instructor should increase, decrease, or make no change in the frequency with which he/she exhibits the behavior in question. Please use the following rating scale in making your judgments:

1=almost never   2=rarely   3=sometimes   4=often   5=almost always

CLARITY: METHOD USED TO EXPLAIN OR CLARIFY CONCEPTS AND PRINCIPLES

- Gives several examples of each concept   1 2 3 4 5
- Uses concrete everyday examples to explain concepts and principles 1 2 3 4 5
- Defines new or unfamiliar terms   1 2 3 4 5
- Repeats difficult ideas several times   1 2 3 4 5
- Stresses most important points by pausing, speaking slowly, raising voice, and so on   1 2 3 4 5
- Uses graphs or diagrams to facilitate explanation   1 2 3 4 5
- Points out practical applications of concepts   1 2 3 4 5
- Answers students' questions thoroughly   1 2 3 4 5
- Suggests ways of memorizing complicated ideas   1 2 3 4 5
- Writes key terms on blackboard or overhead screen   1 2 3 4 5
- Explains subject matter in familiar colloquial language   1 2 3 4 5

ENTHUSIASM: NON-VERBAL BEHAVIOR TO GAIN STUDENT ATTENTION/INTEREST

- Speaks in a dramatic or expressive way   1 2 3 4 5
- Moves about while lecturing   1 2 3 4 5
- Gestures with hands or arms   1 2 3 4 5
- Exhibits facial gestures or expressions   1 2 3 4 5
- Maintains eye contact with students   1 2 3 4 5
- Walks up aisles beside students   1 2 3 4 5
- Gestures with head or body   1 2 3 4 5
- Tells jokes or humorous anecdotes   1 2 3 4 5
- Teaches informally rather than verbatim from prepared notes   1 2 3 4 5
- Smiles or laughs while teaching   1 2 3 4 5
- Avoids distracting mannerisms   1 2 3 4 5

INTERACTION: TECHNIQUES USED TO FOSTER STUDENTS' PARTICIPATION

- Encourages students' questions and comments during lectures   1 2 3 4 5
- Allows students to make errors   1 2 3 4 5

- Praises students for good ideas   1 2 3 4 5
- Asks questions of individual students   1 2 3 4 5
- Asks questions of class as a whole   1 2 3 4 5
- Incorporates students' ideas into lecture   1 2 3 4 5
- Presents challenging, thought-provoking ideas   1 2 3 4 5
- Uses a variety of media and activities in class   1 2 3 4 5
- Asks rhetorical questions   1 2 3 4 5

ORGANIZATION: WAYS OF ORGANIZING OR STRUCTURING SUBJECT MATTER
- Uses headings and subheadings to organize lectures   1 2 3 4 5
- Puts outline of lecture on blackboard or overhead screen   1 2 3 4 5
- Clearly indicates transition from one topic to the next   1 2 3 4 5
- Gives preliminary overview of lecture at beginning of class   1 2 3 4 5
- Explains how each topic fits into the course as a whole   1 2 3 4 5
- Begins class with a review of topics covered last time   1 2 3 4 5
- Periodically summarizes points previously made   1 2 3 4 5

PACING: RATE OF INFORMATION PRESENTATION AND EFFICIENT USE OF TIME
- Covers obvious points quickly   1 2 3 4 5
- Stays with major theme of lecture   1 2 3 4 5
- Covers planned material in class sessions   1 2 3 4 5
- Asks if students understand before proceeding to next topic   1 2 3 4 5
- Sticks to the point in answering students' questions   1 2 3 4 5

DISCLOSURE: CLARITY CONCERNING COURSE REQUIREMENTS AND GRADING
- Advises students as to how to prepare for tests or exams   1 2 3 4 5
- Provides sample exam questions   1 2 3 4 5
- Tells students exactly what is expected of them on tests,
  essays or assignments   1 2 3 4 5
- States objectives of each lecture   1 2 3 4 5
- Reminds students of test dates or assignment dates   1 2 3 4 5
- States objectives of course as a whole   1 2 3 4 5

SPEECH: CHARACTERISTICS OF VOICE RELEVANT TO CLASSROOM TEACHING
- Avoids stuttering, mumbling, and slurring of words   1 2 3 4 5
- Speaks at appropriate volume   1 2 3 4 5
- Speaks clearly   1 2 3 4 5
- Speaks at appropriate pace   1 2 3 4 5
- Avoids "um" or "ah"   1 2 3 4 5
- Varies voice pitch (avoids speaking in monotone)   1 2 3 4 5

RAPPORT: QUALITY OF RELATIONSHIP BETWEEN TEACHER AND STUDENTS
- Addresses individual students by name   1 2 3 4 5
- Announces availability for consultation outside of class   1 2 3 4 5
- Offers to help students with problems   1 2 3 4 5
- Shows tolerance of other points of view   1 2 3 4 5
- Talks with students before or after class   1 2 3 4 5

Reprinted from *The Teaching Professor* (October 1988) published by Magna Publications, Inc., 2718 Dryden Drive, Madison, Wisconsin 53704 (800-433-0444). Used by permission.

A Teacher-Building Test

Marlene D. LaFever

As a teacher, how well do you know yourself? What are the appropriate questions for determining "how you're doing?" Your score on this quiz is not as critical as the insights gained in the process. So get to know you!

Evaluate your growth the way you think your students would. Give yourself a ten for perfection, nine for excellent, eight for good, and so on down the line. A one would indicate that you feel a need for total improvement in that area. Work on your low scores. It's important for you to know yourself.

MENTAL GROWTH

1. I have many interests.　　　　　　　　　　　　　　1. _____
2. I would describe myself as having a growing mind.　2. _____
3. I understand the current educational trends and how they will influence the students I teach.　3. _____
4. I am a good teacher and getting better.　4. _____
5. I look for new ways to do things.　5. _____
6. I enjoy thinking about spiritual things and grappling with difficult concepts contained in Scripture.　6. _____
7. I am a student of God's Word. I am teaching nothing that I'm not attempting to put into practice.　7. _____
8. I can admit to myself that I am creative.　8. _____
9. I could list the ten key concerns or problems of the age level I teach. I have informed opinions about each area.　9. _____
10. I keep up with current events.　10. _____
11. I know in what areas I'm not growing spiritually.　11. _____
12. I know how to lead a peer to Christ.　12. _____
13. I read.　13. _____
14. Jesus has control of what my mind thinks about in its "down" or fallow time.　14. _____
15. I respect the age level I teach.　15. _____
16. I can accept ideas from my students as well as give them.　16. _____
17. I am doing my best to nurture my students and, where appropriate, help them develop their spiritual gifts and talents for God's use.　17. _____

EMOTIONAL GROWTH

18. I am excited about the next five years of my life.　18. _____
19. I am fun to be around.　19. _____
20. I like to converse with people my own age.　20. _____

21. I know how to listen. I can empathize with other
people's problems and joys.   21. _____
22. I have no problems talking with my peers about my
relationship with Christ—what He's doing for me and
how I'm growing in my understanding of Him.   22. _____
23. I accept myself as an adult among my students.   23. _____
24. I am able to admit my weaknesses to myself and,
when appropriate, to my students.   24. _____

PHYSICAL GROWTH

25. I am pleased with the way God made me.   25. _____
26. I am as physically attractive as possible.   26. _____
27. My dress reflects my Christianity.   27. _____
28. I work at being physically fit.   28. _____
29. My students aren't ashamed of the way I look or act.   29. _____

SOCIAL GROWTH

30. I get along with my own family members.   30. _____
31. I have a healthy relationship with my spouse (or,
if unmarried, my roommate or close friends).   31. _____
32. I am concerned about my children.   32. _____
33. My own children love and respect me.   33. _____
34. My peers enjoy being around me.   34. _____
35. I don't have to be the center of attention to have a good time. 35. _____
36. Christ is part of all my social activities.   36. _____
37. I am careful to do nothing that would damage the Christian
growth of my students.   37. _____
38. The family God gave me comes before my church activities. 38. _____

■ Excerpted from Marlene D. LaFever's *Creative Teaching Methods*, David C. Cook Publishing Co., 1985. Used by permission.

Excellence in Sunday School Teaching

Carl Shafer

A teacher unfamiliar with Gregory's Seven Laws of Teaching is like a New Testament scholar being unfamiliar with the epistles of Paul. Carl Shafer applies Gregory's laws to the Sunday school setting.

Most teachers, even those with formal education, have never heard of the *Seven Laws of Teaching*. This was my experience after completing a doctorate in education. The *Seven Laws of Teaching*, written over one hundred years ago by John Milton Gregory, are like the original scrolls of education, holding the secrets of effective and excellent teaching. Gregory, educated as a lawyer, was a Baptist minister as well as a distinguished educator. He served as superintendent of public instruction in Michigan (1859-1865), then was president of Kalamazoo College and the first president of the University of Illinois.

Gregory's *Seven Laws of Teaching,* first published as a book in 1884, are clear and simple factors governing the skill and art of teaching. The laws are like seven hilltops of different height, scattered over the landscape. As one climbs each hill, various points in the landscape can be seen with additional perspective. My abridgement of his work are efforts to make Gregory's thoughts and language more available, readable, and understandable to teachers today.

AN INTRODUCTION TO THE SEVEN LAWS

The Seven Laws of Teaching are so simple and natural that they almost suggest themselves, yet the laws are profound even to experienced teachers.

1. The teacher must know the lesson, truth, or art to be taught.
2. The learner must show interest in the lesson.
3. The language used as a medium between the teacher and the learner must be common to both.
4. The lesson to be mastered must be given in terms of truth already known by the learner—the unknown must be explained by means of the known.
5. Teaching must arouse the students to learn things for themselves.
6. Learning is thinking into one's own understanding a new idea or truth, or working a new art or skill into a habit.
7. Teaching must be completed, confirmed, and tested by review, rethinking, and application.

These fundamental laws are even more clearly seen when they are stated as rules and summarized for teaching.

1. THE LAW OF THE TEACHER

Know thoroughly and be very familiar with the lesson you wish to teach—teach with a full mind and clear understanding.

A teacher's ready and evident knowledge gives her students confidence and helps inspire their love of study. In practice, the teacher works with four levels of knowledge.

1. Your students gain a faint recognition of the knowledge presented.
2. Your students gain the ability to recall and describe the knowledge in a general way.

3. Your students develop the power to explain the knowledge—even prove it or illustrate it.
4. Your students acquire an appreciation of the deeper meaning, gaining ability to apply and act upon it.

Ideally, your teaching is geared to move your students to the fourth level: understanding deeper meanings, apply, and act upon them. Teaching of this competence helps learners move from being "hearers" only to being "doers" also.

Applying this rule, then, an excellent teacher will:

- Study the lesson afresh each time.
- Study in advance and acquire books and study aids to build practical knowledge.
- Seek and use illustrations from real life.
- Gain clear thought about the subject so that she can explain clearly.
- Utilize a natural order from the simple to complex in the presentation of the knowledge and subject.

Without adequate study and preparation, you are like a messenger without a message. Knowledge provides power and enthusiasm for teaching. Some teachers fall into the trap of using sham practices. They parade their own fancies before students; they talk in pompous pretenses, and issue solemn platitudes in wise and pretentious tones. Such practices detract from excellent teaching.

2. THE LAW OF THE LEARNER

Gain and keep the attention and interest of your students. Do not try to teach without student attention.

The interest and attention of your students interact with each other. Master the art and skill of gaining and keeping attention. Several actions will help carry out this rule.

- Begin teaching when your students are physically present and preclude any distractions.
- Adapt lesson length to the ages and attention span of your students.
- Utilize a variety of teaching techniques: visual aids, stories, illustrations, questions, and discussion.
- Move about the class. Maintain eye contact and be animated with natural gestures.

Remember, your enthusiasm is contagious! Old and impractical knowledge results in dull and uninteresting teaching. Routine teaching results in routine learning.

3. THE LAW OF THE LANGUAGE

Use words which you and your students will understand in the same way. Use clear and vivid language.

Your words, language, and aids must be clearly understood by your students. Unfamiliar words, unless explained, reduce your success. Some ideas for excellent communication:

- Study your student's language level and knowledge.
- Use the smallest number of words to communicate ideas. Use short sentences and strive for simplicity in communication.
- Define and illustrate the new knowledge, relating it to the listeners' experience. When they understand, proceed.
- Natural objects, visual aids, illustrations, pictures, and discussion are helpful teaching tools to expand word meaning and understanding.

- Remember that interested looks don't assure understanding. Students may profess understanding for approval.

Topics and knowledge in Sunday school classes are often outside the language and life of students. Consider that Jesus, the Master Teacher, used parables about common life experiences to teach significant truths. Your language and knowledge, then, should also interact with common life experiences to generate student interest and excellent learning.

4. THE LAW OF THE LESSON

Begin with what is already well-known to the students or has been experienced, and proceed to the new material by single, easy, and natural steps, letting the known explain the unknown.

To apply this law for excellent teaching:

- Be sure your knowledge interacts with your students. They can then follow your advance.
- Use natural progression by relating the new to earlier lessons.
- Entrench the new firmly in mind with student questions and discussion.
- Size the lesson and progression to age, concentration, and attainment of students.

Practical knowledge solves real life problems and is usable in life's experience. Show that thinking clearly in Sunday school provides opportunities beyond the classroom.

5. THE LAW OF THE TEACHING PROCESS

Stimulate your students' minds to action. Encourage students to think of themselves as discoverers.

Excellent teaching awakens the students' self-activity. That is, knowledge given must be recognized, rethought, and relived in a student's mind.

- Find a contact point in the life of each student.
- Use practical exercises and assignments involving students' minds, hands, and lives.
- Assign real investigations outside of class.
- Use thinking questions and discussion. Repress the desire to tell all you know.
- Be a student also. Join the search for facts, principles, and skills.

Often, simply telling facts precludes student thinking and knowledge. Expecting the exact words from the text or your lips prohibits real and useful remembering. Real knowledge results from mind and life use.

Lead the march of learning! Transform your classroom into a busy life laboratory. Get your students thinking and discovering for themselves; make them students of life.

6. THE LAW OF THE LEARNING PROCESS

Require your students to reproduce the lesson in thought and action, to work it out in its various phases and applications until it is expressed in the students' own languages and actions.

This law in action in students' learning and lives is the result of the previous law well practiced. Additional action ideas include:

- Help students form a clear idea of the work to be done. Persist until the whole idea is expressed in their words.
- Encourage your students to develop a profound regard for truth searching.

- Stimulate student self-questioning and answering.

Hasty, imperfect, and fragmentary lessons prevent time for original thinking, student power of expression, and practical student work. Remember that giving and expecting only factual knowledge results in education falling short of effectiveness and real excellence in teaching.

7. THE LAW OF REVIEW AND APPLICATION

Review, review, review, reproducing the old, introducing new thoughts to deepen the impression made, add fresh meaning, find new applications, correct any false ideas and complete the true.

Review is the process which completes excellent teaching. Good review is like the finishing touch of the master to the painting. Here are some ways to review:

- Review frequently, thoughtfully, and interestingly.
- Use a variety of fresh conceptions and new associations.
- Bring new light to old lessons.
- Have students use their hands as well as their minds in review.

Lifeless, colorless repetitions of questions and answers constitute review in name only. Also, hurried, impatient, and inadequate reviews, during and at the end of the course, do not complete and support excellent teaching.

Excellent reviews complete excellent teaching. Reviews plug the leaks common in learning. Without review, students' minds leak knowledge without useful application or retention. Students living a variety of reviews with their teacher begin to think review is important and worthwhile. They also develop a desire to master the subject.

■ Excerpted from Carl Shafer's *Excellence in Teaching With the Seven Laws* (Baker Book House, 1985). Used by permission.

Build Your Library for Effective Bible Study

James F. Stitzinger

Would a plumber go to work without his wrench? A carpenter without his hammer? Presented here are some tools of the Christian teacher, and how they can be accumulated and used efficiently and economically.

Spurgeon once lamented over Bible students who didn't see the value of other men's writings: "It seems odd, that certain men who talk so much of what the Holy Spirit reveals to themselves, should think so little of what he had revealed to others." Some of God's choice servants gave their lives to studying the Word and recording their findings for the benefit of others. A well-chosen library of Bible study tools allows us to enjoy what these men have discovered in their study of Scripture. Their work can help us as we study God's Word and seek the illuminating power of the Holy Spirit.

THE BENEFITS

A well-chosen library will be of benefit in several ways:

Efficient Study. It makes a wealth of material on a passage or subject readily available. If you can reduce the time required to understand a passage, you can devote more time to applying its truth to your life.

Light on Difficult Passages. Although each believer must decide the meaning of Scripture for himself, a good book can clarify a hard passage and give you the fruit of other men's study.

Personal Application. Books offer a wealth of biblical truth for your personal growth. All the devotional classics, biographies, and histories of missions illustrate great truths of Scripture in a vivid way. They can give you insight into your own needs by revealing what God has taught others.

THE BASIC BOOKS

Here are four basic tools every Bible student should own:

1. A Study Bible. A study Bible with good cross references, notes, and indexes is essential. What Bible version should you buy? The King James Version is valuable, but you also need a good, modern translation such as the *New American Standard Bible* or the *New International Version*. A paraphrase or expanded translation such as The Amplified Bible can also be helpful. Remember, however, that paraphrases will reflect the interpretation of their author or editor and should be read with discernment.

2. A One-Volume Commentary. You need a concise commentary that covers every verse of Scripture and summarizes the thought of each verse or paragraph of Scripture. Such commentaries condense a lifetime of study into a brief, succinct format. The older work of Jamieson, Fausset, and Brown is still helpful, and the more recent *Wycliffe Bible Commentary* and *Bible Knowledge Commentary* (2 vols.) are excellent.

3. A Bible Dictionary or Encyclopedia A Bible dictionary discusses specific biblical terms, people, and places. Those by Smith, Davis, and Unger are most helpful.

A Bible encyclopedia is also worthwhile because it goes beyond the words of Scripture and discusses related topics. Articles tend to be longer and include archaeological findings, theological issues, and a bibliography for further reading. Encyclopedias are frequently multi-volume sets. Two of the best are *The International Standard Bible Encyclopedia* and the *The Zondervan Pictorial Bible Encyclopedia*.

4. A Concordance. Get a good exhaustive concordance that accesses every occurrence of every word. Both Strong's and Young's concordances are especially helpful because they encode the Hebrew and Greek words with numbers, providing limited study of the original languages for those who know only English. Several Greek and Hebrew word-study books are now keyed to the numbers in Strong's for easy access.

If you have a personal computer, you can benefit from a computer-based concordance. This tool allows you to search for individual words or group of words. Some programs are available in different translations, and some are keyed to Strong's numbers as well.

A WELL-ROUNDED LIBRARY

Expand your library by collecting several good books in each of the important areas of theological study:

- Reference works in theology, church history, world religions, and ethics.
- Bible-study aids, including a topical textbook such as Torrey's *A New Topical Textbook*, a phrase concordance, a Bible handbook, and a guide to parallel passages such as Torrey's *Treasury of Scripture Knowledge*.
- Word-study books, including those by W. E. Vine, Colin Brown, and Harris, Waltke, and Archer. Although those works are somewhat technical, they are still valuable even to those unfamiliar with Greek and Hebrew.
- Commentaries. Be warned that commentary sets are often mixed in quality, so select individual commentaries; don't just buy whole sets. However, it is often wise to purchase one set of commentaries on the Old and New Testaments, such as the *Tyndale Commentary Series*, so that your library covers every book of the Bible. Then purchase primarily individual volumes.
- Theology books. A clear dictionary of theology, such as the recent *Dictionary of Theology* edited by Elwell, is very helpful. Also include a book on Bible doctrines or systematic theology.
- Special interest books, including Bible geography, Bible characters, and manners and customs in Bible times are helpful.
- Cassette tapes of teaching that has benefited you can be an important addition to your library.

SOURCES FOR BUILDING A LIBRARY

Although price should not always be the determining factor in building a library, it is only wise to seek the best price. Subscribe to the monthly catalogs of several discount book houses not only to shop for good prices, but also to stay aware of new books. Try to locate books secondhand. A small want ad in the local paper may turn up a retired pastor's library that can be purchased very reasonably. Most institutional libraries have duplicates available for those who ask. Used book stores are another possible source.

A WORKING PLAN

Having surveyed what a library should include, let's now formulate a plan of action. Develop a list of books you would like in your library. A trusted book such as

A Basic Library for Bible Students by Warren Wiersbe is helpful for that purpose. Also find two or three friends, pastors, or teachers who can recommend good books for your library. A book that has become valuable to you will often refer you to other good books to consider.

• Prioritize your buying list according to those books that are most important and those that can wait. Buy the highest priority books first, and wait to buy the others. Share your wish list with your family and close friends; it makes an excellent Christmas or birthday gift list. A book for your library can be much more beneficial than another tie for the closet!

• Purchase the books on your list. Remember, your library should be a collection of books you need, rather than a collection of what you could find for a bargain. By developing a list of books you want, you can get the best books available, rather than merely accumulating the selections your local bookstore carries.

• Set aside money in your budget for books. Even if it is a small amount, you can systematically build your library from month to month. If something new looks good, put it on your list to think about for awhile. Don't alter your priorities without careful thought. Buy what you are looking for when it goes on sale.

• Browse through Christian bookstores to become aware of newly published materials, but seek a recommendation before you buy. You can also keep up with new books by reading Christian magazines.

SOME GUIDING PRINCIPLES

Here are several steps to follow in building and using a library:

1. **Seek the best books on a particular subject.** Note that the best book is not always the newest or the most expensive. It takes a little time to find out which are the best, but your time will be well rewarded. Visit the library of a trusted friend and take good notes.

2. **Learn to look for trusted authors.** It is rarely possible to judge the quality of a book by its title or publisher. It is important to learn something about the faith, convictions, and theological mind-set of the author so you know how he approaches Scripture. Remember that "the wise in heart are called discerning" (Proverbs 16:21, NIV).

3. **Practice the principle of courtship before marriage.** In other words, examine a book before you buy it. Use a library copy or that of a friend to be sure it will benefit you. A good book may not be good for you. Also, publishers are often caught between publishing what will sell and publishing what is truly worth reading.

4. **Be careful how you allow a book to shape your thinking.** Develop the skill of thinking through a passage or issue yourself before you read about it. Learn to ask the book a question and then read it for the answer, rather than allowing it to think for you.

5. **Use your books.** Many avid book collectors never use their books. Buy only what you will use—use what you buy.

Careful, consistent reading of the Bible itself comes first, but time spent in a library of good books will expand your knowledge of God's Word even further.

■ Excerpted from James F. Stitzinger's "Build Your Library for Effective Bible Study," *Masterpiece* 1, no. 2 (Fall 1988), pp. 18-21. Used by permission.

Discouragement: Its Cause and Cure

Charles R. Swindoll

Overwhelming odds, pressures, and problems combine to intimidate teachers: Is it worth it? Am I making a difference? Let a pastor's pastor show you why discouragement "is not a terminal disease."

f we look closely, we will discover four causes for discouragement when Nehemiah led Israel to rebuild the walls of Jerusalem.

CAUSES OF DISCOURAGEMENT

1. Loss of strength.

Nehemiah 4:10 reads: "Thus in Judah it was said, 'The strength of the burden bearers is failing.'" See the word *failing?* The original text says stumbling—tottering—staggering. "These people, Nehemiah, have been working a long time, and they are getting tired." The newness had worn off.

Let me make it even more practical. Let's say you have undertaken a difficult project of redecorating your home When is the most discouraging time? Usually it's when you are halfway through and the mess gets to be more than you can handle. Halfway is discouraging! A lost of strength takes an emotional toll on our bodies.

2. A loss of vision.

Did you notice what Judah said? "Yet there is much rubbish" (4:10). The burden bearers' strength was expended and began to fail; yet, in spite of all the work, there's a lot of rubbish. "We look around, Nehemiah, and all we can see is debris—dirt, broken stones, hard, dried chunks of mortar. It's getting tiring. There's too much rubbish."

The builders had lost the vision of the completed wall. A perfect illustration of this myopic outlook is the young mother who has changed what seems to be fifty or sixty diapers in one day. She looks at the situation and says, "There's too much rubbish, too much mess, too many diapers, too much work." What has she lost? She has lost her whole sense of fulfillment in the motherhood role because of the current "rubbish."

3. A loss of confidence.

Perhaps the most devastating cause of discouragement is an obvious loss of confidence. Nehemiah's workers became weary and disillusioned. The wall was halfway up. They voiced their feelings by sadly observing, "We ourselves are unable to rebuild the wall" (v. 10). When you lose strength and you lose vision, then you lose confidence. And when you've lost confidence, discouragement is winking at you around the corner. When you lose your confidence, you lose your heart; you lose your motivation.

4. A loss of security.

The final cause for discouragement in the case of these Jews was a loss of their feelings of security. Verse 11 reads: "And our enemies said, 'They will not know or see until we come among them, kill them, and put a stop to the work.'"

What a scare tactic! The enemy said, "We've got a plan. No, we're not going to tell anybody what the plan is; but, when you least expect it, wham! We'll slip in and that will be it. We will handle the job so fast and so thoroughly that you'll never know we are even there." The laborers suddenly slumped into discouragement when they lost their security.

There are many areas of life that we hang onto for tangible security. Maybe you are standing before the door of opportunity or change. You've lost your strength. You've lost your confidence. You've lost your vision. And you've lost your security. There's that feeling deep down within you that says, "It isn't worth it." But wait! You could be on the verge of the greatest years of your entire life.

HOW CAN WE DEAL WITH DISCOURAGEMENT?

Building that Jerusalem wall was certainly turning out to be no easy feat! Discouragement ran rampant. Satan must have been having a field day. But Nehemiah didn't ignore the discouragement. (You can't ignore discouragement. It's like ignoring a flat tire. Pray all you want to; drive all you want to; you never will get air back into it. You've got to fix it. That's the way it is with discouragement.)

Nehemiah rolled up his sleeves like a good leader and dealt with the discouragement. I find five techniques he employed that worked for him and will still work today.

1. Unify your efforts toward a goal. "I stationed men in the lowest parts of the space behind the wall, the exposed places, and I stationed the people in families with their swords, spears, and bows." (Nehemiah 4:13)

Now that is significant. The builders have been scattered all over Jerusalem working together with stones, water, and mortar, and yet separated from their families. Nehemiah unified them according to families and gave each one a common goal—preservation. He turned their attention from themselves to the enemy. Notice what happened in the process of uniting his people: Nehemiah stopped the work. Sometimes the very best thing to do when you are discouraged is to take some time off. There's an old Greek motto that says, "You will break the bow if you keep it always bent." How tight is your bow? When is the last time you loosened the bow and got away for a couple of days?

2. Direct your attention to the Lord.

Next, he directed their attention to the Lord (v. 14). They were looking at the rubbish. They needed to be looking to the Lord. "When I saw their fear, I rose and spoke . . .'Do not be afraid of them; remember the Lord who is great and awesome.'"

The phrase, "Remember the Lord," sounds good, but how do you do it? You can begin by calling to mind the things the Lord has said. You actually put in your mind some of the statements God has made. Call to mind right now five or six good solid promises that you could claim. When the devil attacks, are you ready with the living words that shoot back—the sword of the Spirit, God's Word? The Christian must know what God has said. So Nehemiah unified them around the same goal. That means he had to stop the work process and get them alone. Then he turned their attention to the Lord.

3. Maintain a balance in your thoughts and actions.

What did Nehemiah do next in his attempt to thwart discouragement? He encouraged the Jews to maintain a balance. He called them to action. "Now, you've got to fight," he commanded. "There's a job to be done. Draw swords!" (vv. 14-17). Guard against the subtle teaching that suggests that God does everything and you step back and do nothing. The Bible continually exhorts us to stand, to contend for the faith, to be strong in the fight, and to be good soldiers. We must balance faith and action.

4. Determine a rallying point.

The fourth thing that Nehemiah did was to provide a rallying point. Let me clarify what I mean. Nehemiah wrote in verse 19 and 20: "And I said to the nobles, the officials, and the rest of the people, 'The work is great and extensive, and we are separated on the wall far from one another. At whatever place you hear the sound of the trumpet, rally to us there. Our God will fight for us.'"

What was the rallying point? First of all, it was a place, but it also suggests a principle. The place was wherever the sound of the trumpet was coming from. Nehemiah ordered, "Whenever you hear that trumpet sound, you come running to the spot where the bugler is standing." The principle: Don't try to fight alone. Don't give up until you can link your soul with another who has a kindred spirit, who cares for your soul and for your needs. You need someone to be your rallying point. Nehemiah said, "When you hear the battle cry, come to where the trumpet is." That's where strength is.

5. Develop a "serving others" ministry.

The fifth and final thing that Nehemiah did to dispel all signs of discouragement among this people was to occupy them in a ministry of serving others. Verses 21 and 22 tell us that they carried on the work. "So we carried on the work with half of them holding spears from dawn until the stars appeared. At that time I also said to the people, 'Let each man with his servant spend the night within Jerusalem so that they may be a guard for us by night and a laborer by day.'"

In essence, Nehemiah was saying, "Hey, we need help. I'm asking you to serve and assist each other. We can't handle it alone." In the pressured days that followed, according to verse 23, they didn't even have time to change clothes! When they went down to the water to bathe, they stayed at the task. They ministered to one another in service and involvement.

How involved are you in others' lives? This week, how much of your life will be spent serving others? Or is it all wrapped in yourself? Everyone of us should take a long look at our short lives, taking special note of our personal investment in the lives of others.

Nehemiah, said, "Let's not sit around and lick our own wounds. We need help from one another. Let's get at the business of caring. Let's serve. Let's minister."

Isn't that what the raw edge of Christianity is all about? Am I not to give up my rights and say no to myself? Discouragement is indeed an internal disease. It starts with the germs of self-doubt. Through fear and negative exaggerations, the germs begin to grow and multiply. Soon we lose our way, we weaken, and we run and hide.

As it continues, we become virtually useless and downright defeated. We become easy prey for the enemy of our souls to take charge and to nullify our efforts. It can happen almost overnight. Glance back over the five techniques Nehemiah used to combat the "blahs" in the camp at ancient Jerusalem. His methods will never be outdated. Discouragement may be tough to handle, but it's certainly not impossible.

Remember: *discouragement is not a terminal disease.*

■Excerpted from Charles R. Swindoll's *Hand Me Another Brick* (Nashville: Thomas Nelson Publishers, 1978), pp. 81-97. Used by permission.

Eleven Practical Secrets of Discipline

Katie Abercrombie

Lost the vision for rebuilding classroom discipline? Lacking the tools as well? Here's a list of "building blocks" which can be used as a starting place. Use these as a checklist—you can reach your goal!

Do your kids hear "don't" more than "do"? Discipline problems are the visible signs of a group that lacks underlying direction. Tear down your negative foundation of "don'ts" and rebuild a positive foundation using simple guidelines.

1. Be positive. When you go over the rules, focus on what group members will do and can do rather than what they won't or can't do. "Dos" should outnumber "don'ts."

2. Make expectations clear. Before a retreat or at the beginning of the year, go over your expectations with group members. Most kids new to your group won't know what the "norms" are for behavior.

3. Keep rules to a minimum. Decide what's important and focus on those issues. Make rules that cover many situations to reduce your rules list. "We will treat one another with respect" covers a lot of ground—putdowns and hitting included—and encourages positive interaction.

4. Let kids experience the consequences of their actions. A natural consequence of misusing play equipment is that the equipment gets broken. A logical response is to put the equipment away until the group either repairs or replaces it. By experiencing consequences, kids learn lessons about life and controlling their behavior.

5. Foster mutual respect. Let your kids know that you respect them, and choose other adult leaders who can model that respect as well. Avoid adult leaders who are power-hungry or have unrealistic expectations of kids' behavior. Look for people who listen to kids, consider their ideas and treat their problems seriously.

6. Avoid putdowns. Often adults subtly tear down kids when they discipline them. Don't berate them for not listening attentively to every word you say or for forgetting the rules. Remember their age, abilities and their precarious self-esteem.

7. Craft a group covenant. Working together, spell out what's expected. Let kids ask why a certain rule is needed, and help them come up with the reasons.

8. Avoid double standards. Often adults don't follow the rules they've made for kids. When your group develops a covenant or list of guidelines, the adults should be expected to follow them also. Mutual compliance builds a sense of community.

9. Program wisely. Meetings should be active and experiential. Have more material available than you can possible use in the allotted time. Free time should be structured—too much time with no planned activities invites problems.

10. Expect the best. Let kids know you expect your activities to go smoothly. show them by your attitude and behavior that you have confidence in their ability to behave.

11. Process failure. When something goes wrong, talk with the group. Figure out what went wrong and decide how to deal with it. Express your feelings and let kids express theirs. Use failure to help kids learn about God's grace and forgiveness.

Perturbing Personalities in Your Class

Neal F. McBride

Does any member of your class or group display a personal tendency—a personality trait, a weakness, or a habit—which hinders the class? Here's how to turn that uniqueness into an asset rather than a liability!

It's frustrating, Barbara," Andy lamented, "everyone in the Bible study really likes Trudy, but she talks too much. She never gives anyone else a chance to say anything. You're the group leader, will you talk to her?"

Let me introduce you to Talker Trudy and several other "extreme" group members. Each of the persons you'll meet displays an excessive behavior pattern . . . behavior reflective of different expectations regarding group participation. But different personalities don't have to hinder your group. Kept under control, the varied emphases brought in by group members can actually enhance the benefits you get from small-group or class time. Here's how to let differences work for you.

Talker Trudy. Our friend Trudy could easily earn the nickname "motor-mouth." Much of what she says is worthwhile, but it often gets lost in a constant stream of words. Trudy answers every question and has an opinion on every topic. Some of her fellow group members suspect she talks just to hear herself talk.

How can a Bible study group or class benefit from a talkative member? One idea is to have her serve as the group "summarizer." Give her the opportunity several times during the course of a study session to summarize what has taken place up to that point. This responsibility will give her the opportunity to talk, while at the same time demanding that she develop good listening skills.

Listener Larry. Not much of a talker, Larry just wants to listen to what the others have to say. Mentally, he is actively involved. And on the rare occasion when he does speak, his comments are thoughtful and well stated. Larry wants other group members to accept his quiet participation.

A lot of people are like Larry. In fact, many of us start out as listeners until we feel accepted and comfortable with the other group members. Since "Larrys" are good listeners, I find it beneficial to ask them to serve as class sounding boards. At the end of a discussion we turn to a "Larry" and ask him to summarize what he has heard us say. This provides valuable feedback and serves as a means of reviewing the main points of the study for that particular evening. Using Larry to provide a session review, coupled with Talker Trudy's periodic summaries, facilitates good group process. Perhaps you could use the "Larry" in your group in a similar manner.

Academic Ann. Next meet Ann. She's an intellectual giant who takes great pleasure in "digging" into Scripture. Her expectations for group Bible study are not met unless every word in the Bible passage is carefully analyzed . . . preferably in the original language. Interpreting the passage is Ann's goal; its application is secondary.

Ask your Ann to prepare beforehand a careful analysis of the passage or material you will be studying. Then give her ten minutes or so at the beginning of the study to present her findings. Encourage her to focus on a clearly presented interpretation of the passage and not get sidetracked examining interesting but secondary issues. Good interpretation is the correct path to valid application.

Application Alex. "How does it apply to me?" is Alex's constant question. Alex is the opposite of Academic Ann. He wants to quickly "experience the text" and draw out the application. Unfortunately, too often Alex jumps to an application before securing a good understanding of the meaning of the passage. And at times, like all of us, Alex intellectualizes the application without actually implementing it in his own life.

Given Alex's bent toward practical application, you can channel his expectations into a more productive level of group involvement. After talking with him and helping him see the importance of both interpretation and application, designate Alex to serve as the group's "application monitor." Have him suggest several specific ways the passage can be individually and corporately applied. Allow other group members to add to his suggestions. Record the ideas. During the week, have Alex call each member and in a nonthreatening fashion encourage them in their application attempts. At the subsequent meeting, ask him to co-lead the group for a brief period in which study members share the joys and battles of application.

Philosopher Phil. Theology and philosophy are Phil's passion. He likes the group to focus on "heavy" issues. A good class, according to Phil, is one that revolves around the leader lecturing on the intricacies of the material. Group discussion is OK—if kept to a minimum—but he would rather debate philosophical issues with the leader.

Phil can be used as a group resource in two ways. First, call on him (having given him advance notice) to explain a difficult concept or doctrine introduced in the material you are studying. Permit him enough time to adequately clarify the issue. In some instances, when time is scarce, you may ask him to prepare a brief handout rather than speaking.

A second way to utilize Phil is to stage a debate. Begin the study with Phil defending one position and you, the group leader, another. Depending on the subject, it may be interesting to not tell the other group members what is happening until after the debate. Then, explain what was happening and proceed with the study.

Social Sidney. Life of the party, that's Sid. He wants to "lighten up" the sessions and have some fun. Sid views the Bible study as an opportunity to be with people, a context to meet his need for social involvement—even though he may not consciously recognize the fact. It seems like Sid puts up with the actual group or class in order to be with people he likes. His clever and witty remarks help relieve tension at times, but on other occasions they're ill-timed and disruptive.

If someone like Sid is in your group, why not tap his personal strengths? Ask him to plan several social get-togethers for your group. Encourage him to channel his energy into constructive activities beneficial to all.

Forced Frank. Frank doesn't have any expectations—he would rather not even be there! If the truth be known, he attends only because he feels forced to. The pressure to attend may come from his demanding spouse, a psychological need to be accepted, some type of ulterior motive, or some other person or situation. There in body but not mind or soul, Frank just wants to be left alone.

First, avoid forcing him to participate. Hold back on calling for his opinion or in any way putting him on the spot. Allow him to become involved at his own pace.

Second, the best way ultimately to make Frank a true group member is found outside the class sessions. One or two of the others need to befriend him and seek to relate to him on a one-on-one basis. This person-to-person strategy offers far better results than a program-to-program approach.

Preacher Patrick. Every Bible study or class is Patrick's pulpit. He eagerly anticipates each meeting. Long hours are spent preparing. And while not the official group leader, he frequently dominates the discussion (if he can out-talk Talker Trudy).

Pat is well-meaning, but gets on the other members' nerves. He wants to shield his friends from the agony he experienced in his tempestuous past. Unfortunately, his strong admonitions tend to go a bit overboard.

Given time and the proper training, individuals like Pat can become excellent group leaders. Pat first needs to be made aware of his overzealous attitude and actions. Next, he should be offered the opportunity to participate in group leadership training while serving under the guidance of an experienced leader. When he has developed the needed skills, encourage him to assume the leadership of his own class.

Counselor Carol and Counselee Clara. Carol sees the Bible study sessions through the eyes of a counselor. She tends to "psychologize" every topic, every discussion. Group members are often treated like clients who are in desperate need of her counsel.

Rather than wanting to help group members, Carol's sister, Clara, yearns to have the group meet her emotional needs. She wants the Bible study to serve as a therapy session. Clara desperately hopes the group will study biblical passages related to one of her many problems.

Carol and Clara present quite a challenge. Carol's case is the more hopeful, if she can be helped to see that her expectations for the group are not appropriate. Her behavior suggests that she may possess the spiritual gifts of helps or exhortation. If this is the case, after talking with her, help her find a ministry where she can exercise her gifts. This needed outlet will satisfy her God-given inclinations and should facilitate her "normal" involvement in the Bible study.

Clara's continuing participation in the Bible study is questionable when her problems go beyond life's normal struggles. She may need professional help. The group should not be put in the position of having to deal with or solve her problems. She needs to be referred to a trained individual capable of giving her assistance. But don't abandon her. The Bible study members should support her through the process.

Most likely you don't have anyone in your group who precisely fits the description of the individuals you've just met. On the other hand, you may encounter other types of difficult individuals not mentioned here. Remember that my suggestions for dealing with the people I presented have been very general. Every situation, every individual will need to be treated as a unique case and handled accordingly.

■ Excerpted from "Taming Talker Trudy. . . and other Perturbing Personalities in Your Bible Study." *Discipleship Journal* 8, no. 1 (January 1988), pp. 34-37. Used by permission.

Help!
I Can't Take It Any Longer!

Daniel E. Weir

Ever felt like throwing in the towel due to discipline problems?
Sometimes simple and basic solutions are overlooked in the search for
high and lofty principles. Daniel Weir takes you back to the basics.

Do you have any riot gear I can use for my class next week? What am I going to do with this class? I've tried to teach—but it's impossible to have any control in there. I can't take it any longer. I QUIT!"

Sound familiar? You're not alone. One of the problems many teachers face is discipline in the classroom. Don't give up; there may be hope. Good discipline does not usually come easily or without work—but it can be won. Let's look at some of the causes of discipline problems—along with a few answers.

TEACHER RELATED DISCIPLINE PROBLEMS

Shallow Knowledge Shelly taught a nursery class crammed in a small room in the basement. The students sat on adult-size chairs around an adult-size table. Shelly had been trying to talk to them for the past fifteen minutes. Of course, the children were restless, tired and bored—and the teacher was frustrated.

Sally apparently did not know:
- That the room was too small for the students. For that age students there should be 35 square feet for each child.
- That the table and chairs were too big for them. The chairs should have been 8 to 10 inches high and the table 18-20 inches high.
- That she was talking too much and too long. The attention span for a two- or three-year-old child is about four to six minutes.

Disorganized Daryl was the teacher of the third graders. Even though he really loved the class, he never had quite enough time to prepare everything. He usually arrived late and often forgot to bring some of his teaching materials. His teaching pictures were not in proper order so he had to stop in the middle of the story to find the next place. No wonder he couldn't keep the children's attention. Daryl could have had an effective class if he had only taken the time to prepare properly.

Heavenly Minded Helen studied the Bible every day. She would read over the next week's lesson as soon as she completed teaching her class. She studied faithfully all week. The problem was that she simply did not know how to apply the lesson to the students' needs. In order to teach we must know our students personally by spending time with them.

Ruling Ralph had ideas about classroom discipline but he didn't use his ideas in the right way. He made rules but didn't tell his students. Even when a "rule" was known, Ralph was inconsistent in applying it. He used discipline for its own sake, not to help his students learn.
- Be sure to make the right rules. "I don't want to see any of you move" is very unrealistic for a first-grade class!

- Let your students know the rules. Rules are often not stated in the class.
- Be consistent in enforcing the rules. The students will soon learn the "real" and "pretend" rules. Don't let frustration or anger be the basis for enforcing a rule.

STUDENT RELATED DISCIPLINE PROBLEMS

There are two basic causes of discipline problems with children:

1. The first problem is immaturity. Many times we adults forget what it's like to be a child. Children do not have the experience, maturity, muscle coordination, or reasoning capabilities that adults have.

2. The second problem is rebellion toward authority.

- Some students may not receive much attention from home and have discovered that negative and defiant behavior gains attention.
- Other students may have no training in the home and any authority will cause them to react.
- The food that the students eat can cause unwanted behavior. Many children react to sugar or food additives, causing them to become "hyper."

Problems caused by a rebellious attitude must be dealt with firmly but lovingly. God tells us that rebellion is "like the sin of divination" (1 Samuel 15:22).

STEPS OF DISCIPLINE

1. Discover why the child is acting the way he is.

- If it is a result of one of the teacher-related discipline problems, then the teacher needs to correct the problem.
- If it is a student problem, discover the basis of the problem—immaturity, a rebellious attitude, or some other issue.
- If it is a rebellious attitude, try to discover why. This may be difficult but a visit to the student's home may reveal a wealth of background information.

2. Remove the cause of unwanted behavior. Distractions? Boredom?

3. Show your love to your students.

4. Talk to the individual. This is usually most productive when it is done privately. Let the student know what is expected and what the consequences will be if he chooses not to follow the rules of the class.

5. Dismiss the student from class activities. Not from your sight, just out of the action. Following the class, speak with the student to assure him of your love.

6. Ignore the behavior. If you feel that the unwanted behavior is a way to receive attention, it may be best to ignore it since it may go away.

7. Recognize and praise good behavior. Many times other students will respond in the same way so they can be praised. Emphasize positive instead of negative reinforcement.

8. Plan times to be together outside of the classroom. A class outing will bring you and the students closer together. Knowing and understanding each other usually results in a more workable group.

9. Don't say things that you don't mean. If you are going to have consequences for negative behavior, make sure that the consequences can be enforced and then follow through.

10. Keep your composure. You are the example of how you want your students to act. You are a model of godliness for them.

■ Excerpted from *Christian Education Today* 38, no. 4 (Fall 1986), pp. 25-26. Used by permission.

Surviving a Troublemaker's Attacks

Ann Cannon

It takes a creative leader to effectively manage the energy level and "creativity" of teens. Here's a battle plan to help youth leaders separate "win" battles from "no win"—making teens and teachers the winners!

Ernie's a good kid one-to-one. But in a youth group setting, he's dynamite in the worst sense of the word. He's sarcastic and pushy, he doesn't follow instructions and he makes fun of other kids. He's like an exploding bomb. And the target is the youth group. Every youth worker has old war stories of times when an "Ernie" successfully sabotaged a youth activity. Attacks may be unexpected. Skirmishes test boundaries. A war of wills heats up as teenagers push their independence against your authority. While you may have survived previous encounters, you also realize there will be future collisions. So approach the troops with a battle plan to produce victory for all.

TROOP COMBAT CAUSES

They seek attention. To make an effective battle plan, understand why kids disrupt meetings. A teenager struggling with personal identity may try on difficult personalities to see how others react. A sexually or physically abused young person may inflict his or her pain, shame, and frustration on others. Or a teenager participating in activities that he or she knows are wrong will "spew off steam at others to avoid listening to his or her noisy heart and guilty conscience," suggests Wade Rowatt, counselor and psychology professor.

They're under stress. Teenagers may have stressful home situations. Adolescents' erratic hormones also create violent mood swings. "My mind wants to do one thing, but my body does another," says Corey, a fifteen-year-old.

They lack social skills. Some kids don't know how to interact with each other. "It's like taming a wild animal," says Barbara Varenhorst, a counseling psychologist. "These undersocialized teenagers must be trained in social skills before they can be an acceptable part of a group." Young people's families may model rude behavior. Without guidance, the kids don't know how to set limits on their mouths or actions.

They're bored. The subject matter may be too difficult or too simple. Inappropriate behavior may also relate to the stages of faith development in your group.

NO-WIN BATTLES

No matter why kids disrupt meetings, don't ignore the attack. Realize, though, that your response may win the confrontation, but lose the battle—and especially the kids. In dealing with troublemakers, several battle plans don't work. Avoid:

Attacking teenagers' self-esteem. A reaction such as yelling at teenagers to "straighten up" in front of the youth group demeans or shames them. Yelling, sarcasm, and putdowns only demonstrate a leader's lack of self-control and ability to lead.

Making empty threats. "If I've told you once, I've told you ten times," tells teenagers you can't carry threats out. They soon recognize your threats as jokes.

Making rules that only please adults. Instead, make rules that please young people. For example, how Margaret appeared to adults was more important than dealing with her group's dynamics. "This group is so rude it embarrasses me in front of the other adults," she said to her youth group. Youth group members immediately saw how unimportant they were.

WINNING THE WAR . . . . WITHOUT LOSING THE TROOPS

Not every battle plan is no-win. Handle troublemakers in these positive ways.

Plan 1: Prevention
- *Build relationships.* Show each teenager you care about and trust him or her. Take time to know each one personally.
- *Use challenging meetings and curricula.* For disruptive, bored teenagers, provide a deeper Bible study with a contract that states the commitment required. Or assign a troublemaker a task where he or she works alone.
- *Involve young people.* Include them in the meeting planning. Have them set group goals and rules and expectations of group members.

Plan 2: Positive Peer Influence
- *Talk openly.* Ask: What can we do to improve our group? Instead of allowing group members to attack the troublemaker, urge them to state the problem and offer alternate actions. Draw up a covenant agreement. Have each person sign an agreement of acceptable behavior and consequences of inappropriate behavior. For example, if a person regularly interrupts a meeting, he or she can't go to a pizza party.
- *Help one another.* Encourage group members to say: "Okay, John, quit clowning around. Let's get started." Remind them to attack the behavior, not the person.
- *Form pairs.* Pair up stronger young people with troublemakers. For example, have the pair work on an assignment or leave the room to talk.
- *Monitor the group's behavior.* Use peer observers. Group members don't know who the observers are until the end of a meeting. "Just knowing their actions are being observed causes kids to be on their best behavior," says Varenhorst. "The unexpected result is the voluntary compliments each person receives from the observers. Positive peer pressure can be very powerful."

Plan 3: Praise
- *Praise teenagers.* They find it difficult to dislike or confront someone who honestly praises them. Say something positive about each young person during the activity.
- *Assign a task.* Ask a disruptive person to write on a poster, demonstrate something or read a Bible passage. Then praise him or her for a job well done.
- *Show something unusual.* When Rowatt is challenged by a troublemaker, he shows the group a rubber band trick. Then he tells the disrupter, "When you can figure out the trick, you can talk" or, "If you'll give me your attention now, I'll show you how to do the trick later."

Plan 4: Know How To React
- *Confront a teenager.* Rowatt attacks the behavior, not the teenager. For example, "Talking while I'm talking makes me angry."
- *Be firm.* Set limits. "Kids really do want the adult to be in charge," says Varenhorst. "Kids hate a group that's out of control even if they're a part of it." For example, Ed reacted to a question with vicious language. I said: "I care about you, but I won't tolerate your language. Don't talk to me like that

again." Ed remained an active participant, never using abusive language again.

• *Remove the troublemaker.* "Your first responsibility is to the total group," says Varenhorst. "If I tell a kid to leave, I make it very clear why that person is being sent from the room." If possible, ask an adult to leave with him or her. Search beyond surface behavior for answers to problems. Ask: What's making your life so painful? How can I help? Don't ask: Why do you talk all the time?

• *Remain calm.* Many out-of-control leaders tend to talk louder and louder in hopes of overpowering the din of disruptions. But it usually backfires. The kids talk louder rather than quiet down and listen. So use silence or speak softly and wait for kids to get the hint and quiet each other.

• *Model appropriate behavior.* Varenhorst says that because groups are becoming more difficult to work with, many leaders take the easy way out. They play games, watch videos or provide entertainment, never letting young people really talk. Knowing group members personally is a key. Teaching them how to interact is another. "Learning how to get along with others is a very important skill to pass on to our teenagers," says Varenhorst. "It requires a lot of patience. And it takes time. But it's part of our mission and service to kids."

The bottom line: You aren't going to win the war until your kids recognize that you care more about them than yourself. Then the victory can be celebrated by everyone!

QUESTIONS FOR YOU, THE COMMANDING OFFICER

While it's easy to blame the troops for disruptive behavior, don't neglect self-inspection. Take these steps:

1. Check your prejudices. Does your body language give away your true feelings about teenagers' dress, mannerisms, language, hair styles, cultural or economic situations? Do preconceived ideas cause you to label kids and result in their living out your expectations?

2. Check your ability to relate and lead. Do you struggle with your own self-esteem? Do you neglect to understand and study topics before presenting them to your youth group?

3. Check your flexibility. Do you stick to a plan, not adjusting when necessary? Do you do what's most comfortable for you and not what's best for group members?

4. Check your stress level. Do you suffer from battle fatigue? For example: Beth had problems at work. She was moving to a new apartment and recovering from a broken relationship. One Sunday morning when teenagers continued to talk about everything but Scripture, Beth loudly announced, "If you're not going to listen, just leave." And the whole class did! A break from teaching gave Beth perspective and rest.

If you answered "yes" to several questions, examine your commanding-officer skills. Then choose at least one to improve.

■ Reprinted by permission from *Group Magazine* 14, no. 8 (October 1988), pp. 12-14. © 1988, Group Publishing Inc., Box 481, Loveland, Colorado 80539.

"Dos and Don'ts" of Discipline

Linda and Keith Burba

Too often in instructional settings we are told either the "do" or the "don't." In this pointed article we're given both at the same time. Give yourself a quick check-up, and make corrections as needed.

Specific "dos and don'ts" in teacher behavior are listed in the following chart:

DON'T	DO
•laugh at a child	•develop a sense of humor
•threaten for misbehavior (makes teacher responsible)	•define limits and consequences (makes child responsible)
•ignore child because he/she behaves badly	•ask yourself, "How do I feel about this child?"
•try to change a child through nagging	•influence him by your own proper attitudes
•expect trust unless you . . .	•first earn the child's respect
•become angry	•*act* in response to his behavior
•be vague in your expectations	•tell the child *exactly* what you want him to do or stop doing.
•constantly make exceptions	•act consistently with expectations and follow-through
•punish; it focuses on past behavior	•enforce consequences; they focus on future good behavior
•be unyielding, insisting on always being right	•say, "I'm sorry," when you are wrong.
•be uninvolved	•get to know each child
•threaten	•act
•criticize efforts	•show appreciation
•try to reason during a crisis	•wait for a calm time to enlist their input for a solution to the problem behavior
•tolerate physical assault on others	•protect all students from harm by whatever measures are necessary.
•allow name calling or labeling	•accept every child just as he is

In summary, there are many reasons for misbehavior in the classroom. The teacher who wishes to gain classroom control needs to be aware of these and look for the following clues when a child misbehaves:

1. Attention-getting (How can I get teacher to notice me?)
2. Power struggle (Who's in charge here?)
3. Revenge (Nobody's gonna make me behave and get by with it!)
4. Assume inability (I can't do what the teacher wants, so why try?)
5. Rejection by peers (Maybe if I act up, my classmates will think I am neat!)
6. Lack of affection at home (Mom and Dad don't care; why should anyone else?)
7. Poor self-image (Nobody thinks I'm any good. I'll show that teacher how bad I really am.)
8. Need to test the limits (Does the teacher really mean what he says?)
9. Unfulfilled needs (I dress as well as the other children; I'll earn their respect by giving the teacher a hard time.)
10. Doesn't understand teacher expectations (What does she mean by, "Be good, and we'll get an early recess"?)
11. Upsetting emotions (Mom and Dad argued nearly all night. What was that I barely heard about us kids?)
12. Uninteresting curriculum (Boring, boring, boring! Who cares what he did when he was a kid?)
13. Inconsistent expectations (One day she says we can sharpen our pencils any time we need to; the next she says we can't. Guess I'll try it. All she can do is yell at me.)

The Christian teacher has the marvelous advantage of the Holy Spirit's guidance as he seeks to understand each child in his classroom. These problems, as with all others, may be talked over with God. He will give the wisdom needed as promised in James 1:5: "If any of you lack wisdom, let him ask of God, that giveth to all men liberally, and upbraideth not; and it shall be given him." A wise teacher is a praying teacher—one who prays before the children misbehave!

■Taken from *Train Up Children* by Linda and Keith Burba. © 1985 by Beacon Hill Press of Kansas City. Used by permission of the publisher.

Ministry and the Spirit's Control

John F. MacArthur, Jr.

As a teacher, do you wonder whether you do or don't have the spiritual gift of teaching? While a good question, a master teacher here reminds us that the scriptural priority is on using, not searching for, gifts.

Every Christian is given a marvelous gift the moment he becomes a Christian. The moment that we believe, we receive the Holy Spirit. He is God, the third Person of the Trinity, who takes up residence in our lives.

From the moment that you believed, the Spirit of God came to live within you. He became your guide, your truth-teacher, and your power supply in order to do all for the glory of God. As a result, the New Testament urges us to behave in a certain way relative to the Spirit. For example, we are to walk in the Spirit (Romans 8:4), live in the Spirit (1 Peter 4:6), be filled with the Spirit (Ephesians 5:18), pray in the Spirit (Ephesians 6:18), manifest the fruit of the Spirit (Galatians 5:22), and to exercise the gifts of the Spirit (1 Corinthians 12:11). On the negative side, we are warned not to grieve the Spirit (Ephesians 4:30), resist the Spirit (Acts 7:51), or quench the Spirit (1 Thessalonians 5:19).

All of this shows us how vitally important it is that we operate in the sphere of the Holy Spirit. The Christian life is a Spirit-dominated, Spirit-directed, and Spirit-controlled existence.

THE RESULTS OF THE SPIRIT'S CONTROL

When we allow the Spirit of God to reign in our lives and have control and give direction, some marvelous results always occur:

Holiness. Under the direction, control, and complete domination of the Spirit of God, our life pattern results in a constant sanctification.

Joy. A constant satisfaction occurs when we walk and live in the Spirit.

Liberty. "Where the Spirit of the Lord is, there is liberty" (2 Corinthians 3:17b). There is a constant sense of freedom.

Confidence. A constant security occurs when we walk in the Spirit.

Victory. There exists a constant strength against the adversary.

Ministry. There is a constant service to the Body of Christ. So, when we walk in the Spirit, not only are there personal results, bur there is another result—we are able to minister to others and to build them up in Christ. As I walk in the Spirit, my gift is ministered to you. As you walk in the Spirit, your gifts are ministered to one another. As we live, move, walk, and are filled with the Spirit, he operates through us via the spiritual gifts we have been given to minister to other believers.

THE ISSUE: WALK IN THE SPIRIT

People often ask me, "How can you know your spiritual gift?" I reply, "That isn't the issue." It doesn't really matter if I have defined my gift. In the first place, it is elusive—I can't always pinpoint it. The issue is: Walk in the Spirit. If I walk, live, and am filled with the Spirit, it is not too important for me to understand the definition of my gift. It isn't an academic issue; it's a matter of getting on your knees and asking the

Spirit of God to dominate and control your life. As you yield to Him, the Spirit of God operates through you. And that will be your area of ministry. So, the best way to know your gifted area is not to figure it out and then do it but to walk in the Spirit and then look back and say, "So that's what I do." Don't worry about definitions. It doesn't matter to me that I have a definition; it only matters that I walk in the Spirit so He can minister through me.

THE PROBLEM: MANY COLORS

Now remember when you try to define your gift, you will run into some problems because there is so much overlapping of the gifts. When I was in high school, a lady wanted to paint my portrait. I remember that she had a palette in her hand and painted with a palette knife. On the palette she had some primary colors, which she had squirted out of some tubes. Then she began to mix all of those colors together. It was amazing to see the various combinations of colors that came out of those primary colors. Finally, she began to paint them on the canvas.

This exactly how spiritual gifts function. The Holy Spirit has a palette. On it are some primary gifts. They are the gifts listed in Scripture. But by the time they are spread around, there is a mixture. Each one of you becomes very stylized, individual, particular, peculiar, unique portrait.

■ Taken from *Spiritual Gifts* by John MacArthur, Jr. © 1985 Moody Bible Institute of Chicago. Moody Press. Used by permission of Moody Press.

Give Them a Choice of Assignments!

Donn McQuirk

What teacher or parent hasn't discovered that "telling" children what to do is quicker and easier than allowing them to learn to make choices? But is it the best way in the long run? Here is excellent food for thought.

No, I don't give a choice of assignments to my students. They take too much time to decide. The main thing is to cover the lesson, so I can't waste time waiting for my students to make up their minds about what they want to do! Discipline problems? Well, yes, I do have some, but doesn't every teacher?

Students who make their own choices at church school are more likely to be involved and less likely to cause disturbances than those who are assigned "unlovely tasks." Forced assignments may have the following outcomes:

- Billy dislikes art work because he thinks he isn't "good at it." When his church school teacher assigns him a picture to draw, the result is frustration and perhaps a feeling of failure. Billy may then start up some unwanted behavior in the classroom.
- Tom, a poor reader, is assigned to look up a Bible passage, read it to the class, and interpret it. Instead of immediately getting down to work, Tom will probably "goof off" and get into trouble.
- Joan, who is quite a good artist, has an idea about a picture she would like to draw to illustrate the lesson. Instead, she is assigned a map study. Joan may not create a disturbance in the classroom, but inside Joan there is a big disturbance!

Compare these two approaches:

"John, your assignment is . . ." and *"Count off by 3's; the 1's will do assignment A; the 2's assignment B . . ."*

with

"Take your choice of . . ." or *"You may choose between . . ."*

In the long run a teacher will probably spend more time dealing with unwanted behavior after making assignments than will be lost as the students make their choices. Teachers themselves have a wide range of alternative ways to give choices to students:

1. Write projects on individual index cards. Place the cards on a table top and allow students to select the one they want. Only one student may choose a particular card. Be sure to have more cards than students so all students have choices.
2. Cut out fish shapes from heavy paper. On each fish write a scripture reference and put a paper clip on the mouth end of the fish. Place all the fish in a box, deep enough so no one can see into it. Make a fishing pole from a dowel rod and string it with a small magnet tied or taped to the end. Students fish for their scripture references. If someone catches more than one fish, he selects the one he wants and throws the other one back.
3. Write each assignment on an index card. (Have a wide variety—some duplication is fine.) Put the card assignments into categories, such as map

study, word study, writing, art work, or scripture study. Mark the back of the cards in each category with the same color. Spread out the cards so students can choose a color category they prefer. Have extra assignments so a student can choose a different one if he really dislikes the assignment he draws, but do not announce this possibility.

4. Using the card assignments (as above, without color), attach a string to each card with a piece of masking tape. Each student chooses a string which he follows to "his" card on the table.

5. Students draw from a box a slip of paper with a number on it. The number matches a number on an assignment sheet.

6. Using the number matches (above), print them randomly on a piece of poster board. Then cover the numbers with either a piece of paper with a drop of rubber cement, a self-adhesive colored circle, or a small piece of masking tape that has been rubbed on a table top to pick up dust and make it easier to remove. Students pull off the covering of the number, which they match with one on the assignment sheet.

7. Display magazine pictures that could in some way illustrate a scripture verse to be studied. Print the scripture reference on the back. Students select pictures they like and then look up the scripture and explain the connection between the two. (The visual generates many ideas and helps make the scripture more easily understood.)

8. Ask students to select one of the displayed pictures and tell how they think the picture could relate to the concept being studied.

9. Collect egg cartons so that you have one cup for each student, with a few extras. Number the cups in sequence and place one assignment, folded very small, in each cup. Students draw numbers and take the corresponding assignment. A refinement is to assign each egg carton a category such as writing, reading/reporting, map study, or art work to allow student choice of categories.

10. Write the assignment on a small piece of paper or a rolled-up card and place it in a balloon, which is then inflated and tied. Each student selects and bursts a balloon to find her assignment.

Although some of these suggestions are admittedly gimmicky, they do add variety and excitement to a class session. While in most cases students do not see the exact assignment they are choosing, they still feel they have some choice.

The more opportunities we can provide for our students to make choices, the more we tell them we respect them as decision-makers. Giving students some freedom of selection helps them to "buy into" what goes on in our classroom. This one concession alone can make a difference in students' attitudes and behavior. The additional time it takes for teacher preparation can make the actual teaching easier and more satisfying.

■ Excerpted from "Give Them a Choice: The Self-Directing Alternative to Assignments," *Church Teachers* 14, no. 5 (March–May 1987). Used with permission from Harper San Francisco, a division of HarperCollins Publisher.

Expectation

LAW TWO

TOPICAL SURVEY

Expecting the Best

Alan Loy McGinnis

An expert on human potential and achievement recounts examples of people who expected the best from others, and the impact of their expectations. Learn from—and imitate—these "people-blossomers!"

Three months after retiring from a direct-sales company where she had worked twenty-five years, Mary Kay Ash decided to start her own company. Her attorney and many friends thought she was crazy to invest her life savings of $5,000 in a foolhardy idea for a cosmetics firm, but Mrs. Ash had some strongly held beliefs that she thought would work in the corporate world.

After only twenty years, the company recorded $323.8 million in sales in 1983, and over the previous five years had averaged more than a 40 percent return on equity. That is among the highest in American industry. One figure for her company is absolutely unique: there are more women earning over $50,000 per year at Mary Kay Cosmetics than at any other company in the world.

What is the secret of such success? In part it lies in the remarkably positive attitude Mrs. Ash displays toward every person on her staff. "I wanted to create a company that would give women an opportunity to accomplish anything they were smart enough to do," she says, and she apparently thinks that the people who work for her are smart enough to do anything. When one enters the gold, glass building which houses the home offices of the firm, larger-than-life photographs of the national sales directors stand out. "While some companies use paintings or sculptures or perhaps images of their products to make a statement," Mary Kay says, "we want our message to be: 'We're a people company.'"

More than anything else, it is our attitude toward the people in our classroom or office that will determine failure or success at motivation. If people know we expect good things from them, they will in most cases go to great lengths to live up to our expectations. If we expect the worst, they will meet those predictions with disappointing accuracy. So rule number one for becoming a good motivator is this:

EXPECT THE BEST FROM PEOPLE YOU LEAD

In George Bernard Shaw's play *Pygmalion* the professor helps a slattern by the name of Eliza Doolittle become an elegant lady. He does this primarily by treating her like a lady at all times until she begins to live up to his expectations of her. Goethe stated the principle this way: "Treat a man as he appears to be, and you make him worse. But treat a man as if he already were what he potentially could be, and you make him what he should be."

A famous study in the classroom by Robert Rosenthal, a Harvard psychologist, and Lenore Jacobson, a San Francisco school principal, furnishes us with a good illustration of this. They asked the question: Do some children perform poorly in school because their teachers expect them to? If so, they surmised, raising the teacher's expectations should raise the children's performances as well. So a group of kindergarten through fifth-grade pupils was given a learning ability test and the next fall the new teachers were casually given the names of five or six children in the new class who were designated as "spurters" with exceptional learning ability. What the teachers did not know was that the test results had been rigged and that the names of these "spurters" had been chosen entirely at random.

At the end of the school year, all the children were retested, with some astonishing results. The pupils whom the teachers thought had the most potential had actually scored far ahead, and had gained as many as 15 to 27 I.Q. points. The teachers described these children as happier, more curious, more affectionate than average, and having a better chance of success in later life. *The only change for the year was the change in attitudes of the teachers. Because they had been led to expect more of certain students, those children came to expect more of themselves.*

"The explanation probably lies in the subtle interaction between teacher and pupils," speculates Rosenthal. "Tone of voice, facial expressions, touch and posture may be the means by which—often unwittingly—teachers communicate their expectations to their pupils. Such communication may help a child by changing his perceptions of himself."

THE PLEASURE OF DISCOVERING HIDDEN TALENT

When we elect such a positive view, lots of buried talent begins to surface. Elbert Hubbard said, "There is something that is much more scarce, something finer far, something rarer than ability. It is the ability to recognize ability." Average people have a way of accomplishing extraordinary things for teachers and leaders who are patient enough to wait until ability becomes apparent.

The history books are full of stories of gifted persons whose talents were overlooked by a procession of people until someone believed in them. Einstein was four years old before he could speak and seven before he could read. Isaac Newton did poorly in grade school. A newspaper editor fired Walt Disney because he had "no good ideas." Leo Tolstoy flunked out of college, and Werner von Braun failed ninth-grade algebra. Haydn gave up ever making a musician of Beethoven, who seemed a slow and plodding young man with no apparent talent—except a belief in music.

There is a lesson in such stories: different people develop at different rates, and the best motivators are always on the lookout for hidden capacities.

A CLIMATE IN WHICH TO GROW

We can provide an environment in which people not only can discover their gifts but also develop them. Theodore Roosevelt wrote, "There are two kinds of success. One is the very rare kind that comes to the man who has the power to do what no one else has the power to do. That is genius. But the average man who wins what we call success is not a genius. He is a man who has merely the ordinary qualities that he shares with his fellows, but who has developed those ordinary qualities to a more than ordinary degree."

THE CAPACITY FOR STRETCHING

When Dwight D. Eisenhower was president of Columbia University, he called John Erskine "the greatest teacher Columbia ever had." Erskine was one of the most versatile men of his era—educator, concert pianist, author of sixty books, head of the Julliard School of Music, popular and witty lecturer. Writing about that remarkable career, his wife Helen attributed it to his "defiant optimism." He was a good teacher, she said, because of "his own excitement for learning and his trust in the future." He would tell her often, "Let's tell our young people that the best books are yet to be written; the best paintings have not yet been painted; the best governments are yet to be formed; the best is yet to be done by them."

CAPITALIZING ON THE DESIRE TO SUCCEED

It may seem an obvious fact, but so many leaders ignore this simple truth that I must state it explicitly: No one wants to be a failure. Nearly all of us want to succeed. "Every man believes that he has a greater possibility," Emerson said, "and all my patients, no matter how depressed and down, seem to believe that they are capable of something better. They may be behaving terribly and performing poorly, but they want to do better, and there are many reasons, they say to themselves, for their present poor performance."

To the scornful, such rationalizations are lame excuses, and it is easy to say that such persons will never live up to their talk. The road to hell is paved with good intentions, such skeptics are fond of saying. But the point is this: Deep in the breast of everyone there is a drive to achieve something, to be somebody. And therein is a wonderful entry point for the motivator. If you will tap into that drive and demonstrate that you believe in people's futures, they will do almost anything to live up to your expectations. And they will work harder for you than for anyone else in the world. Bill Hewlett, one of the founders of Hewlett-Packard, said, "Our policy flows from the belief that men and women want to do a good job, a creative job, and that if they are provided with the proper environment they will do so."

SHE WANTED ME TO SUCCEED MORE THAN I DID

I was one waiting to speak at a sales conference when the year's awards were being given to the outstanding salespeople. One woman, who had performed spectacularly that year and who had made an extraordinary amount of money, gave all the credit to her sales manager. As she stood before a crowd of three thousand people, clutching the award for best producer of the year, she recalled the slump she had been in two years previously. The future had looked so bleak that she was ready to resign and had even called her supervisor several times to quit. But the manager kept persuading her that she had not tried long enough, that she would not have been hired if there had not been unusual potential in her. Her voice cracked as she related that story. Then she made this insightful remark: "For all those months when I wanted to quit and didn't think I had any future, Joan believed in me more than I believed in myself. She wanted me to succeed even more than I did."

That sales manager had effectively employed the first rule of motivation: Expect the best from people you lead.

■ Reprinted from *Bringing Out the Best in People* by Alan Loy McGinnis, © 1985. Used by permission of Augsburg Fortress.

How to Inspire Others

Janet Dunn

Perhaps no other factor in human development is so overlooked and underused as the power of inspiration through personal praise. This article will motivate you to want to blossom others through praise!

How can you help others achieve their highest potentials in life? In the backyard scene of Act 3 of William Gibson's play *The Miracle Worker,* Helen Keller's teacher, Anne Sullivan, tries again to teach the concept of words. This gifted teacher, totally committed to her student, worked tirelessly to draw out of Helen all the treasurers buried deep inside her. Again and again she willed Helen to succeed. Watching this powerful play, I saw Helen blossom in the warm vibrance of Anne's potent love.

Over the years I've watched other scenes, scenes in real life. I've been awed by the powerful effect people have on people. I'm convinced God uses the encouraging words, positive actions, and edifying attitudes we direct at each other to strengthen our inner resolve to succeed.

PRAISE BUILDS SELF-ESTEEM

To be effective, praise should be immediate, specific, and genuine. Dr. William Mayo, co-founder of the Mayo Clinic, used praise to encourage young doctors. One young doctor said, "You'd read a paper at a staff meeting and afterwards he'd see you in the elevator or the hall, and would shake hands, or put his hand on your shoulder with a quiet 'good work' and a straight, warm look that made you think he meant it. Or perhaps a day or two later you'd get a note from him, just a short one, saying something like, 'Dear ____ , I learned more about ____ from that paper of yours the other night than I ever knew before. It was a good job.' Believe me, a fellow prized those notes."[1]

ACTIONS THAT EDIFY

Actions that pave the way for another person to succeed are powerful motivators. When I was a college freshman, I wanted to tell others about Christ, but I didn't know how. Chris, my Bible study leader, sensed my struggle and started coaching me one-on-one. First she helped me write out my testimony. Then she gave me key verses to memorize and taught me a simple illustration to explain the plan of salvation.

A few weeks later, she took me with her for a coffee date with two non-Christian freshmen she was befriending. Over ice cream, Chris skillfully guided the conversation onto spiritual issues. When one of the girls asked, "How does a person become a Christian?" Chris turned to me and said, "Janet, why don't you answer that?"

I was so excited that I talked and talked and talked. I told them all they wanted to know and a lot they didn't want to know. But Chris was willing to let me blow this excellent opportunity because she knew I needed to learn by doing. Chris' consistent love in action, her step-by-step practical help, strengthened my resolve to learn to share my faith.

ATTITUDES ARE THE KEY

More than words or actions, our positive attitudes have a powerful effect on others. The woman caught in adultery is a graphic case in point (John 8). It's clear from the passage how the Pharisees viewed her. "Moses commanded us to stone such women," they told Jesus. How different Jesus' attitude was! He looked at her and said, "Woman, where are they? Has no one condemned you?" She said, "No one, sir." Jesus said, "Then neither do I condemn you. . . . Go now and leave your life of sin." I can't help thinking that the woman in this story spent the rest of her life living up to the view Jesus held of her.

A few months ago, in a deep discussion with a close friend about an area of my life I wanted to change, I said, "But what if it's too late? What if that area is like a house plant that totally withered and died for lack of watering?"

My friend looked at me with surprise and deep compassion. "But you're not a house plant! You have a soul and that never dies!"

Those words, said with conviction, soaked into my heart like warm spring rain. I could feel hope begin to push up through the soil of my heart. My friend believed in my capacity for comeback and that faith gave new life to mine.

ENCOURAGE ONE ANOTHER DAY AFTER DAY

The mandate to "encourage one another," "build each other up," "spur one another on to love and good works" is woven all through the New Testament. All of us have savored the enriching effects of affirmation. Why is it, then, that we sometimes pocket the praise we should pass on to others or side-step the practical help we could offer to open the way for another to succeed?

Sometimes it's simply because we are lazy or selfish or fall into the habit of taking people for granted. Sometimes it's just easier to find fault. At times we underestimate the encouragement our words and actions can be to another person, or we assume our approval is obvious. Occasionally people fear that praise might be a stumbling block, triggering pride in another person. Jesus didn't fear that when He hailed Nathanael: "Here is a true Israelite, in whom there is nothing false" (John 1:47). What a compliment!

Today why not ask God for an opportunity to offer genuine praise to someone in your world? Ask Him to use you to run alongside another person and encourage him toward his goal. Praise, practical help, encouragement—all of these flow out of us naturally and genuinely when we begin to see, as Anne Sullivan saw, the untapped potential buried inside each individual.

Notes

1. Helen Clapesattle, *The Doctors Mayo* (Minneapolis: University of Minnesota Press, 1941), 384.

■ Excerpted from "Inspiring Others," *Discipleship Journal* 5, no. 4 (July 1985), pp. 26-29. Used by permission.

You Are Not a Nobody!

Charles R. Swindoll

When you wonder whether history will be different because of your teaching, recall this article. You may have the next world-changer in your class! You are SOMEBODY—a teacher of world-changers!

You are YOU. There is only one YOU. And YOU are important. Want to start feeling better? Really desire to dispel discouragement? I can say it all in three words: Start being YOU.

Pull a sheet of scratch paper out of your memory bank and see how well you do with the following questions:

1. Who taught Martin Luther his theology and inspired his translation of the New Testament?
2. Who visited Dwight L. Moody at a shoe store and spoke to him about Christ?
3. Who worked alongside and encouraged Harry Ironside as his associate pastor?
4. Who was the wife of Charles Haddon Spurgeon?
5. Who was the elderly woman who prayed faithfully for Billy Graham for over twenty years?
6. Who financed William Carey's ministry in India?
7. Who refreshed the apostle Paul in that Roman dungeon as he wrote his last letter to Timothy?
8. Who helped Charles Wesley to get underway as a composer of hymns?
9. Who found the Dead Sea Scrolls?
10. Who personally taught G. Campbell Morgan, the "peerless expositor," his techniques in the pulpit?
11. Who followed Hudson Taylor and gave the China Inland Mission its remarkable vision and direction?
12. Who discipled George Müller and snatched him as a young man from a sinful lifestyle?
13. Who were the parents of the godly and gifted prophet Daniel?

Okay, how did you do? Over fifty percent? Maybe twenty-five percent? Not quite that good?

Before you excuse your inability to answer the questions by calling the quiz "trivia," better stop and think. Had it not been for those unknown people—those "nobodies"—a huge chunk of church history would be missing. And a lot of lives would have been untouched.

Nobodies.

What a necessary band of men and women . . . servants of the King . . . yet nameless in the kingdom! Men and women who, with silent heroism, yet faithful diligence, relinquish the limelight and live in the shade of public figures.

What was it Jim Elliot, the martyred messenger of the gospel to the Aucas, once called missionaries? Something like a bunch of nobodies trying to exalt Somebody. But don't mistake anonymous for unnecessary. Otherwise, the whole Body gets crippled . . . even paralyzed . . . or, at best, terribly dizzy as the majority of the members within the Body become diseased with self-pity and discouragement. Face it, friend, the Head of the Body calls the shots. It is His prerogative to publicize some and hide others. Don't ask me why He chooses whom He uses.

If it's His desire to use you as a Melanchthon rather than a Luther . . . or a Kimball rather than a Moody . . . or an Onesiphorus rather than a Paul . . . or a Hoste rather than a Taylor, relax!

Better than that, give God praise! You're among that elite group mentioned in 1 Corinthians 12 as:

> . . . some of the parts that seem weakest and least important are really the most necessary. . . . So God has put the body together in such a way that extra honor and care are given to those parts that might otherwise seem less important (vv. 22, 24, TLB).

If it weren't for the heroic "nobodies," we wouldn't have top-notch officers to give a church its leadership. Or quality sound when everyone shows up to worship. Or janitors who clean when everyone is long gone. Or committees to provide dozens of services behind the scenes. Or mission volunteers who staff offices at home or work in obscurity overseas with only a handful of people. Come to think of it, if it weren't for the faithful "nobodies," you wouldn't even have this book in your hands right now.

Nobodies . . . exalting Somebody.

Are you one? Listen to me! It's the "nobodies" Somebody chooses so carefully. And when He has selected you for that role, He does not consider you a nobody.

Be encouraged!

The Law of Encouragement

Howard G. Hendricks

*Would you like to know what one of the world's greatest motivators
thinks about the subject of motivation? Here is a chance to learn from
one who has spent a lifetime motivating students—SUCCESSFULLY!*

The number one problem in education today is the failure to motivate
learners—to get them off the dime and into action. The longer I
teach, the more convinced I am that a person's M.Q.—his Motivation Quotient—is
more important than his I.Q.

Teaching tends to be most effective when the learner is properly motivated.
Underline the word *properly* in that definition, because it tells us there is such a thing
as improper motivation—illegitimate motivation that can bring devastating results.

One form of it is what I call lollipop motivation: "Son, behave yourself in church
this morning and I'll buy you an ice cream cone." Or, "Memorize two hundred verses
of Scripture and we'll send you to camp for a week." Now those sound good, and they
can make students do good things. But it's altogether possible that those good things
will not have good results.

Another improper motivation is guilt. That is another reason many people
memorize Scripture: I can't be a first-class Christian if I don't memorize these verses. In
fact, this is probably one of the most common motivations some Christian communicators use. They keep piling the guilt higher and higher, and the people keep making
the formations and salivating when you ring the bell. But for all the wrong reasons.

Yet another improper motivation involves deceit—intentional or unintentional. If I
told you I knew a success formula and convinced you that if you tried it immediately it
would totally revolutionize your life, you probably would give it a shot, but only once. It
had better work the first time, or that would be the last thing you would listen to from me.

So friend, let's stop promising people more than Christianity promises them, more
than the Scriptures promise them. Don't say, "If you come to Christ, all your problems
will be solved." That is how people get disillusioned. Sure, Christ will meet their needs,
but not according to your script, or in your time, or in your way.

TWO LEVELS OF MOTIVATION

There are two levels of motivation. The first is extrinsic motivation—motivation
from without. The second is more significant—intrinsic motivation which comes from
within. Your task in all extrinsic motivation is to trigger intrinsic motivation. You wish
you could crawl inside a student, rummage around, find his hot button and press it. But
you can't. You have to work on the outside to get something to happen on the inside.

We have too many parents and teachers who think their primary goal with a child
is to rear a good boy or a good girl. But their job is to rear a good man or a good
woman—that is, a self-starter who is internally loaded. We have too many people at
age forty-six who are still good boys and girls. As a teacher you want to help people
develop into selfstarters. You want them to do what they do not because you ask them or
you twist their arm, but because they themselves have chosen to do it. One of the best
ways to trigger this choice is to help the learner become aware of his need.

I once met a seminary student on his way to give an evangelistic talk at a fraternity house on a university campus. He asked for my prayers.

"What do you want me to pray for?" I asked. "Pray they won't go for my jugular," he said. I told him I was going to pray they did exactly that. The next day he said, "The Lord answered your prayer." They shredded him. But today he has one of the best ministries to college students in America, and he looks back to that day in the fraternity as the point when he really got the picture—when he discovered how much he didn't know.

MOTIVATION THROUGH TRAINING

You motivate people by correctly structuring their training experience. Training involves four major stages:

1. The *telling* stage

The first is the *telling* stage, and we are usually strongest here. I always recommend in this stage that the content be recorded both in writing and on tape. Don't make learners depend on just one exposure to the content, but put it in a form they can review repeatedly. Only then will they begin to catch on.

2. The *showing* stage

The next stage is the *showing* stage. You provide a model. What does it look like? Flesh it out. Let them watch you out there in the alligator pits, sweating it out, relating truth to your life. When they see it in action, they will say, "Hey, that's what I want."

We often miss it here. In our Sunday school teacher training courses we say, "Come next week for a very important session on storytelling." Next week they come, and the instructor gets up and says, "Stories are very important. Jesus told stories. All the great teachers have told stories. There are five major parts to a story and here they are . . . " Then he comes to the end of the presentation and says, "Anyone have a question?" But who would? They wouldn't know a story if they fell over it. "Come back next week for another exciting teacher training session," we say, and they stay away in droves.

3. and 4. The *doing* stages: controlled and uncontrolled

Stages three and four involve *doing*—but in different ways: first in a controlled situation, then in uncontrolled, real-life situations. I have never heard of a correspondence course in swimming. No, you learn to swim by swimming, not by reading books and not by watching the pros go up and down the pool. You have got to get wet.

I think I have taken seven courses in personal evangelism. I thought about that one day and counted them up. Honesty compels me to say not one of them did a blessed thing for me. In one course in college, we memorized a list of Scripture verses matched with common objections people have to the gospel. Then they sent us to Union Station in Chicago. The first guy I talked with brought up an objection that wasn't on that list. And I was hung!

TRAINING BY RESPONSIBILITY WITH ACCOUNTABILITY

Another mark of good training is giving people responsibility with accountability. Our problem in the churches is that we don't do that. The United States Government takes multi-million dollar planes and puts them in the hands of kids nineteen years old; and when those same kids come to church, we don't even let them take up the offering.

Ever been in a courtroom where a will is being read? The reader is mumbling his way over the legal jargon, and everyone else in the room is half asleep—everyone, that is, except the person named in the will as the beneficiary.

The application: When your teaching has the learner's name written all over it—

when he sees that, in effect, his name occurs throughout the Book, and it's personal—it will make a big difference in his level of motivation. Some of the best motivators I know never work in a classroom. They are teachers without the label—men and women who are doing discipleship and changing the lives and the perspectives of other people. Why? Because they are willing to flow into other people's lives.

I am convinced that everyone—no exception—can be motivated to learn. But not at the same time, and not by the same person, and not in the same way. The timing is crucial. Teaching is the assembling of a time bomb in a classroom, marked for explosion at a later date and in a different location. That is why you need to walk by faith to be a good teacher, and you need a lot of patience. And you aren't God's answer to every individual. That is what the body of Christ is all about. You can teach people I couldn't touch with a twenty-foot pole, and someone else can teach others whom neither you nor I could.

I have had the privilege of teaching high school students as well as adults of every age. I have taught professional career people and people who are underprivileged. I have taught groups of men and groups of women. I have taught doctors and lawyers, and I have taught children. And every one of these groups brings to the class a different set of interests that can be creatively harnessed. Take teenagers, for example. "We can't get these kids excited about the Word of God," I hear. But I don't believe that. Our problem is that we aren't willing enough to put our creative hooks into the area of their interests and abilities.

ARE *YOU* MOTIVATED?

I'm asked over and over again, "How do you get a person motivated?" I answer, "When you sock someone with twenty thousand volts of electricity, they don't turn to you and ask, 'Did you say something?' No, they move." The key question is, "Are *you* motivated?" Because motivated people become change agents.

In his book *The Crisis in the University*, Sir Walter Moberly cites the failure of evangelicals to penetrate university campuses with the gospel. To those who claim to follow Christ he says, "If one-tenth of what you believe is true, you ought to be ten times as excited as you are." So many people in our churches have never become impassioned about the only thing ultimately worth getting impassioned about. So if it's exciting, get excited!

■ Excerpted from *Journal of Christian Camping* 20, no. 4 (July–August 1988), pp. 26-35, official publication of Christian Camping International/USA. © July–August, 1988, Christian Camping International/USA.

The Art of Incidental Praise

Joan Rae Mills

Small, consistent steps usually produce greater progress than the infrequent leap. The same is true with praise. The consistent use of incidental praise can change the life of the recipient. Try it and see!

When my high school creative writing teacher returned a poem I had written with the words, "You write some good poetry" scrawled at the bottom, my self-confidence soared. The note took him less than ten seconds, yet ten years later I still draw strength from his remark. Little did he know the effect he had on me. And little did he realize the seed he had planted would bloom so that when I became a teacher, I would attempt to encourage my students in the same way.

Praise is something everyone needs. It is true "soul food." No one grows up healthy without it. And who is in a better position to give praise than a teacher? Our students are with us week after week—often coming to Sunday school and church hungry for a bit of recognition and encouragement.

This affirming seems time-consuming, but if we work at it, we can do it easily and naturally, making it a part of our regular contacts. Brief compliments can be given in a casual way, even as you pass a child in the hallway. Stickers have become quite a craze lately, and they offer another alternative. Stick them on a piece of paper, jot a note to a student and hand it to him discreetly. Special notes or comments written directly on a notebook page or take-home paper work well, especially for students to whom public praise may be embarrassing. It also allows them to savor the moment a bit longer.

But what about the rebellious or uncooperative students? Look for something they do right, even if it's the obvious, the expected. I remember one junior high boy who was ordinary—and restless. He didn't walk into the room, he skidded. Sensing this show-off routine as "hunger pangs," I searched for something to say. Then I thought, "He's on time." So although this is only expected behavior, I told him as he was leaving for the day, "I like the way you're on time." The next day the young man was early, quietly sitting in his seat, and had arrived by simply walking!

Perhaps you could praise a student for neat writing, another for always studying his lesson; still another for being friendly to a newcomer. Or you could create a situation by asking a student to run an errand and then praise her for the way she did it. Just knowing that someone notices the good they do gives students more encouragement and hope than we will ever realize.

The benefits of praising children are reason enough to do it. But true to the laws of sowing and reaping, benefits return. My joy was great when recently a student passed me a note with a few words of praise on it.

Did he know what he was doing for me by his praise?

Excerpted from *Christian Education Today* 38, no. 2 (Spring 1986), p. 21. Used by permission.

How to Speak with Emotion

The World's Greatest Teachers!

What if every sunset or sunrise was a battleship gray—every day? Unfortunately, our speech is often that uninspiring. Imitate God's style by building colorful variety into your speech. Become a verbal sunrise!

When you speak, do you convey emotion? What color are your words? What temperature? What mood is conveyed? In short, do you know how to speak *emotionally*? The following examples of "feeling" and "expectation" words will help you communicate with maximum effect.

"FEELING" WORDS

The focus here is the emotional response or reaction to another's positive behavior; how I feel about what they've accomplished.

I feel (. . . . .) in light of what you've done!

accepted	encouraged	joyful	sobered
affirmed	energetic	lighthearted	sociable
aglow	envious	loved	special
alive	excited	lucky	spiritual
amused	exhilarated	motherly	stimulated
appreciated	expectant	motivated	sunny
approachable	fascinated	natural	supported
astonished	respectful	needed	supportive
attractive	fatherly	nurtured	surprised
awed	forgiven	optimistic	tearful
brave	fortunate	peaceful	tender
brotherly	genuine	pleased	thankful
bubbly	glad	positive	thoughtful
calm	good	proud	thrilled
challenged	grateful	quiet	understanding
cheerful	gratified	reflective	understood
childlike	grown up	refreshed	unique
clean	happy	relaxed	uplifted
comfortable	honored	relieved	valued
committed	hopeful	responsive	virtuous
competent	humbled	rewarded	warm inside
confident	independent	satisfied	whole
content	influential	secure	wonderful
courageous	intelligent	sentimental	worshipful
creative	intimate	serene	worthwhile
determined	involved	significant	youthful

"EXPECTATION" WORDS

The focus here is on the development of general character and maturity traits; what I see a person's character becoming which will insure their success in any endeavor.

I see you as a person who is (. . . .) in light of what you have done!

- achieving new heights in
- becoming better at
- becoming more consistent
- becoming wiser
- demonstrating maturity in
- desirous of
- discovering
- increasingly able to
- increasingly secure in
- learning
- more and more willing to
- more confident in
- more dedicated to
- more relaxed in
- showing
- so skilled at
- the kind of person who
- unusually unique

I see you as a person who is making great progress in your (. . . .)

- ability to be an asset wherever you are
- choice of values
- choosing of friends
- commitment to
- difficult decisions
- discernment in
- following through on hard jobs
- fruit of the Spirit
- handling of money
- hard work in
- humility
- involvements in church (community, school, academic, athletic, leadership) achievements
- leadership traits
- loyalty to friends/family
- mental, physical, spiritual purity
- perseverance in trials
- perspective on worldly things
- resistance to temptation
- respect for authority
- self-control
- setting of priorities
- spiritual disciplines

The Power of Encouraging Words

Donald Bubna with Al Janssen

Every parent and teacher has personally witnessed the power of words to encourage or discourage. Our challenge is to become encouragers. Let a pastor known for encouragement encourage you—to encourage!

Words that encourage are words that say "I believe in you. You are of great importance. God has given you great abilities."

Watermelon season was one of my favorite times of year when I was a boy. Rather than buy our melons at the market where they were sold by the pound, we usually bought ours right off a farmer's truck. One summer day, as our family was taking a walk, we saw a farmer selling his truckload of watermelons. They were the first ones of the season.

Dad picked a nice ripe one. "Can I carry it?" I asked. "I'll carry it," said my father in his normal, abrupt manner. My father, a product of the work ethic, did not express himself well verbally. To him, what one did spoke louder than anything said. I didn't understand this as a boy.

I was very conscious of my skinniness and knew I wasn't physically as well built as most boys my age. Dad's rebuff was painful to my ego. Again I asked, "Please, Dad, let me carry the watermelon." "You're not big enough," he said. My ego was shattered. I began to whimper. "Why don't you let him try?" my mother suggested.

"All right," he said, and he plunked the melon in my arms. I had no idea that watermelons were so heavy, and I wasn't prepared for the sudden weight. It slid right through my arms and cracked open on the pavement below.

"See, I knew you couldn't do it," said my father as he bent over to retrieve the pieces. Inwardly I felt as crushed as the broken watermelon on the pavement.

Sounds like an innocent comment, doesn't it. I'm sure my dad forgot it within the hour. But so many years later I still remember the pain of that moment, though I fully realize my father in no way meant to hurt me.

God has given each of us a tongue—a simple, basic tool to help us encourage one another. It has been given to all—young and old, rich and poor, wise and foolish. It is a tool we can use to discourage or to encourage. Too often we use the tongue to tear down people rather than to build them up. And it is in the closest relationships that we are usually the most critical. Criticism done in the wrong spirit undermines a person's self-esteem. It can make that person become critical of others.

We also hurt people with our ridicule and sarcasm. "What makes you think you're so smart?" or, "That's the stupidest question I've ever heard." Laughing at another's mistakes, making fun of a person, and labeling people as "klutz," "lazy," "sloppy," "stupid," or "fatty" may get a laugh from others, and even from the victim, but such words often leave painful wounds. We can discourage people by trying to show off our superior knowledge.

Sometimes we hurt people just by talking too much, leaving them no time to express themselves. It gives others the impression that what they have to say is relatively unimportant compared with our words of wisdom.

WHEN WORDS HEAL

I saw the contrast between negative and positive input in high school. My high school typing teacher didn't like me. I'm glad I don't remember her name. "You'll never pass this course," she said to me one day. "You're behind! I don't care if you were sick. You're not going to make it."

Frustrated by her words, I mentioned my problem to the school counselor. "She's not going to give you a chance," the counselor said when we were alone. "Drop the course and come here each day at that period and help me with a major project. I could use your skills." She helped me develop a sense of confidence in myself as I worked with her in the school office for the rest of the semester. Her affirmation put me far ahead of where I would have been had I continued to struggle in that typing class. Later I made up the typing course with another teacher.

That counselor was one of the reasons I even attended college. "You have the potential and can do college work," she said. She wasn't concerned about the fact that no one else on either side of my family had ever completed college. She believed in me, and that was enough to encourage me to make much better grades in college than I had in high school.

A FEW WELL-CHOSEN WORDS

When I think of the power of a few well-chosen words, I think of people like Bill Ward, my Sunday school teacher in the primary grades. I can't remember a specific lesson he taught or even one book of the Bible we studied. But I remember he once observed how I made a tough decision and commented, "You are a courageous young man. You can stand alone." You never know how a simple, well-placed word of encouragement might change a person's life!

Words that encourage are words that communicate: "I believe in you. You are of great importance. God has given you great abilities." We often have the opportunity to speak a positive or affirming word but hesitate to do so because it can sound like flattery. People may think we are trying to get on the good side of someone who can advance our position.

Angela, a third grader, was struggling and her teacher knew it. She handed in a writing assignment that had nearly every word misspelled. The wise teacher had caught something of "the wisdom that is from above," and chose to say, "Angela, you've done a good job staying in the margins. And your letters are very clear and easy to read."

"Thank you, teacher!" said Angela with a big smile. "And now I'm going to work on my spelling!" Proverbs says, "Words fitly spoken are like apples of gold." Because that statement is true, we are amply equipped to pour out great riches to those around us.

WRITE IT!

Verbal words of encouragement can do so much, but an even better way to encourage someone is to write a note. There is something about a personal note that communicates, "You are special." Many reasons can be given for writing instead of waiting to tell the person.

- **It assures getting it done.** We may not see that person for a couple of weeks. We can easily put off a phone call, or the line may be busy, or the person might not be home. What we want to say may be hazy by the time we see her or talk to him. Besides, often a written note is less of an interruption than a phone call, and it also takes less time.

- **It shows love and forethought.** Taking time out to write even a brief word communicates a deliberate act of love, not something that accidentally came out of a conversation.
- **A note is preserved for remembrance and review.** When people receive notes of encouragement, particularly hand-written notes, they read them and reread them, save them and savor them for a long time.
- **Letters go to faraway places.** Writing allows us to encourage people who live a long way from us, or with whom, for whatever reason, we are not able to make any other kind of contact.

PRACTICAL TIPS

- **Whom to write.** Friends who mean a lot to us should be told just how much they mean. Family members and relatives need to hear our words of encouragement. May we never have to say, "I meant to tell them while they were alive. . . ." Short notes are a means of making new friends. A simple note that says, "I enjoyed meeting you," or "I hope you enjoyed our group (or class, or service) today" makes for a great start. A timely note to a leader can encourage them to persevere when they might otherwise be discouraged.
- **When to write.** Write whenever someone comes to mind. It helps to carry around a supply of postcards. Then, as you think of people, it is easy to get off a quick note. Special occasions such as birthdays are good times for note writing. I enjoy receiving greeting cards, but I'm always a little disappointed if the senders don't also write at least a line of their own. When we are feeling down ourselves, writing someone else might help to get our attention off our own situation and give someone else a lift.
- **How to write.** It's best to be brief. One of the advantages of using cards is that it forces us to be brief. The limited space forces me to say my message in two or three sentences. Use warm and affirming words written in your own handwriting. If your penmanship isn't good, you might type a note. Even then, a short, handwritten note at the bottom makes it much more personal. Be careful about using Bible verses. A thoughtfully selected verse can be significant if you share what the verse has meant in your own life, rather than using it to preach. Be careful about using Romans 8:28—"We know that in all things God works for the good of those who love him." Of course it is true, but it may not be immediately fitting in the face of tragedy.

The Power of a Hug

Kathy Paterson

Scientific studies on both human and animal young have documented the negative developmental impact of the absence of touch. Are there some around us whose self-esteem awaits the stimulus of a loving hug?

I once had the exhilarating experience of working with a group of academically unmotivated—but decidedly street-wise—twelve-year-olds. As their teacher, I spent more of my time monitoring their behavior and playing counselor, mediator, and facilitator for them and the authorities (with whom they always seemed to be in conflict) than I did "teaching" in the true sense of the word.

THE POWER OF A HUG

Unfortunately, the traditional methods of dealing with angry or upset students simply didn't work with these kids. They laughed at the behavior modification attempts, refuted positive reinforcement, and were unaffected and unperturbed by detentions or additional assignments (which they didn't do anyway).

To their credit, however, they were completely, undeniably loyal to anyone lucky enough to establish rapport with them and gain their respect. Needless to say, doing so was a difficult task, and one with which I was still realizing only shaky success on the memorable day in November when "hug therapy" was introduced to our classroom.

A particularly surly boy was having another particularly bad day. I had exhausted all the intervention tactics I knew, and still he stormed around, refusing to do anything constructive. Finally, in desperation, I said to him, "I don't know what to do with you or for you! What is it you want me to do?" He looked at me defiantly and spat out, "How should I know?" Without thinking, I blurted out, "Well, how about a hug, then?"

He stopped pacing instantly and looked at me with unabashed surprise. Then, without warning, he literally threw his arms around me and held on. I hugged him tightly for about ten seconds.

The effect was incredible. He rewarded me with a beautiful smile and said simply, "Thanks." Then he returned to his desk and sat down quietly. I'd like to report that he then started working, but that would not be true. However, he did calm down, and his interference with the rest of the class stopped.

THE EFFECT OF A HUG

That was the beginning! Hugs became a common intervention method in my class. One of the kids brought me a large orange pin that read, "I want a hug." I left it on my desk, and kids would often pick it up and "wear" it—their way of saying that they were having a bad day.

No one misused this technique, and I witnessed positive behavior changes in many of the kids. For some, a hug was simply a bandage—a quick treatment for the prevention of inappropriate behavior escalation, or a small dose of "tender, loving care" for the blues. For others, it had a more lasting, calming effect. One of these was the boy I have just spoken of, who regularly came for a hug at the onset of a day, and seldom again displayed the impossible behavior with which he had begun the year.

I realized that hugging twelve-year-olds, many of whom were physically bigger than I was, was a potentially dangerous action. Our 1980s "hands off" approach decrees that a teacher shall not touch a student in any way. In fact, our entire society appears to have gone overboard on the "touching as sexual abuse" issue, to the point where the simple expression of affection or caring is seriously frowned upon.

THE NEED FOR A HUG

Certainly it is true that children must be protected from inappropriate sexual advances, but I wonder if, in our zeal to "protect," we have not taken away a very valuable and necessary ingredient of life and the growing-up process—that of physical closeness. Children, particularly pre-adolescents and adolescents, are notoriously insecure and thus are fraught with feelings of uncertainty. Are we really helping them by denying them the wonderful virtues of a hug, which can instantly, if temporarily, remove or alleviate these feelings?

Literature and industry constantly avow the merits of the hug, and we have all heard heartbreaking reports of children who were raised in environments in which they were deprived physical contact and who subsequently did not develop as well as their "handled" counterparts. The consumer market is swamped with posters recognizing the value of, and in fact the indispensability of, the hug.

The simple hug has long been recognized as an understated, powerful action. Yet, teachers are sometimes strictly forbidden to hug their students, kids with whom they spend as much or more time during the school term as do any other adults.

Granted, the hug can be misused—hence, the current overcautiousness about sexual abuse. But why not think positively by having faith in human nature, replace pessimism and suspicion with optimism, and learn again to demonstrate genuine affection with a hug when it is warranted?

A hug is simply a hug, nothing more, nothing less. Given with warmth and unconditional regard, it holds no devious, underlying sexual connotations. Rather, it is an expression of humanity and caring, a form of nonverbal communication that can be understood by even the most distraught child and a confirmation of support when words are not enough. How magnificent that so simple a gesture can mean so much! How unfortunate that adults today are cautioned to withhold this demonstration of affection, or to give it with a disquieting sense of trepidation.

THE DECISION TO HUG

It was my conscious choice, in my classroom, to overcome my personal hesitancies (which were not actually mine anyway, but those imposed on me by current societal beliefs) and provide hugs where needed. I never once regretted that decision, and it never once became a problem.

In fact, I believe sincerely that my willingness to hug led to better student performance and improved harmony and classroom cohesiveness. An ancient proverb says that love makes all hearts gentle. My classroom experience led me to believe that this is true.

Individuals, of course, are just that—individual—and what works for one, or even the majority, does not work for all. This is also true of hugging. Some kids simply do not like or want to be touched, and the compassionate adult must quickly discern and respect this message. I found such kids to be in the minority, and, in fact, most of them had demonstrated a definite "warming trend" by the end of the term.

One of the highlights of my teaching career came on the last day of school when a boy who had initially shown severe distaste for any form of physical closeness honored me with a mammoth bear hug. No words could ever have expressed so perfectly his thoughts at that time.

But just as students differ, so do teachers, and I realize that not all educators are comfortable with the physical expression of appreciation or affection. So be it! Certainly, hugging cannot be forced, for kids are quick to recognize and reject superficiality. These teachers have their own ways of communicating their feelings to the students. However, for those of us whose natural instinct is to share a hug, for whatever reason, the benefits of this action should be recognized rather than rebuffed.

Another proverb suggests that "Hearts may agree though heads differ." If we examine the hug from the heart, surely its innocuous and beneficial status can be confirmed, and teachers can, once again, feel free "to hug or not to hug."

■ From *The Education Digest* 69 (1988), pp. 17-19, Ann Arbor, Michigan. Used by permission.

Three Proven Ways to Motivate Children

Gary Smalley

If you had to list three proven techniques to motivate children, what would they be? Have you considered "salting their oats?" How about their natural bent? Do you use word pictures? This expert uses all three!

True motivation comes from one or (a combination of) two factors: a desire for gain or fear of loss.

Working with young children, teenagers, and college-age young people for more than thirty years has made me aware of over twenty ways to motivate children. At the heart of each of these methods is the desire for gain and the fear of loss. In this article, we will focus on three of the most powerful ways to motivate children.

1. USE A CHILD'S NATURAL BENT.

Often there is a combination of personality types in a child, but usually one is predominant. When motivating a child by using his or her "natural bent" it is important to learn the child's basic interests and talents. Our daughter Kari's strong interest is to become a school teacher. We have used this goal to motivate her to eat healthier foods, play on the high school basketball team, and study more diligently in school by showing her that she will be better prepared physically and mentally to be a good teacher.

Our son, Greg, wants to be a zoo keeper. We have visited different zoos and talked about what it takes to be a good zoo keeper. Because a zoo must be neat and orderly, we have motivated Greg to keep his room more neatly arranged. We have given him books about animals to encourage him to be a better reader which has motivated him to do well in school. He's enjoyed doing several research papers because of his strong interest in animals.

When you use children's interests to motivate them, the resulting progress is often amazing. Motivating a child through his interests is effective because it comes from within him. It reflects his bent.

2. USE THE SALT PRINCIPLE

We are all familiar with the saying, "You can lead a horse to water but you can't make him drink." But that's not necessarily true. If you dump salt in the horse's oats, he will become thirsty and want to drink. The more salt you dump on his oats, the thirstier he becomes and the more he wants to drink.

The Salt Principle motivates children to listen carefully and thereby learn some important truths about life. It can be used to teach children many important lessons. Here are some guidelines for using salt effectively:

1. Clearly identify what you wish to communicate.
2. Identify your listener's most important interests.
3. Using their areas of high interest, share just enough of your idea to stimulate curiosity to hear more.
4. Use questions to increase curiosity.

5. Communicate your important information or idea only after you see you have your child's full interest and attention.

Not long ago, I wanted to teach my son Mike an important lesson. If I had said, "Hey, how about a Bible lesson together, just the two of us?" you can imagine the response: "Yeah Dad, maybe later, OK?" or perhaps, "Oh no, not one of those again." We are an ordinary family and I realize that my children often are not interested in what I consider to be important for their lives. But I can salt their interest by relating to things they are interested in. Here's how I used it with Mike:

"Hey, Mike? Want me to tell you a story?" I asked.

"No, Dad. I'm playing right now. Maybe later."

"Well OK, then I won't tell you about a crazy, wild man who lived in the mountains, and he was so strong he could break chains and no one could hold him down and he made these horrible screams so no one would get near him."

I paused and Mike immediately piped up, "That's in the Bible?"

"Yes. And you won't believe what happened to him. Maybe sometime I'll tell you the story."

"No, tell me now, please!" So I proceeded to tell Mike the story about how Jesus healed the demoniac in the region of the Gerasenes.

I had a high school English teacher who used salt to motivate us to read books. He would read to the class from a book. Then just when he got to the most exciting part, he'd stop reading and close the book. Naturally, we'd all say, "What happened?"

"It's in the book," would be his reply.

"What page?" we'd beg.

"You'll find it."

And so we'd dash to the library to check out the book, and many times we'd read the entire book to find out what happened. Norma used the same method to motivate our children to read fifty books one summer.

Look around and see how many people use salt. Television shows twenty– or thirty–second previews of upcoming programs. They show you the most exciting scenes, but don't let you know how they are resolved. They'll show a car flying over a barrier in a chase scene, but in order to find out if it lands or crashes, you have to watch the show.

It's important to remember that the Salt Principle stems from a desire to serve a child's real or felt needs and interests. It guides that child toward fulfillment of his goals, while helping him gain important information that is vital to becoming a mature adult.

The next area is as equally effective in motivation as using a child's natural bent and using the Salt Principle. However, using it not only motivates a child, but I have never used anything more effective to communicate with children. This is the best method I've found for causing positive adjustments between parents and children.

3. USE EMOTIONAL WORD PICTURES.

Using word pictures to motivate others is identifying with them emotionally. It's motivating on an emotional level. Jesus Christ was a master at using emotional word pictures. He used natural things and experiences to teach truth. He said things like, "The kingdom of God is like finding a valuable pearl." Or "Unless we fall to the ground like a seed and die, we will never produce the true fruit of life." "I am the good shepherd." "Faith is like a mustard seed." "I am the light of the world." These word pictures illustrate truths that are understandable to man because they are put in the context of human experience and emotions.

I've witnessed the power and effectiveness of emotional word pictures in my own home. It took five minutes to help my son change an irritating habit. I travel frequently throughout the country and am often gone for several days at a time. When I arrive home, the whole family usually greets me. It is an encouragement when they rush out to hug me and yell, "Welcome home, Dad!" When our son Greg was twelve, he would usually join in the welcome, but there was a time when, after the initial greeting, he would avoid me for an hour or two. I would try to touch him or ask him what He'd done while I was gone, but he'd say, "Just leave me alone, I don't want to talk."

That bothered me. He was acting like his spirit was closed toward me, but I hadn't done anything to him. I asked Norma what she thought was wrong and she explained that Greg was probably angry because I had been gone, and this was his way of punishing me.

I wanted Greg to understand how his rejection hurt me, so one evening a couple of days after I'd returned from a trip, I took him out for dinner just the two of us. After dinner, I made up a story relating to his participation on the school basketball team.

"Greg, suppose you made first string on the basketball team and you were playing well, and suddenly you got an injury. We took you to the doctor and he said you couldn't play for two weeks so the injury would heal. So you don't play, but you show up at practices. Then after two weeks, you're ready to play again, but the rest of the players and the coach just ignore you. They act like you aren't even there. How would that make you feel?"

"Dad, that would really hurt. I wouldn't want to go through that."

"That's somewhat how I feel when I come home from a trip and you welcome me home, but then reject me for an hour or two. I want to get back on the family team, but I feel you are ignoring me."

"I didn't know that," he said. "That really makes sense. I won't do it anymore."

About two weeks later, I left for a trip. As I was getting into the car after saying goodbye to my family, Greg yelled, "Have a great trip, Dad. And get ready to be rejected when you get home." We all laughed, but he remembered, and never again did he reject me when I returned home.

Emotional word pictures can be used with anyone. Try using emotional word pictures with your mate or a good friend before trying it on your children. The more you practice, the better you will become, and you will see that this simple motivating force is very powerful.

■ Excerpted from Gary Smalley's book *The Key to Your Child's Heart,* © 1984 Word Books, Dallas, Texas. Used by permission.

Secrets to Building Confident Youth

Margaret Houk

Words like "fragile" and "precarious" are used to describe the emotional and spiritual state of youth in the teen years. Here is practical help for those called to nurture, teach, and blossom these tender ones.

There is nothing teens need more than self-esteem. They want it. God wants it for them. But it is very hard to come by during those trying years of gawky legs and social awkwardness.

You can't give a person self-esteem. It is something people have to give themselves, a true do-it-yourself job. But there are ways by which those who live and work with teens can help them along the road.

LISTEN TO THEM

Nothings convinces a human being that he or she is important and valued as much as getting the undivided time and attention of another human being, even if it is only for a brief two-minute conversation.

Good listening requires that we listen non-judgmentally and that we appreciate the messages we hear, no matter how hard they might be to accept. Vivacious free-souled Sarah blurted out in eighth grade class one day, "How do we know God loves us? How do we know that isn't just a story our parents are telling us?"

Teen messages are sometimes plenty far-out. One of my imaginative young friends once said, "I think God is an alien. He is from outer space, isn't he?"

Sometimes the messages can be disheartening. Fourteen-year-old Steve said one night, "I don't believe in God anymore. I've decided to become an atheist." His parents had just separated.

The honesty and searching that teens get into is not so much a threat as it is an opportunity to build a strong foundation of their own with the Lord. Noted Christian author Catherine Marshall once said that we must all "throw off" the faith of our fathers in order to take on our very own. Startling teenage comments can be door openers, helping teens think through who and what God is and what they should do about that. In others, their remarks give every evidence that they are on a colorful road to spiritual maturity.

AFFIRM THEM

Everybody needs praise, but no one more so than a teenager. With bodies that are growing fast, interests that suddenly shift gears, and emotions that run rampant, they are bound to goof up. But they also have moments of glorious sunlight.

Teens have varied gifts from God—personality traits that they can use in service to the Lord. One might have strong leadership skills, another the ability to follow. Some teens are aggressive, others quiet and retiring. Because society tends to reserve its rewards for leaders, we need to emphasize to teens that all traits are equally important to God.

To affirm your students, identify an outstanding characteristics in each one of them and mention it one-on-one as often as opportunity allows. Point out things that happen during class to "prove" the affirmation.

HELP THEM AFFIRM THEMSELVES

Teens wanting to feel good about themselves are fighting a gigantic battle. They are extremely and often excessively self-critical. But they fight many external sources of put-me-down messages as well.

We live in a self-deprecating society. So many of us, when we receive a compliment, say, "Oh, it was nothing!" We are also bombarded with subtle messages that tell us we are either too young or too old, too skinny or too fat, or not quite "cool."

To help your teens rise above this, teach them to screen what they are seeing and hearing and to replace negative messages with positive ones. Once is not enough. With self-image assault coming at them steadily from all directions, teens need to affirm themselves frequently and regularly.

GIVE THEM RESPONSIBILITY

When my third daughter left home, barely eighteen, to move into her own apartment, she was terrified. A high school course had led her to believe it would take $4,000 a year more than she was making to support herself. Her big fear was, "I can't make it on my own!"

This is a very common reaction among teens going independent. In a complex social and economic structure such as ours, the fear has some validity. Independent teens need elaborate independent living skills—care of self, home, car, money, and time planning. Add to this the decisions they must make frequently about their responsibilities toward others and toward God. Anything teens can do to prepare themselves for the big day—care of their possessions, household chores, leadership duties—not only sets a firm foundation, but also raises their confidence.

LET THEM FAIL

Parents and adult leaders often take on responsibilities teens could handle because teens sometimes forget, goof up the job, or don't get things done fast enough. Letting teens do things themselves takes more adult time, involves aggravation, and subjects situations to failure. But teens need the experience of slipping and falling once in a while.

Soon no one will be there to pick up after them. The road to adulthood is easier if we allow them the painful consequences of irresponsibility. The more often they have to take hold lest they let somebody down, the faster they are able to face the world with grace.

When they fail, let them correct the situation, if at all possible. This is education for independent living. But don't let them get so down on themselves that they lose heart. Be firm, but keep it light: "I'm sorry you forgot to call your list about the hayride. That happens sometimes at your age. Why don't you call your friends and apologize? I think you'll feel better about it. And I'm sure they'll understand. They forget things, too, once in a while."

After a failure, encourage teens to forgive themselves and go on. Teens often hang on to their mistakes in bouts of rehashed guilt, self-pity, and self-condemnation. God wants us to sincerely regret our mistakes, to ask forgiveness of those we have offended, to make amends as best we can, and then to accept his forgiveness, and get on with our lives. We must do that so that we have more energy for helping others.

To help your teens cross this bridge, point out that, after they put goofs behind them, they are far more fun to be around, and their friends enjoy them more.

ENCOURAGE THEM TO TREASURE THEIR RELATIONSHIPS

Joy is sweeter and sorrow diminished when two share the burden of one. Our relationships with other people bring our greatest joys and deepest sorrows. Essential to self-esteem, then, is the building and maintaining of satisfying relationships.

Encourage teens to communicate in healthy ways. Twisted messages, those based on what the teen thinks others want to hear rather than on genuine ideas and feelings, foul up relationships. So do messages that pressure or manipulate others. Honest, straightforward communication not only clears the air, but also works better and feels better.

Communication is a skilled art, one that is never perfectly learned. No matter how hard people try, sooner or later they run into conflict. Urge your teens to resolve their conflicts quickly in a spirit of lovingkindness. Point out that the aim is to heal a treasured, damaged relationship, not to prove who is right or wrong.

There are many ways of settling differences, but teens in conflict usually see only two: my way and your way. Suggest that they try compromise, finding middle ground, or trading off. (Finding a middle ground is finding a solution that both parties like. Trading off is following the one person's choice one time, the other person's the next.)

Psychologists say that we must love ourselves if we are to love other people God's way—unselfishly. To accomplish this we need self-esteem. By listening to teens, affirming them, helping them plant seeds of self-affirmation, expecting responsible behavior, letting them fail, and showing them how to get along with others, you can and will help them on their way.

The Language of Love

Gary Smalley and John Trent

While a picture may be worth a thousand words, a few well-chosen words can produce a masterpiece of results! Let these actual word pictures stimulate your verbal palette as you speak to your students.

CAPTURING THE JOYS OF MARRIAGE

1. My husband treats me like a roomful of priceless antiques. He walks in, picks me up, and holds me with great care and tenderness. I often feel like I'm the most precious thing in our home. He saves the best hours and his best effort for me, not T.V.

2. I felt like an acorn that was tossed into a pile of rocks. I never had the right amount of light or the proper soil, and so I grew into an oak tree that was bent and crooked. But in nine years of marriage, I feel that you've done the impossible. You've transplanted me to a place in the sun where I can at last grow straight and tall.

3. There have been times over the years when I've faced hailstorms that I thought would turn into tornadoes. But like the shelter of a storm cellar, I can always run to my husband to protect me from hardship. He's solid as a rock, and I know he'll always be there when the storm clouds blow into my life.

4. I feel like the kids and I are a valuable piece of farmland with dark, rich soil that would quickly become overgrown with brambles and thorns if it weren't cared for properly. Fortunately, my wife is like a master gardener. Every day, in many ways, she lovingly nurtures and cares for me. Primarily because of her skills at planting and raising an intimate relationship, we've got a garden that's the envy of all our neighbors.

EXPRESSING THE JOYS AND CHALLENGES OF PARENTING

1. When I see my daughters and how well they're doing in life, pride swells within me like the snow-capped Rockies above a beautiful mountain valley. It's a feeling like I'm on top of the world. My children have moved away now, and most of the time the mountains stand at quite a distance. Yet, even from afar, looking at them fills me with wonder and thankfulness.

2. When I come home from a busy day, I often feel like a woman stranded in a barren desert. Exhausted and thirsty, I long for a quiet, cool, peaceful oasis. My husband and son give me that place of rest and refreshment I need so much, by both their pleasurable company and their sacrificial willingness to help with duties around the home. I feel like I have two angels that are also my great friends, good helpers, and loving encouragers.

3. Because of my children's constant affirmation, I feel like a beautiful, well-groomed show horse. My coat shines and my beautiful mane dances as I parade about. I often go out for a run with other show horses, and many of them feel abused and misused by their children. I'm so thankful for the kids I've got, and the way they reflect even more love than I give them.

TELLING SOMEONE HOW I FEEL TODAY

1. I feel like a green tree progressing through the seasons. Winter sometimes brings cold, harsh people who hurt me. But spring always returns, and with it come

new green leaves. I keep growing!

2. I feel like a salmon fighting its way upstream, with an occasional stop in a calm eddy of friendship. Those cool waters always refresh me for the next part of my journey into the mainstream of life. With these pools of friendship along the way, I know I can continue to swim for as long as I have to.

3. I feel like a beautiful old car that was in need of repair. An expert mechanic has been working to correct the problems. Though much of the work has been painful, I can tell the car rides better already! Change is never easy, but I feel that my time in counseling has helped me rebuild my engine and get back on the road.

4. As I reflect on my seventieth birthday, my travel through life has been like a trip to a faraway land. It's been full of excitement and uncertainty, which is sometimes scary but never boring. Through it all, I've met many new, interesting people and seen God's faithfulness displayed in ways I never thought possible. I've had a great life!

TELLING OTHERS HOW MUCH THEY MEAN TO ME

1. Returning home to you from a trip is like taking a quiet drive in the country after having driven a taxi in New York City for a week. No one is cutting me off or yelling at me. There are no red lights to frustrate me nor any crummy drivers to swerve into my path. Coming home is like driving on a country road where people actually wave because they like me and are glad to see me, not because they're mad.

2. Marrying you was like getting a release from life's prison of loneliness. For thirty-six years, I spent every night in solitary confinement. I now spend each night in a garden of love, with the one I love sleeping next to me.

3. You're as beautiful and delicate to me as the most expensive piece of Waterford crystal. Looking at you is like looking at a work of art, skillfully crafted by masters. Your every facet is unique and perfect in its own way. You sparkle in a rainbow of light, and every day I catch a new reflection of why I love you so much.

4. Being with you is as fulfilling as the first and only time I received a standing ovation from a class of students. As a teacher, I work so hard and rarely get any praise. But when that class showed its genuine appreciation by standing to applaud, it made all the work and long hours seem worthwhile. Honey, your encouragement and loving words make me feel like I come home to a standing ovation. Even when I haven't put in the time and don't deserve it, you support me like the best class I've ever had.

Application

LAW THREE

TOPICAL SURVEY

From Application to Action

David R. Mains

*One of America's beloved church and radio pastors talks about provi-
ding bridges for listeners—bridges to help them travel the path from
hearing the Word to doing the Word. Become a bridge-builder yourself!*

I listen to a lot of other preachers—carefully, too. It's more than professional curiosity; I want to learn from both their strengths and their weaknesses.

WHAT TO DO?

I can usually determine the subject of the sermons I listen to. But often I'm confused about what I'm supposed to do or to stop doing. That's frustrating, especially since it's a rare text that doesn't call for an explicit response.

Sometimes I work with student preachers. Once they choose a text, I tell them to look for two things: the subject and the response being called for. I ask them to identify these two elements before they look for anything else in the passage. Why? Because the success of their preaching hinges on imparting not only the meaning but the imperative of a text.

When lay people tell me they heard a preacher and say, "Oh, he was good!" I often respond, "I'm pleased. Tell me, what was his subject?" Usually, with varying degrees of accuracy, they can answer. "And what did he want you to do or to stop doing?" Now we're on a desert journey without water. Most people can't remember. Most likely, the preacher never stated the desired response. The major component necessary for better preaching, I believe, is the imperative—the call for specific action.

SCRIBES OR PREACHERS?

Scribes tend to be fascinated with information. By contrast, preachers, like Christ, are more action oriented. For them, the word "sermon" means a thrust. "It's a thrust from the sword of the Spirit," writes Simon Blocker in *The Secret of Pulpit Power*. "And the preacher knows whether or not his thrust has been driven home."

I'm convinced many people say they like certain preachers not because they're helped to be different but because they found that speaker interesting, clever, able to project personality into his sermon. Their bottom line: He wasn't boring and I enjoyed listening to him. But were preachers meant to be entertainers?

If someone wants to know how to play music, it does little good for me to talk about the lives of famous composers, or to compare in detail the various instruments in the orchestra, or review how violins are made. It may make me sound learned and wise, but this person needs to be told, "Lesson one is on how to hold your flute. Between now and when we meet next week, I want you to practice holding it like this."

PROFUNDITY OR SIMPLICITY?

Most Christians I know don't need more information or "deeper truths." They haven't processed a fraction of the ones they already know. Profundity is not the crying need but simplicity coupled with directness: "Here's what my text is about, and it's calling for us to do this."

I want my preaching to communicate specific responses to genuine needs felt by real people. And they respond favorably to such down-to-earth preaching anchored in their world. They don't particularly want more ideas. They aren't enamored with brilliant analysis or formal essays. I can't even assume they have a great love for theology or a vast reservoir of biblical knowledge.

I always ask the question: "What practical suggestions can I give to help people respond to what is said?" That's a watershed question. If I adequately address that question, my listeners will appreciate what they hear. And they'll be helped by it.

BRIDGES TO BEHAVIOR

To make sure I am communicating, I have tried various methods, like brain-storming my sermons on Wednesday nights with a random group of parishioners invited to my home, or holding a pastor's class after Sunday worship to discuss the sermon. The people who have most shaped my sermons have not been ministers but parishioners gracious enough to not only listen but also critique what they heard.

In discussing my sermons with listeners, I've found it doesn't take long before they agree that the subject is relevant and the response called for in the passage is legitimate. But they say they need help with the "how tos." That's what the serious Christian comes to a sermon to hear.

"Don't say any more about the subject," they tell me. "I already agree with the biblical challenge to respond. Tell me how to pull it off! Can't you use your time building a bridge for me to get into this coveted new land?"

THE ART OF BRIDGE-BUILDING

We preachers must build practical bridges. We need to list the first steps necessary to respond to what Scripture requires, and then we have to walk people over those bridges, step by step, to get them to that point.

For example, when Billy Graham preaches about conversion—being born again— he challenges his hearers to follow Christ. That's his desired response. Now how are they to do this? What's his bridge?

"What I want you to do," he tells them, "is to get up from where you are sitting and to walk down here to the front." He knows trained counselors are ready to talk with these people and lead them to Christ. It's a good bridge—"Here's how to do what I've been telling you about."

Some people find an immediate public response intimidating. They intend to respond—the Word has done its work—but making such a sudden decision and walking in front of all those people seems out of the question. For them I might devise bridges less threatening in a congregational setting, such as:

- Printing my phone number in the bulletin with specific hours I will be at the phone with the sole purpose of taking calls from those wanting to investigate the implications of becoming a Christian.
- Providing cards on which they can write their phone number so I can call them.
- Arranging a meeting after the service, sometimes over lunch, for any who want to continue working toward a decision.
- Making inexpensive books available to borrow or buy after the service.
- Challenging people to talk with a Christian of their choice about any decision they have made.
- Making available cassette tapes to those who have made decisions, again getting their names for follow-up.

Each of these alternatives builds a bridge to action. People can walk away from a service knowing something concrete to do if they have made a decision. They have their first steps outlined for them.

WHAT KIND OF BRIDGE IS BEST?

The use of bridges, however, is not limited to evangelistic sermons. Every sermon can benefit from suggested steps to action. Since the type of bridge depends on the response intended by the text, there are countless possibilities. When trying to determine what bridge to use for a particular sermon, the questions to ask are: What response does the text demand? How can I best move the people toward the response?

1. Thought-probing bridges

When preaching on prayer, for example, I wanted people to learn to pray thankfully. I might have left it at that: "When you pray, be thankful." But that would have left most of them at a loss: Thankful for what? How do I pray thankfully?

So I provided a bridge. I asked them to take a few minutes later that day to write out ten things they were thankful for. The next day they were to write out ten more, not repeating any from the first day, and on the third day ten more, until the week was up and they had a list of seventy blessings. I asked them to bring the list the next week, when we would talk about it some more. By the next Sunday, they were ready to hear more because they had acted on the first sermon.

2. Habit-breaking, choice-making bridges

For a sermon on addiction to pornographic materials, I asked the congregation if during the next week they were willing to throw away questionable mail before opening it, to destroy that hidden stash of unseemly materials, to avoid particular book racks and magazines and theater marquees. Since pornography can be an addiction, I asked them to consider one more step they felt they could take to break its hold. The bridge took them from knowing what is bad to determining what to do in response.

3. Accountability bridges

A sermon by John Huffman at the Congress on Biblical Exposition stands out for me because he told me what to do and also provided me a bridge. His bridge was simple: Get into an accountability group. He told how he had done it and what it meant to him and his preaching. He shared his weakness and his need for counsel. I came away from his sermon with an idea of what he wanted me to do and how to do it.

4. Scriptural bridges

Supply a short list of scriptures to be memorized; print a card with the sermon theme for people to carry in their wallets; suggest they evaluate a certain television show for its secular or Christian message; put a question in the bulletin for people to discuss over Sunday dinner—the bridges are varied. The common denominator is their specific practicality. They can be done immediately as a way to begin to put the sermon's message to work.

WHAT TO DO NOW

I have found through years of lay/preacher dialogue that if I can't tell my listeners what to do, if I can't construct good bridges for people, they probably won't figure out applications for themselves. I don't worry about sounding "Mickey Mouse." The specifics, the how tos, the practicalities belong in great exposition every bit as much as in Sunday school handouts.

When approaching a text, I can preach or teach best by . . .

First, zeroing in on the text's subject;

Second, extracting from Scripture the response being called for; and

Third, from my Christian understanding, constructing a bridge that will help people get from where they are to where this text teaches they should be. I want to help them respond to the challenge of the passage.

According to a 1985 poll, 42 percent of the adults in America attend religious services in a typical week. If we can get those four in ten adults to leave our preaching services saying, "I know what God wants me to do and I have been given a reasonable way to begin the process. I'm going to do it!" and if we can pull this off Sunday after Sunday, then our preaching will fulfill its purpose: God's Word will equip his people to begin doing his will.

■ From *Leadership* 4 (Fall 1986), pp. 64-68. Used by permission.

Why Use Illustrations?

David Gudgel

Illustrations—what are they really for? Often knowing why something should be used increases our willingness and desire to use it. Twelve great teachers give seven great reasons for using illustrations in teaching.

M ost pastors are convinced they need to use illustrations when preaching. But many, like myself, have been given little help in learning the basics of using them. Seminaries often assume you simply know these things. Yet that is like assuming every home mechanic knows how to find a speedometer cable.

For the first few years after seminary, I tried to do it myself—putting illustrations in here and there. Finally I got frustrated enough to seek help. I needed a few clear principles to work with. The library offered little help, so I wrote to twelve men whom I considered gifted communicators and asked them why and when they illustrate.

1. TO CAPTURE ATTENTION

It would be nice to believe our congregations come to the service with hearts and minds prepared to soak up God's Word. But sometimes even we have a hard time forgetting about the football game that starts at 1:00 P.M. or the fight the kids had in the car.

An illustration at the beginning of a sermon can transfer the listener's attention to the desired subject. Bruce Wilkinson, president of Walk Thru the Bible Ministries, says, "An illustration, whether humorous, biblical, personal, or imaginary, is often the best way to capture the attention of the audience."

Chuck Swindoll is a master at this. I still remember how he introduced a sermon on Nehemiah 6 with a story about quarterback Sonny Jurgensen. After the Washington Redskins had lost a game, a sportswriter asked, "Sonny, doesn't it make you want to quit when people throw things at you?" Sonny leaned back, smiled, and said, "No, not really. I don't want to quit. I've been in this game long enough to know that every quarterback, every week of the season, spends his time either in the penthouse or the outhouse."

Such a story, or sometimes just a popular quote, is all that's needed to draw people into the message.

2. FOR PERSONAL IDENTIFICATION

A couple of summers ago, my family and I tried something new for our vacation—being chaplain for a week at a state campground. We were looking forward to blending in for a week, and then worshiping God with other campers in an outdoor amphitheater on Sunday.

At the park entrance we were warmly greeted and given directions to our campsite. Peace and quiet, here we come! We turned the corner and looked for our site. You couldn't miss it.

There stood a sign that clearly read "Park Chaplain." So much for blending in. All week we felt like animals at the zoo. As people went by, they would look at the sign, then at us, then back at the sign. It gave us plenty of time to think about how God has intended we live a lifestyle that will "stand out."

Personal illustrations, like that sign, help to open up our lives to our congregations. Howard Hendricks of Dallas Theological Seminary suggests that illustrations provide contact with the congregation in two ways: They enable a speaker to identify with his congregation and his congregation to identify with him.

Illustrations will help you see the truths of the message from the listener's perspective and identify with his needs and problems. They help you preach in a way that is relevant rather than preaching at them.

And illustrations enable a congregation to "relate to me as a speaker," says David Hocking, pastor of Calvary Church, Santa Anna, California. If they can see how the truth has worked in your life, they'll be motivated to let it work in theirs, too.

3. FOR NEEDED CLARIFICATION

Perhaps the most basic principle is to illustrate when the biblical truth needs clarification. Ray Stedman, pastor of Peninsula Bible Church, Palo Alto, California, says you should illustrate "whenever you feel what you are attempting to convey requires it. It may be difficult to understand, it may lack color and appeal, it may need dramatization in order to be fully understood."

Illustrations can be a window to let light in, a bridge to connect two points separated by an obstacle. We must help the listener understand the meaning and relevance of the Word of God in today's context. For listeners to understand, we must describe the unknown in terms that are known.

I used to work at Pittsburgh Plate Glass. The best way to understand how glass is made is to get a job there or take a tour of the plant. But for those who can't, someone who's been there can describe glass making in all its particulars. Accurately described, what has been an abstract idea can come alive.

We would do well to apply Swindoll's plan of attack: "Illustrate whenever an issue is perhaps a bit unclear or too theoretical. Follow a simple plan—use the well-known and the familiar to shed light on the unknown and unfamiliar."

4. TO HOLD ATTENTION

Hendricks hit the nail on the head when he said, "The nature of our culture is highly visual and poorly verbal. Listening skills are rapidly deteriorating under the input of TV, and therefore one has to paint more pictures and change his pace more frequently than ever before."

A pastor needs to evaluate the attention span of his congregation and intersperse his illustrations accordingly. As Joe Aldrich, president of Multnomah School of the Bible, says, "Those who have 'wandered' usually return when a good illustration is introduced into the message."

I found myself in such a state at a conference where John Walvoord of Dallas Theological Seminary was speaking on the Second Coming. He was laying a foundation for his arguments from 1 Thessalonians 4. We had driven five hours that afternoon to get there, and I was tired. The information was familiar, so I found myself thinking about other things. But then he used a short illustration. He said he had seen a bumper sticker that reminded him of his text. It said, "Those who stay physically fit die healthier." That got back my attention!

5. FOR SPECIFIC APPLICATION

The purpose of a teaching or preaching ministry is to see the Word of God transform lives, to move people from simply hearing God's Word to acting upon it. Illustrations are essential for this. They shorten the distance between God's truth and its application in our lives. And the shorter the distance, the greater the impact.

Gordon MacDonald, past president of Inter-Varsity Christian Fellowship, says, "What good is this evangelical community of ours with all of its sermon notes of doctrinal facts when it doesn't know how to humanize it into real life? Much doctrinal preaching is built on this premise: Explain the facts, and people will believe and therefore act. With few exceptions this simply isn't so. Stories open people to truth and show how the truth has been utilized in the past and infers significance in the present."

Recently I was preaching on the love of God through Paul. I felt I had a handle on the text and was able to show several ways Paul demonstrated love through his life, but I was missing a final punch.

I finally used a song from the musical *Fiddler on the Roof.* Tevye had asked Golde for the first time if she loved him. Her reply: "Do I love you? For twenty-five years I've washed your clothes, cooked your meals, cleaned your house, given you children, milked the cow. After twenty-five years, why talk about love right now? . . . For twenty-five years I've lived with him, fought with him, starved with him. Twenty-five years my bed is his; if that's not love, what is?!"

"I love you" had never been spoken. But the actions of love were all there. In a similar way, Paul's love was expressed in actions, not just words.

6. FOR FRESH REPETITION

It's well-known that a preacher must first "tell his congregation what he's going to tell them, tell them, and then tell them what he told them." Illustrations are a key to saying the same thing over again without it sounding the same.

The Old Testament is an excellent source for illustrating New Testament principles (1 Corinthians 10:11). For instance, a way to point out our culture's moral degradation is to examine Baal worship. Such worship was characterized by temple prostitution, human mutilation, and human sacrifice. Sound familiar? Think of prostitution, abortion, and suicide.

Sometimes an illustration gets at a familiar topic in a way that will draw out the needed application. When speaking on faith, you could tell a story of a pilot having difficulty landing his plane because of fog, so the control tower decided to bring him in by radar. As he was receiving the directions, he remembered a tall pole in the flight path and appealed in panic to change his course. The tower replied, "You obey instructions, we'll take care of obstructions."

7. TO IMPROVE RETENTION

I heard Hendricks speak a year ago. I don't remember all the details of his sermon, but I'll never forget this illustration and the principle it teaches:

Bud Wilkinson, former football coach at the University of Oklahoma, was in Dallas for a series of lectures on physical fitness. A reporter asked him, "What is the contribution of modern football to physical fitness?" Wilkinson answered, "Absolutely nothing. . . . I define football as twenty-two men on the field who desperately need rest and fifty thousand people in the grandstand who desperately need exercise."

Hendricks went on to say, "That's an apt picture of the church today: a few compulsive people running around the field while the mass of the people rest in the stands." If a story like that can aid in remembering a message, use it.

Stedman says, "The primary reason for illustrations is that God has made our minds to respond both to cognitive and visual information. Doctrinal preaching is basically cognitive, appealing to the mind, while illustrations are visual, speaking primarily to the emotions. Good preaching finds its impact in combining an appeal to the mind and the emotions in order to reach the will."

If sermons were preached only to be comprehended, illustrations might be optional. Instead, sermons are meant to be remembered and translated into action. The speed with which people can forget a message is appalling.

John MacArthur, Jr., pastor, seminary president, and radio Bible teacher, likens it to parishioners filling up their thimble of truth during the worship service and after the service, upon reaching the car, dumping it out before driving home. Because illustrations linger in the mind, God may use them to help believers recall the truth and take appropriate action.

8. JESUS' USE OF ILLUSTRATIONS

Jesus illustrates how to use illustrations. He used them for personal identification when He spoke to the woman at the well of her need for physical water and her deeper need for spiritual water. She was immediately able to identify with His use of this natural medium.

At times, Jesus would use an illustration when clarification was needed. When the lawyer asked Him what he must do to inherit eternal life, Jesus told him to do what is within the Law (Luke 10:25-28). To make it clear to him who his neighbor was, Jesus told the story of the good Samaritan (vv. 29-37).

The Sermon on the Mount (Matthew 5-7) is one long series of illustrations. It demonstrates that Christ considered illustrations important in getting the truth to men and holding their attention.

Christ would often use an illustration for explicit application. Wishing to teach His disciples that they need to pray persistently, He told the parable of the unrighteous judge (Luke 18:1-8). When asked by Peter how often one should forgive his brother who sins against him, He told the parable of the unmerciful slave (Matthew 18:21-35).

He also used illustrations as a means for fresh repetition. The entire fifteenth chapter of Luke demonstrates this. His primary purpose was to teach the Pharisees and the scribes the inestimable value of the sinner who turns to God. He taught this single lesson in a repetitive way through the parables of the lost sheep, the lost coin, and the lost son.

Finally, Jesus used illustrations to improve retention. It was His desire to see the truth change people's lives. Their ability to recall the truth through the power of the Spirit would ensure change.

The most effective preachers are those who follow Christ's example and use illustrations to communicate truth. Telling stories and illustrations from the pulpit or podium is not a waste of time, but a necessary tool to draw your congregation into the topic, keep them tuned in, and help them understand, remember, and apply the message of God's Word.

■ From *Moody Monthly* 86, no. 11 (July–August, 1986), pp. 76-78. Used by permission.

Storytelling:
Lifechange through Imagination

Reg Grant

Many of the greatest truths in Scripture are communicated through stories such as parables, proverbs, and word pictures. Discover here why stories communicate so effectively, and how to tell them.

Good things happen when you tell a story. You begin with, "It was the time of year when kings buckled on their armor, saddled their horses and rode off to battle . . ." As you start, you notice chattering slows to a tentative stop, movement freezes, and all eyes refocus on you, the storyteller. You have hooked their imagination with a sharply defined picture: kings, horses, armor. You enhanced the image with movement: buckling, saddling, riding. You crossed a threshold from this time back to an age of rattling swords, flashing spears, and the acrid smell of war. You constructed your time machine from nouns and verbs that shimmer and echo in the mind; they magically transport your listeners to 1000 B.C., the time of David, the king. Your listeners are interested because they are involved. They are involved because you have engaged their imagination with a story.

IMMERSE YOURSELF IN THE STORY

You must immerse yourself in the story, believe in it, see it for yourself. If you don't see it, they never will. You begin the immersion process by reading the biblical story through several times. Your goal is not to memorize the story word for word, but to note how the story begins, how it develops, and how it ends. Once you can remember the basic structure of the story, try repeating it to yourself in your own words.

INTERPRET THE STORY

Now it's time to ask an interpretive question. "What lesson does God teach us through this story?" In the story of David's sin with Bathsheba in the first part of 2 Samuel 11, the lesson may be something along these lines: "During times of idleness we need to be spiritually alert to temptation." Once you have discovered the lesson of the story, you will want to read other Bible passages which speak to the same theme as well as trusted Bible commentaries on your passage. Make sure there is general agreement on your understanding of the story's message.

ENHANCE THE STORY

Now that you have validated your interpretation, you will be able to enhance those details of the story which reinforce the lesson. For example, in telling the story of David and Bathsheba, you would probably want to highlight the fact that David was idle when he should have been busy, but you would probably not want to spend much time talking about historical backgrounds. Adding unnecessary detail will often obscure the lesson the story is trying to get across.

INTERPRET THE STORY IN YOUR OWN WORDS

Write out the story in your own words. Highlight some key words in the Bible story that you will want to weave into the fabric of your manuscript. Some of the important words in the David and Bathsheba narrative include "saw" [" . . . and up on the roof he saw a woman bathing, . . . " (11:2)], "he inquired" ["So David sent and inquired, . . . " (11:4)], "he took" ["And David sent a messenger and took her, . . . " (11:4)], and "lay" [" . . . he lay with her, . . . " (11:4)]. Notice how these important verbs reveal the sequence in the story. At first David sees, then he inquires, then he takes, and finally he lies with Bathsheba. Here you have the structure of the story.

As you write the story in your own words, you can use synonyms to reinforce the meaning of these important Biblical words. David doesn't just "see," he "leers." He doesn't "take," he "steals." He spies, he lusts, he seduces. Choose your words carefully to buttress your word usage.

INVOLVE YOUR AUDIENCE IN THE STORY

When you begin telling the story, begin firmly. The first words should be clear and a bit louder than normal to help the audience focus their attention. Take time to paint the picture for them. You can visualize the story taking place just over their heads on an imaginary screen. Your focus should shift periodically from the person on your make-believe screen to direct eye contact with audience members.

Try to look at individuals for a few seconds at a time. When you tell stories to individuals, you will find that everyone in the class feels as if you are speaking privately to him or her. At the end of the story, pause, look at the audience, and exit the storytelling area. This movement physically reinforces the fact that the storytelling time is over.

When you finish the story, resist the temptation to moralize. A good storyteller doesn't mix conventional didactic teaching methods with storytelling. If the story has been told well, the moral will be clear.

INSTRUCT THROUGH THE STORY

Storytelling encourages us to relive a small portion of the great story of the Bible. As we journey back to the days of the Bible, we discover timeless truths which inform our minds and transform our living for today. In David's story for example, we found a man subject to the same kinds of temptations we face every day at the office, at home, and in school. His story provides warnings against immorality, admonitions to guard our hearts, and encouragement to keep our eyes on the Lord.

But David is just one among hundreds of the Bible's characters who provide lessons for our instruction. Immerse yourself in scriptures that tell their stories. Baptize your imagination in the truth of God's Word. Search out and share the lessons that will change lives now and forever.

■ From *Christian Education Today* 41, no. 4 (Fall 1989), pp. 20-21. Used by permission.

How Great Communicators Illustrate

Daniel W. Pawley

Welcome to an unusual setting. You have the privilege of joining the distinguished group of communicators listed below as they talk about how to illustrate truth. Get ready to take notes—they're just beginning!

The following speakers and preachers are among the most listened to in America. Their thoughts on the task of illustrating truth follows.

- James Boice, pastor, Tenth Presbyterian Church, Philadelphia, Pennsylvania
- Herschel Hobbs, past president, Southern Baptist Convention
- Oswald Hoffmann, speaker, Lutheran Hour radio broadcast
- David Hubbard, president, Fuller Theological Seminary
- Calvin Miller, author, pastor, Westside Baptist Church, Omaha, Nebraska
- Norman Vincent Peale, pastor, Marble Collegiate Church, New York City
- Paul Rees, editor at large, World Vision
- Haddon Robinson, professor of homiletics, Gordon-Conwell Seminary
- Paul Smith, pastor, Peoples Church, Toronto, Canada
- Charles Swindoll, pastor, First Evangelical Free Church, Fullerton, California

THE NEED FOR ILLUSTRATIONS

Robinson: "Good pulpit communication moves back and forth from the abstract to the concrete. Each time the preacher states a deep, broad, general truth, the mind of the audience asks, 'For instance?' That's when you need an 'abstraction lighter,' a concrete example which applies the truth."

Hubbard: "I have to confess that illustrations are hard for me when I'm thinking conceptually about theology. Often I will construct a tight sermon outline only to struggle with how to open a window that lets light and air into my sermon so it doesn't sound too cerebral, too propositional, too closely reasoned."

Rees: "Early in my ministry I wasted a lot of time with illustration books. I feel they were bland and not relevant to my life."

Hobbs: "It's not only that pre-packaged illustrations are usually dead and out of date, but psychologically they lose their sense of immediacy. I have a hard time getting excited about sharing someone else's illustration in my sermon."

Robinson: "Every preacher knows the value of a good story: it gets attention, it's concrete, people listen. But right there lies the danger. The tendency is to tell the story for its own sake and not for what it illustrates. An illustration is like a row of footlights that shed light on what is presented on the stage. If you turn the lights into the audience, they blind the people."

OBSERVE THE ORDINARY

Hoffmann: "The preacher needs to be a constant observer of ordinary things that happen around him. One night my wife and I were sitting outside, and our dog Mack stood barking at us. Suddenly my wife said, 'The children must have been playing with Mack because he's off his chain.' But the dog didn't know it, and he would go only to the spot where the chain usually yanked him back. We watched to see how long it would take him to realize he was free. After about ten minutes, he discovered he was not held by the chain, and he bounded happily to us. It occurred to me right then that this was a picture of how people live: we live shackled by our passions and prejudices and pride. The Lord died to set us free, but as long as we think we're bound by chains, then we really are. When we realize freedom is ours by faith in Christ—the shackles have been broken—then we are free indeed. The story brings to life a major point on which the whole sermon is built: freedom in Christ."

BE SENSITIVE TO NATURE

Rees: "Beyond the shimmering line of white foam, a sheen of burnished gold stretches until the blue sky dips to touch the ocean. All the while the sun seems to be saying, 'Don't look at me, look at the glories I'm revealing to you.' So it is with the Holy Spirit as he reveals and magnifies our Lord."

Peale: Preaching the funeral service of magazine publisher DeWitt Wallace, Peale carefully integrated an illustration from nature into his sermon: "It is the end of March and the beginning of April, and this wind that we feel signifies the rebirth of the earth. I know what beautiful flowers are here in summer, even though the ground looks barren now. But there's life underneath these barren twigs and leaves and grass. The sun will overcome the wind and cold and soon it will be spring. This is precisely what DeWitt Wallace believed about life. He was a Christian; he believed in the Bible; he accepted Jesus as his Lord and his Saviour. I want to tell you we are in the presence of immortality here."

Hubbard: Immerses himself in the *National Geographic*. "Perhaps I'll see an article about the Amazon River and use it to illustrate the river glorious, which is the peace and love of God."

READ WIDELY

Rees: "You don't read just to cull stories. You read for enrichment, keeping an eye open for illustrations, but selecting them only as they become relevant to your experience and sermon topics."

Rees: "People are usually interested in the lives of great people. But you have to remember two things: 1) The biographical character has to relate in some meaningful way to the life experience of your audience; 2) There needs to be a close, recognizable relationship between what you're pulling out of a person's life, and the point you're trying to make."

Boice: "Most people are interested in history that directly connects with their lives. When a preacher reads a biography of Luther, for instance, he is sitting on illustrations that apply to the Christian life in total." In a sermon about prayer, Boice wanted to counter the statement, "If it be thy will," a line he says Christians use when we don't really believe anything is going to happen. "In the heat of the Reformation, Luther received word that his friend Fredrick Marconius was dying. Luther wrote back, 'I forbid you to die. This is my will, may my will be done; the Lord will never let me hear that you are dead because of the work of the Reformation.' Marconius was too weak to hear or speak, but eventually he did recover and outlived Luther by several years."

USE SCIENCE

Swindoll: "A researcher built a cage to house 160 mice. All their needs were met: plenty of food and water and the right climate. He let the population increase, much more than normal, and in less than three years the mice population reached 2,200. At that point the colony began to disintegrate. The adults formed groups of about twelve each; each mouse played a particular role, but there was no role for the healthy young mice, so they began to disrupt the society. The males who had once protected their territory withdrew. The females became aggressive and forced out the young. The young mice became self-indulgent, eating and sleeping. Later, courtship or mating ceased, and in five years all the mice died, even though there was plenty of food and water, no disease, and an ideal climate.

"Now the scientist who did this research suggested that overcrowding humanity in such an inescapable environment might have similar effects: 'First, we would cease to reproduce our ideas, then our goals; finally, our values and priorities would be lost.' But the church has to minister in a different way. We experience the same things, face the same societal problems, but we think differently, and we can't use the world's methods. Our priorities and values must come directly from the Word."

Boice and Hubbard: Both issued strong warnings to make sure your facts are correct when you're talking about science. If Hubbard cannot verify the accuracy of a scientific illustration, he will scrap it. Boice sometimes contacts experts in his congregation. Last Easter, for instance, part of his sermon probed different theories on death. The afternoon before he preached, he verified his illustrations with one of his parishioners, a nurse with knowledge on the subject, and he wound up reworking much of his sermon.

DISCOVER HUMOR AND IMAGINATION

Swindoll: "When you tell a good story, immediately there is interest because your audience is asking, 'What's going to happen now?' Humor adds an interesting twist, but slapstick, joke book humor is not good. Good humor exists in real-life stories and predictable situations."

Peale: "If there's humor in a story, let the humor come out, but don't force it."

Hubbard: "I keep my eyes open all the time for events, situations, statements that my imagination can caricature into a creative illustration."

Smith: Says he stumbled onto one image-evoking statement by Helmut Thielicke: ". . . the fact that the salt is there doesn't mean everyone is going to turn into a Christian, any more than when you put salt into a bowl of soup the soup turns into salt." Smith used his imagination to inject life into it: "In my illustration I have a kitchen table, a salt shaker, and a bowl of soup. I call the salt shaker 'the ecclesiastical salt shaker,' and I describe it as the church, which is a good thing. The soup represents the world and the salt's objective is to get into the soup. I imagine two grains of salt having a conversation, and one is exuberant about enjoying the fellowship. 'We're both the same size, same color, we like each other, we've got these walls of glass around us and it's all kind of neat.' Then the other grain says, 'Yeah, but at some point, I think we're supposed to be dumped into the soup.'"

Hubbard: Says the preacher has to use some degree of "impressionistic portraiture," but it should be done within reason: "It's like an ice cream sundae; you have to use chocolate sauce with discrimination. If the whole sundae becomes chocolate sauce, then the sauce loses its effect."

Robinson: "Every preacher enters into a kind of covenant relationship with his audience. In the covenant are unspoken agreements about sermon length, depth of scholarship, and authenticity of illustrations. Violating that covenant in any way can mean losing your listeners."

Peale: "People relate most completely to what others have gone through. When they see their own experiences of frustrations, sufferings, and joys against the background of the gospel, they are moved in action and commitment."

Robinson: "Good sermons happen when flint strikes steel—when the flint of a person's experience strikes the steel of the Word of God. That's when you get the spark."

FIND YOUR OWN WAY

Although the importance of good sermon illustrations was clearly emphasized, the conclusion was that there really aren't a lot of hard-and-fast rules for coming up with them. In fact, sticking rigidly to a do-and-don't code for sermon illustrations may choke off the creation of good ones. "Some preachers make illustrations their magnificent obsession," one interviewee noted. "All that does is nag them to collect more and more and more." Robert Frost once compared creative writing to playing tennis with the net down. You know that rules exist, but you don't necessarily have to use them."

The same holds true for the art of illustrating sermons. Each preacher ultimately must find his or her own way, accepting some suggestions, rejecting others. What does seem to be important is the cultivation of a constantly perceptive mindset. Reading extensively, observing with a penetrating eye, keeping track of personal experiences that happen to those around you—all are necessary to produce creative and authentic illustrations. As summarized by Haddon Robinson, "It's the way you look at life that makes the difference."

■Excerpted from *Leadership* 2, no. 3 (Summer 1981), pp. 41-48. Used by permission.

How To Find Personal Applications

James C. Galvin

So you're convinced that illustrations and applications are critical to the teaching process? The next question is obviously, How do I develop effective applications? We're glad you asked—the answer begins here!

After a stressful day at the office and a satisfying dinner, Ed helped Sue wash the dishes and put the children to bed. Later, he sat down in his recliner in the living room, picked up a newspaper and, as usual, turned on the radio to listen to one of his favorite Bible teachers. As he skimmed the paper, he heard the teacher read the text from 1 Samuel 24:1-15.

As Ed listened, the account gripped him. Folding the paper, he picked up his Bible and followed along. As the preacher skillfully explained the story of David's refusal to kill Saul, the king of Israel whom the Lord had anointed, Ed felt he understood what was happening. He wondered what he would learn from this account that he could apply to his own life. At that moment, the preacher concluded, "Neither should we lift our hands against the Lord's anointed. This is an important thought of crucial significance for us today. Let's pray."

Ed sat up in his recliner. "Wait a minute!" he said, glaring at the radio. "So what? I'm not plotting to assassinate any government leaders! I'm not out to undermine my pastor! What does lifting a hand against the Lord's anointed have to do with me?"

Ed felt cheated. His frustration made him more determined to find out if this passage related to his life. He read the text again and again. No applications came to mind. He pulled two thick commentaries down from his bookshelves but found no answers for his questions. Yet he couldn't shake the feeling that there was something important here for him to know and put into practice. He just didn't know how to get at it. He was stuck.

Perhaps you get stuck like this once in a while. Some portions of the Bible are difficult to apply. How do you respond when you want to know what to do and cannot find an answer? Where can you go for help when you honestly ask, "So what?"

Application does not always come easily or naturally. Whether or not it does, three important techniques have been proven useful for digging personal applications out of puzzling passages. These tools will help you discover the parallels with your own life and know more clearly what you should do about what you learn.

STEP 1: IDENTIFY WITH THE PEOPLE

The first step is to identify with the people in the passage. Granted, the stories in the Bible took place thousands of years ago in a completely different culture. But if you try to understand the people and what they were going through, you will often find connections between their lives and ours. To identify with the people in a passage, ask these questions:

- Who are all of the people involved in this passage?
- How are these people like people in my world?
- What characteristics in myself do I see represented in these people?

Don't forget to include the author and the original audience; they are the "people," too. In narrative sections such as Genesis or Matthew, this step is straightforward.

When Ed tried this, he immediately identified with David. Both he and David were men under pressure. David waited patiently for the throne that was rightfully his; Ed was waiting for his long-deserved promotion at work. While Ed could not identify personally with Saul he couldn't help but notice similarities between Saul and some men at his office. As he thought about other characters in the story, he saw a parallel between himself and the men who advised David to kill Saul. He had learned to take quick advantage of significant opportunities that arose at work and home. As he was fond of saying, "There are only two types of leaders—the quick and the dead." By asking himself these questions, Ed successfully identified with the people in the story.

STEP 2: REDISCOVER THE PLOT

The second tool is to connect what happened in the story with what is happening in your life. To rediscover the plot, ask,

- What is happening in this story or teaching?
- What is the conflict or tension?
- What would I have done in this situation?
- How is this similar to what is happening in my life or in the world today?

Summarizing the plot is an easy way to do this. The questions listed here go further to help you explore the parallels to your own life. The plot is easy to unravel in a gospel or any historical book. But what if a story line is not clearly apparent, as in 2 or 3 John? In this case, check through commentaries and other Bible resources and try to determine the conflict that underlies the passage. Every book in the Bible either contains a story with conflict or speaks directly to one, and understanding this conflict will help unlock additional applications.

The Bible teacher had helped Ed understand what was happening in the passage. Ed now had to find the connections with his own life. He was not being threatened by a king, nor was he hiding out from any authorities. But as he thought about how this might apply, he realized that his pressure at work was remarkably similar to David's in this story. The manager had been making life difficult for Ed's team and demoralizing the entire division. In the opinion of many workers, Ed was better qualified for the position, and they wanted him to be the manager.

Recently some of Ed's key people had come to him with a plan to undermine the manager in a technically permissible but ethically questionable way. They reasoned that it would be best for the company in the long run if Ed had that position. All week, Ed had felt the pressure to go along with their plan. He was qualified for the position and had been waiting a long time for a promotion. Besides that, he needed the money.

Although the manager was clearly hurting the company, Ed did not feel right about undermining his boss's authority. David's inner turmoil in this story was compelling to him: David was under pressure to get rid of the one man standing between him and what he rightfully deserved. Ed was in a strikingly similar situation— and was about to give in to the pressure from his team. But how could he hold his people back?

STEP 3: MAKE THE TIMELESS TRUTHS TIMELY

The third step is to transfer the truth in the story from the "then and there" to the "here and now" by identifying the biblical principles in a passage and bringing them into our world. Ask,

- What is the message for all of mankind?

• What is the moral of the story?
• What does this mean for our society and culture?
• How is this relevant to my situation?

You may find one or more transferable principles in each Bible passage that you study. These principles are the essence of a passage. Discovering these principles can be as exhilarating as reaching the top of a mountain after a long climb. The view is so inspiring that you might feel tempted to end your journey at the top. But to apply the Bible you must go down the other side, carrying the truth back into daily life. Just as a mountain peak has only one point, but many trails ultimately leading down, so each Bible passage will have one interpretation, but many applications.

The Bible teacher had correctly identified an important principle from the passage: Do not lift your hand against the Lord's anointed. Ed had to bring the truth to bear on his particular situation. He decided that his boss may not be anointed, but the Lord had allowed him to be appointed to this position, and it was certainly Ed's duty to be a faithful employee. Any move to get his boss fired or reassigned, even if he didn't break corporate rules, could be considered "lifting his hand against him."

Ed realized in a new way that opportunity does not make a wrong thing right. He also knew that if he undercut his boss, he would plant seeds for further dissension in the future and possibly his own undoing. But Ed, a man of action also knew that doing nothing could mean an intolerably long wait for his own promotion.

He needed to pray for patience and restraint for himself, as well as for the wisdom to know how to persuade his team to stay in line. He thought, *Perhaps I can tell them of my desire for a position like this and of my appreciation for their confidence in me, but also let them know my convictions about faithfully serving those in authority.* With David's inspiring example of successfully resisting pressure indelibly etched in his mind, Ed began to make some notes for a special meeting with his department.

An insight from your study of the Bible will not make a difference in your life until you take it personally. Bible knowledge alone is insufficient. For a changed life, you must also think, pray, and plan to put it into practice. Application is the process of carrying the principles and timeless truths of the Bible back to where you live. I hope you will find these three techniques helpful in applying the Bible to your life. Who knows . . . they might even come in handy as you listen to the radio some night!

■ Excerpted from *Discipleship Journal* 2, no. 2 (March–April 1990), pp. 47-49. Used by permission.

Applying God's Word Today

Roy B. Zuck

Wouldn't it be incredibly helpful to have a list of nine steps to insure accurate application of the Bible to today's needs, along with specific biblical examples from which to learn? Look no further than this article!

The following nine steps are suggested as ways to apply the Bible properly to our lives.

STEP 1. BUILD APPLICATION ON INTERPRETATION

If a text is interpreted incorrectly, then the application may be faulty as well. Interpretation asks, *What does this passage mean?* Application asks, *What does this passage mean to me?* If we have not accurately determined the meaning of the passage for the initial hearers, we may not accurately apply that meaning to today.

For example if we say in our interpretation that *every* reference to oil in the Bible refers to the Holy Spirit, then we end up interpreting the story of the widow's lack of oil in 2 Kings 4:1-7 as meaning that she lacked the Holy Spirit. In turn this wrong interpretation would then lead to a faulty application if we said that believers today are not indwelt by the Holy Spirit.

STEP 2. DETERMINE WHAT WAS EXPECTED OF THE ORIGINAL AUDIENCE

It is important as a first step in application to ask what application(s) the writers expected from their initial readers.

Sometimes commands are given in the New Testament that are clearly indicated as being for all Church-age believers. In Ephesus the Christians to whom Paul wrote Ephesians were members of the body of Christ, just as are believers today. Therefore much of what Paul wrote in that epistle is directly applicable to present-day Christians. The commands, admonitions, and exhortations for the Ephesians are also directives for all generations of believers since then.

The commands, prohibitions, exhortations, wishes, and permissions give instruction for direct application, whereas the others are more indirect. For example many of the verses in Proverbs tell of the benefits of following certain actions or the undesirable consequences of following other actions. Not direct commands, they nevertheless give commands indirectly or implicitly. The many verses that state the consequences of not controlling one's temper imply the command, "control your temper." These passages then *inform* the reader whereas others basically direct the reader.

STEP 3. BASE APPLICATIONS ON ELEMENTS PRESENT-DAY READERS SHARE WITH THE ORIGINAL AUDIENCE

The commonality between the original audiences and people today is the basis for valid applications. Both belong to the universal church, and both depend on apostolic authority for guidance in faith and practice. The command in Colossians 3:2, "set your minds on things above," and the command in verse 9, "do not lie to each other," are as relevant and authoritative for Christians today as for believers in Colosse two thousand years ago. The two audiences have much in common, though separated by time and geography. However, God's command to Israel in the wilderness to pick up manna six days each week is obviously a specific historical instance in which Israel and the church have little in common other than the fact that they both are people of God.

STEP 4. RECOGNIZE HOW GOD'S WORKING VARIES IN DIFFERENT AGES

Since God's dealings with mankind have differed from one dispensation to another, we need to be aware of those differences as we seek to apply the Bible. Of course some matters never change. For example the command to love one's neighbor is given not only in the Old Testament Law but also in the New Testament. This command was first given in Leviticus 19:18, and is repeated in Matthew 5:43, 19:19, 22:39; Romans 13:9; Galatians 5:14; and James 2:8. In addition nine of the Ten Commandments are repeated in the New Testament, and yet when repeated they are given with higher standards. The Mosaic Law commanded, "You shall not murder" (Exodus 20:13), but the New Testament church age command prohibits not only murder (Matthew 5:21) but even hatred ("Anyone who hates his brother is a murderer," 1 John 3:15).

Of course some regulations in the Old Testament Law have been annulled for believers in the present age. An example is the prohibition against eating certain foods (Leviticus 11), which Peter learned is no longer valid (Acts 10:9-16; cf. 1 Timothy 4:4).

STEP 5. DETERMINE WHAT IS NORMATIVE FOR TODAY

Because God has done something in the past for an individual does not mean we can expect Him to do the same for us. If what happened to someone in Bible times is considered normative for all believers, it must be in harmony with what is taught elsewhere in Scripture.

Abraham, Jacob, David, and others had more than one wife. Does this mean polygamy is acceptable, as some believe? No, this is not an acceptable practice. Even though God did not specifically condemn them individually for such a practice, as far as the scriptural record is concerned, we know polygamy is wrong because God gave Adam one wife. He said, "For this reason a man will leave his father and mother and be united to his wife, and they will become one flesh" (Genesis 2:24). Numerous passages in the New Testament speak of marital fidelity to one's *wife* (singular), e.g., Matthew 5:27, 31-32; 1 Corinthians 7:2-3; Ephesians 5:22-33; Colossians 3:18-19; 1 Thessalonians 4:3-7).

STEP 6. SEE THE PRINCIPLE INHERENT IN THE TEXT

Sometimes the Scriptures give specific commands, directives specified for all believers, as discussed earlier. However, other times such declarations are not explicit. Therefore we look for principles inherent within the text.[1] "When Jesus said, 'If someone forces you to go one mile, go with him two miles' (Matthew 5:41), He was putting a general principle into concrete terms. The application goes far beyond the particular situation."[2] What if someone were to force us to travel with him *two* miles? Would Jesus' words then no longer apply? No, the point is that when we are forced in this way we ought not retaliate but should do the opposite.

Principles, to be valid, must be affirmed elsewhere in Scripture. How does God's sending ravens to feed Elijah during a drought (1 Kings 17:6) apply to us today? Obviously this does not mean God desires to feed Christians by means of birds. Instead the principle is that God sometimes meets human needs by unusual means. The application of this principle is that believers can trust the Lord to supply their needs.

From these examples two points become clear. First, we should derive principles directly from the text. Second, we should be sure the principle is consistent with Scripture elsewhere.

STEP 7. THINK OF THE PRINCIPLE AS AN IMPLICATION (OR EXTRAPOLATION) OF THE TEXT, AND AS A BRIDGE TO APPLICATION

Seeing the principle in a text is an essential step in drawing out what is legitimately intended or implied in Scripture, and in formulating a bridge by which to relate Scripture to present-day contexts or situations.

For example, Christians in Antioch took an offering for poor believers in Judea (Acts 27-30). What does that situation almost two thousand years ago have to do with us? A principle that can be seen in this action on the part of the believers in Antioch is this: Christians in one locale should help meet the needs of Christians in other areas. Obviously this thought is not explicitly stated in Acts 11, but it is certainly implied. Therefore the principle serves as a bridge between interpretation and application. The application for today could be stated as follows: I will send money this week to help poor believers in Haiti (or some other needy country or area).

STEP 8. WRITE OUT SPECIFIC ACTION-RESPONSES

As you study the Bible, note ways you can apply the truth. Think of application in terms of relationships: your relationship to God, to Satan, to others (at home, church, work, school), to the world, and to yourself. Recognize that application can be in the form of improved attitudes as well as in improved actions. Make your applications personal. Use the words *I, me, my, mine,* not *we, us, our.* Application statements that remain in the "we" category are too general

Also be specific. Rather than saying, "I should love my wife more," be specific, by saying something like this: "I will take my wife out to dinner this Friday evening." Adding a time element, such as Friday evening, Thursday, or this weekend helps insure that the application is not delayed indefinitely.

In writing "I will . . . " application sentences you may want to choose from the following list of ninety action verbs for completing those sentences (see p. 104).

STEP 9. RELY ON THE HOLY SPIRIT

We must be sure that in the entire process of studying, interpreting, and applying the Bible, we are relying on the Holy Spirit to guide us. We need to ask the Holy Spirit to show us areas in our lives where application is needed, and then to make us sensitive to that need, and to give us the desire to change by appropriating the truth. In applying God's Word we need to ask the Holy Spirit to work in us to bring about changes in our lives that will make us more Christlike. It is not enough to perceive the truth; we must also receive it, by responding as God would have us to do.

Application, the crowning step in Bible study, can be exciting, as you see the Scripture working in your own life. As the Word of God penetrates our souls, it enables us to see areas where improvement is needed and enables us also to overcome weaknesses by the Holy Spirit's enabling and to "grow thereby" (1 Peter 2:2, KJV). Knowing the truth of God is essential, but blessing comes from *doing* it. As Johann Bengel wrote in 1742, "Apply yourself wholly to the text and apply the text wholly to yourself."

Action/Application Verbs

Accept	Discuss	Memorize	Spend time
Admit	Do	Organize	Stay away
Analyze	Eliminate	Plan out	Stop
Ask	Encourage	Pray	Study
Ask myself	Enjoy	Pray about	Substitute
Avoid	Evaluate	Pray to	Take
Be sensitive	Exemplify	Pray with	Talk with
Be willing	Experiment	Prefer	Teach
Build	Find	Pursue	Telephone
Buy	Follow	Read	Thank
Choose	Give	Realize	Think about
Claim	Go	Record	Value
Collect	Guard	Rejoice	Visit
Commit	Help	Repair	Wait
Compliment	Invite	Respond	Wake up
Comply	Isolate	Sacrifice	Walk
Confess	Keep	Save	Watch
Control	List	Schedule	Witness
Count	Listen	Select	Work on
Create	Look for	Send	Write down
Decide	Look up	Share	Write to
Develop	Love	Show	
Direct	Meet with	Sing	

Notes

1. Fred L. Fisher, *How to Interpret the New Testament* (Philadelphia: Westminster Press, 1966), 167-168.

2. Zuck, "Application in Biblical Hermeneutics and Exposition," in *Walvoord: A Tribute*, ed. Donald K. Campbell (Chicago: Moody Press, 1982), 27.

■ Reprinted with permission from Roy B. Zuck, *Basic Bible Interpretation* (Wheaton: Victor Books, 1991).

Applying the Lesson

Kenneth O. Gangel

If you as a teacher are committed to only one thing, let it be this: "The real test of teaching is not what students learn, but what they become." Let a teacher's teacher explain how to pass this test in your teaching.

The basic purpose of all Bible teaching is to effect change for good in the lives of students. The real test of teaching is not what students learn, but what they become. Education includes both the acquisition of knowledge and its use. For this reason, teachers should not be satisfied with their teaching unless students not only learn Bible truths but begin to apply them to their lives.

IMPORTANCE OF APPLICATION

You are responsible to help shape the lives of your students. To do this, you teach the Word of God. However, the task is not completed when you have imparted Bible knowledge. You must help your students develop godly character and maturity as well.

Character Building. It is impossible to separate Christian character from Christian living. Christian character is developed by living and expressed through living. The outward Christian life is the result of the Christ-formed character within. When Christ is acknowledged as Lord, the learner will be mastered by God's truth and will establish habits of study, prayer, reverence, worship, obedience, and unselfishness. An urgent desire to cultivate these habits should motivate Christian teachers.

Christian Growth. Christian character grows by expression—not through dreaming or wishing or talking. The habit of doing nothing is as devastating as the habit of doing wrong. If instruction and inspiration are not expressed in action, they will destroy spiritual sensitivity and make response to the Holy Spirit's leading extremely difficult. Incorporating expressional activities in the teaching program will encourage positive, active Christian character.

Christ's teaching methods included a strong emphasis on application. "By their fruits ye shall know them" (Matthew 7:20). He taught his disciples that the inner spiritual condition is manifested by outward deeds and actions. They did not learn this truth in a formal schoolroom, they learned it by sharing his life and work. They lived as he lived. They learned right attitudes toward God and their fellow men. They sensed his motives and the urgency of his ministry. Then he sent them out to complete their training by practical experience in everyday life.

People develop Christian behavior patterns in the same way. They learn to pray, not by defining or describing prayer, but by entering actively into prayer. They learn how to study God's Word by actual use of the Bible. They become reverent, obedient, and unselfish by practicing these virtues.

Spiritual Foundation. The Word of God provides the foundation for Christian living. It is useless to attempt to build Christian character independent of instruction in it. The Bible deals with life by recognizing sin and supplying God's remedy. It touches every inner and outer area—sports, social activities, home, school, church.

YOUR EXAMPLE

The Spirit of God applies the truths of the Word to students' lives. However, the Spirit often uses teachers to clarify the meaning of a lesson both by actions and attitude.

Actions. Teachers cannot successfully relate truth until they have applied it to their own lives. Students must constantly see exemplified in you the biblical truth you wish them to apply to their lives. This is a categorical imperative in Christian teaching.

The Lord Jesus accompanied his teaching by a constant demonstration of the truth. He exemplified meekness by girding himself and washing the disciples' feet (John 13:4-17). He frequently taught forgiveness (Matthew 6:15; 18:21-22), but it was in His look of forgiveness that Peter learned its real meaning after he had denied his Lord.

Attitudes. A recent study demonstrates that the attitude of junior high students toward God is not dependent on the amount of their Bible knowledge. Their attitudes are dependent on those expressed by their parents. Teachers also transmit attitudes through frequent relationships with students. Often teachers will be more influential in the lives of their students by the attitudes they evidence than by what they say. Many young people have testified that while they forgot the verbal instruction received in their youth, they could never forget the exemplary lives of godly teachers.

PLANNING FOR APPLICATION

Personalize the Lesson. Among specific procedures which help personalize a lesson are: ask probing questions; confront the class with alternatives; lead students into actual or imaginative predicaments that require the application of the truth; focus attention on sub-Christian attitudes and activities; allow the class members to express doubt, wonder, skepticism, and curiosity about points of application; help students interpret their own experiences.

Relate to Life. Until early adolescence, students have a limited power of generalization. They do not readily see the underlying principles of biblical teachings which apply to many different situations. For example, students may learn and be able to respond accurately to testing about the principle that a Christian should not steal. Yet when a store clerk returns too much change they may not understand keeping the extra change is a form of stealing. Use examples like this to help students apply what they learn to their own life situations.

Involve Students. Learning will be more effective when students participate in making the application. Sometimes the entire class can agree to select a certain behavior pattern, an attitude, or an activity which reflects the emphasis of the lesson. They may agree to follow this behavior pattern or set of values during the coming week. This can be followed by an evaluation of results in the review of the lesson the following week.

EMPHASES OF APPLICATION

There are several areas of spiritual development in which application of lesson content should be evident.

Salvation. It is imperative that all students understand their personal responsibility when making a decision for Christ. Instruction should train them in the truths and procedures that will prepare for personal acceptance of Jesus Christ as Savior and Lord. Have as a primary goal the leading of every one of your students to Christ.

Spirituality. The aim of spirituality is the mature person in Christ. "Till we all come in the unity of the faith, and of the knowledge of the Son of God, unto a perfect man, unto the measure of the stature of the fullness of Christ" (Ephesians 4:13). As the reality of Christ increases by faith, the fruits of the Spirit will also become more evident (Galatians 5:22, 23).

Stewardship. The development of spiritual life also involves the students' personal responsibility for their use of time, abilities, and possessions. They should be taught to support the entire program of the church and to contribute their own money. The actual sharing of possessions provides the best learning.

Service. An adequate curriculum, properly taught, should lead students to a personal responsibility for their talents. Capture every opportunity to direct students to worthwhile activities. Make your instruction a laboratory course in Christian service as a stimulus for lifetime surrender to Christ in the home, in the church, in the community, in the world.

SUMMARY

The final test of all teaching is in the changed lives of students. This requires application of the truth, for applying the truth builds character and provides for Christian growth and a spiritual foundation.

Much learning takes place through relationships. Students learn from what teachers are. Knowledge can be transmitted by an effective teaching process; however, life changes take place when a teacher's actions and attitudes corroborate their words.

Successful translation of truth into life requires deliberate planning on the part of teachers. They must constantly strive to personalize biblical truth, relate it to the life situations which students are facing, and then involve them in action. The evidences of successful application are salvation, spirituality, stewardship, and service.

■ Reprinted from Chapter 11 of Kenneth O. Gangel's *Teaching Techniques for Church Education* (Evangelical Training Association, 1983). Used by permission.

Applying Scripture in Sunday School

Terry Hall

Here's a presentation of some creative ways to help Sunday school students personalize and apply a passage of Scripture. You can use these immediately—how about this Sunday morning?

Revelation demands a response. Scripture was given not just to satisfy our curiosity but to change our lives. If we aim for a life response, we're more likely to hit it.

Don't give students spiritual indigestion by stopping with the facts of Scripture. To make a difference in our lives, God's word needs to work in three areas: our minds, emotions, and wills. Ask, "What do I want my pupils to know, feel, and do as a result of this lesson?" Don't leave pupils the same. Take them from where they are to some new goal in life.

Here are several options to help students (and teachers) discover what God expects from them.

SORTING OUT

One meaningful way to find personal application is to sort out God's responsibilities from ours.

Begin by drawing two vertical lines on a chalkboard or transparency, dividing it into three columns. Title the left column "My Duties" and the right "God's Duties." The middle column will be labeled "Results."

Using verses from the lesson, fill in the columns. (Note: not every verse will have all three elements.) From the "My Duties" column, ask each student to write down one thing he plans to do from his assigned responsibilities. After the chosen item, he should write out two or three specific action steps to accomplish it. Action steps for "keep my way pure," for example, might be: Stop reading a certain magazine; walk away from groups telling off-color stories; or, when lustful thoughts come, thank God for making girls.

Use what has been written into the three columns as a basis for conversational prayer. Ask God to help us carry out our specific duties, and thank Him for the results and for fulfilling His responsibilities.

PERSONALIZE GOD'S LETTERS

Turn a Bible passage into a first-person prayer. For example, compare this first-person prayer to James 1:1-8:

> Father, I thank you that James was your servant as well as the servant of the Lord Jesus Christ. Thank you for using James to send greetings to the twelve dispersed tribes. Lord, I also want to be known as one of your servants. Please help me to bring your good news to other people.
>
> When I face trials of many kinds, help me to consider it pure joy. Help me to realize in such times that the testing of my faith develops

perseverance. Please help me to let perseverance finish its work so I may be mature and complete, not lacking anything.

Dear Father, when I lack wisdom, remind me to ask you. Thank you that you give generously to me without finding fault. Please help me to believe and not doubt when I ask you for help and wisdom with my problems and decisions. I don't want to be like a wave of the sea, blown and tossed by the wind. I want to receive what I ask from you. I don't want to be a double-minded person who is unstable in all he does. In the name of Jesus. Amen.

Note how restating God's Word as a personal prayer brings its truths out of the ancient world right into our lives. Practice turning a portion of the Bible into a personal prayer, continuing with James 1 or using another passage.

"SPECS" TO SEE BETTER

Have your students read a Scripture portion and make notes on a sheet of paper with the five letters **SPECS** (Sins to avoid, Promises to claim, Examples to follow, Commands to obey, Stumbling Blocks to avoid) spaced vertically down the left side.

- •Sins are attitudes or actions that displease the Lord and should be forsaken.
- •Promises are assurances or benefits from God to be claimed, but there are often conditions attached.
- •Examples are good attitudes or actions to imitate. Bad ones would be listed as sins or stumbling blocks.
- •Commands are directions from God to obey.
- •Stumbling blocks are things God warns us to avoid. Decide on one specific action to put into practice from this passage.

DEAR ME

Distribute an envelope, stationery, and postage stamp to each member to write a letter to himself about what this quarter's study (or a particular Bible portion) has meant to him, what he wants to change in his life as a result, and how he plans to pursue this new goal.

When collecting the self-addressed, stamped, sealed letters, assure writers you won't peek, but will mail them in about six months.

Optionally write to a Bible author, expressing gratitude for his writing, asking any questions, and stating how his writing has affected our lives.

Or write a letter to God and thank Him for what He has written and for what He has done, is doing, and has promised to do. Specifically ask His help to live the Christian life, admitting any sins or shortcomings His Word has pointed out. Allow time for each to actually send (by praying silently) his letter to God.

YES OR NO?

Help your pupils create a yes or no quiz from a Bible passage, each asking if what God says is true of him or not. Here are some sample yes or no questions from James 1:1-8:

- •Am I a servant of God?
- •Am I a servant of the Lord Jesus Christ?

•Do I ever give God's greetings to others?

•Do I face trials of many kinds?

•Do I consider it pure joy when I face them?

•Do I know that the testing of my faith develops perseverance?

•Am I becoming mature and complete through perseverance?

•When I lack wisdom, do I first turn to God?

•Do I view God as One who gives to me generously without finding fault?

•When I ask God for wisdom, do I ask doubting or believing?

•Am I double-minded and unstable in my ways?

BASIC PRINCIPLES

Ask what lessons for life God teaches through this week's Bible story or portion. Principles are like the "moral of the story" and may be directly stated or strongly implied. The more historical the passage (relating events), the more principles are implied. The more doctrinal the passage (relating ideas), the more principles are explicitly stated.

We can't find an exact quotation of an implied principle because it's woven in as an underlying theme. When we see an implied principle, we are on good ground if we find that idea clearly taught in two or three different Bible passages. Consult the cross-references printed in many Bibles or look in a topical Bible such as *Nave's Topical Bible* (Moody Press), an index to Bible subjects.

Looking for principles in the Bible makes ancient passages seem more relevant.

GET SPECIFIC

Don't assume anything when it comes to application of truth to life. Our lesson goal is not met if each student leaves knowing only a memory verse or central thought of a Bible text. Each must also know something specific God wants him to do as a result of exposure to His Word.

Christian teaching is a dynamic cooperation with God. The same Holy Spirit who indwells the teacher indwells every Christian student and convicts every nonbelieving one. The Holy Spirit of God is the great Motivator. Christian students leave our classroom with the Teacher living within them.

As teachers, we prepare, pray, and teach, but God is the only One who can effect life change. Pray for your pupils individually through the week, asking the Holy Spirit to motivate them to alter their lives to fit His Word.

Following our Lord's example, teaching for life response will help you to be the best Sunday school teacher you can be.

Preach and Teach with Practical Application

Elmer L. Towns

These ten guidelines for making effective application should be copied and kept right with your lessons. Read over them afresh each time you prepare a lesson—biblical or academic—to relate truth to life effectively.

Practical application integrates sermons or lessons with members' past experience. Preachers or teachers can take ten steps to ensure that their message is practically applied in the lifestyles of their students.

1. Relate each Bible passage to the whole of Scripture. A lesson is like a spoke in a wheel; each is necessary for the whole. Teaching should relate a Bible chapter to an entire book, then each book to the whole Bible.

2. Relate each lesson to the whole of members' lives. When members see how the message relates to aspects of their lives and sees how things fit together, they listen and learn.

3. Use real illustrations from modern life. The computer generation may not be able to relate to horse-pulled plows and houses without electricity. When illustrations solve modern problems, members can identify with people in the story and apply the answers to their lives.

4. Use positive role models from Scripture. God communicates His principles for us through the lives of people in Scripture.

5. Identify positive role models from members' lives. Role models must have discernible strength in the area where they are used as an example and members must have positive attitudes toward the role models.

6. Solve problems. Teaching that is effective is functional. When we identify problems in the lives of members and give them answers, they will transfer the lessons into their lives.

7. Point out relationships. Teaching is not just giving facts, but showing the relationship between facts so members remember the connection.

8. Point out principles. God wants us to live by biblical principles. The teacher should point out these principles and help members see the relationship between them and their lesson as well as the relationship between their lives and the principles.

9. Motivate students to establish and/or live by principles. Teachers who want to permanently influence the lives of their students will use every motivational technique possible to get them to recognize and live by the principles existing in their lives.

10. Relate new principles to those already known. Teaching is relating things to each other and guiding learning activities. One of the most effective learning activities is relating facts, principles, and concepts to life.

Adapted from Elmer Towns' *Towns on Teacher Training,* © 1989 Church Growth Institute, Lynchburg, Virginia. Used by permission.

Teacher: Face the Future As a Change Agent

Harold J. Westing

Most teachers will agree that teaching is for lifechange. But are people always eager to change? Does this make teaching harder? Think through this issue as you prepare to "face the future as a change agent."

Have you ever noticed how people reject change? Over the years I've noticed there is a growing resentment among teachers of adults and youth, and among the students themselves, about the idea that their lives need to change. It may have grown out of their fear of being manipulated by psychobiology, or B.F. Skinner's "behavioral modification." After all, we have discovered that we can create an environment to help foster that kind of change in society. Or perhaps they identify with the Human Rights movement which is strongly built upon the assumption that one person should not seek to change another. We all have built into us psychological reactants which make us antagonistic toward anyone who is trying to change us!

When adult Sunday School students talk about the course they prefer to take, it seems they tend to choose one of two kinds of subjects: one they have studied many times and feel familiar with; or current winds that tend to be blowing through the evangelical world. One might conclude that they are not really interested in changing their lives, but only in either feeling comfortable in the classroom, or in gathering additional information.

WHAT DOES THE BIBLE SAY ABOUT CHANGE?

A biblical Christian education cornerstone, Colossians 1:28, instructs that we should be teaching in all wisdom to bring people to maturity in Christ. This suggests that the ultimate goal of Christian education is to help people come to maturity, which immediately suggests spiritual development, or CHANGE. God intends the growing believer to move away from carnality toward godliness.

It will take every bit of wisdom we can muster to help students make the transition from immaturity to maturity in Jesus Christ. Hebrews 10:24-25 affirms one of the major reasons the church ought to be involved in an educational program which concentrates on change. The statement behind the passage suggests that people don't normally get together as believers, and even when they do very little productivity comes out of the meeting.

The writer of Hebrews implies that there ought to be a kind of dialogue among believers which draws the greatest potential of love and good works out of each other. The same writer says in 13:17 that we need to keep watch over the students who are assigned to us. James 5:19-20 also offers an admonition to bring about change. Teachers are greatly "congratulated" for turning someone back from the error of his ways. Again, a change of direction in spiritual life is intimated here.

These passages refer to the church at study, and I am consequently assuming that a major focus of education is to produce change in the classroom; and to be constantly exercising ourselves unto a new position of godliness (see 1 Timothy 4:7-8).

The major reasons we need to be engaged in such endeavors is that we all have a bent toward depravity and carnality, even though we are new persons in Christ. A strong underlying statement in both Old and New Testaments is that "growth necessitates change." 1 Peter 2:2 admonishes us to grow by partaking of the pure milk of the Word of God. Not only does Peter challenge us to grow, but Paul's letters to the various churches repeatedly emphasizes the need for growth in faith, hope, and love. The major theme of each one of those epistles has to do with the process that believers need to go through to gain a new level of maturity.

As we consider what Scripture says concerning the necessity of change in the members of the body of Christ, we need to keep in mind that *indoctrination* is significantly different than *persuasion*, although at times they look very much alike. Manipulation forces one to go against his own will so that another person will benefit from it. That is why Paul tells the church at Thessalonica that he did not use flattering words with pretext of greed. He rejected "cunning craftiness" to get them to change against their will, but tried to motivate them toward higher spiritual gains. (See 1 Thessalonians 2:4-5).

Change is so important to God that He has gifted certain people in the church to help bring it about. Pastors, teachers and evangelists are given the specific task of equipping the saints so they might be able to function with a higher level of efficiency in bringing all of the body of Christ to maturity (Ephesians 4:11-16).

HOW CAN TEACHERS FACILITATE CHANGE?

As we look at the various texts reminding us to be engaged in the change agent role, we notice how they imply that teachers and leaders need to be skilled in the art of persuasion. First, they have to know exactly what godliness looks like. Where does this individual student need to move next? But teachers also need to possess the skill required to get them there!

The following suggestions should help you in becoming a skillful "spiritual persuader":

1. As often as possible help people make their own choices. Keep in mind that teaching is not really giving people anything; the learning they achieve is what they take for themselves. Unfortunately, the older they get the greater the resistance to change. That's why we teach adults differently than we teach children.

It might help to remember that when Jesus taught He did not reduce reason and moral conscience but increased them. He did not come to lighten the burden of thought, but to make it more active. He didn't come to settle minds, but to provoke them. He didn't come to make life easier; He came to help men to learn (Matthew 10:34).

Since this is true, you need to become skilled in asking questions. I constantly try to keep this little formula in mind as I ask questions in class:

    a. The student who asks questions and finds the answers himself
        will be engaged in the best kind of learning.
    b. The student who asks questions and is given answers is
        engaged in the second best kind of learning.
    c. The student who is asked questions and finds answers will learn
        in the third best fashion.
    d. The student who is asked questions and given answers
        learns the least.

2. A change agent teacher will be effective when he recognizes that spirituality basically has three component parts. A spiritual person is someone who *knows the content of Scripture, feels properly about that content* and *responds accordingly.* Therefore, the teacher deals with the student's mind, his emotions and his will. Too many teachers are masters at loading minds with Scripture but they have a difficult time getting their students to respond. Perhaps such teachers have not fully understood that as change agents they wrestle with people's emotions, as well as giving them content. We are to help build the "muscle of the will" so that it can be sufficiently strong to act in accordance with the Word of God.

At times you may make your students feel uncomfortable—not so much with what they know, but how they behave. You may have to create a state of "disequilibrium" (throw them off balance a bit). You should feel satisfied only when their wills are properly exercised in carrying out a new command from Scripture—and that's change. Knowing what it means to lift another person's burden is not enough; they must practice that Christian behavior toward other people.

3. A good change agent recognizes the necessity of involvement-type methods in his teaching process. All the research in how people learn gives strong indication that such techniques as role-playing, case studies, and field experiences produce the best kind of learning. I often like to think of the Christian life as a whole system of habits—habits which are both internal and external. I "habit" to exercise my will to say "no" to sin. I "habit" to keep my mouth quiet when I am tempted to slander.

When a Christian businessman is confronted in his Sunday School class with a value decision about his encounters in the business world, he is far more apt to develop a habit (habituate) to live that way on the job. Change agent teachers of teens develop programs which consistently help the teens to resist the temptations they are confronting every day in scores of different areas. Of course, this immediately suggests the necessity of a certain level of accountability to the change agent teacher, their peers, or some other significant individual.

4. Changed attitudes follow changed behavior. Change agent teachers program their lessons to include behavioral activities. They understand that the sooner you put into practice a truth which you have learned, the more apt you are to actually "own" that truth.

■ Taken from Harold J. Westing, "Teacher: Face the Future As a Change Agent," *Christian Education Today* 38, no. 4 (Fall 1986), pp. 14-15. Used by permission.

Closure: The Fine Art of Making Learning Stick

LuOuida Vinson Phillips

You've spent the hour communicating: good content, effective illustrations, challenging applications. But how do you make it stick? Here are five proven techniques for bringing closure in your class.

On Monday you're confident that the lesson on fractions is a success, but on Tuesday, when you ask kids to summarize what they learned, you get blank stares and vague answers. When you reassess Monday's presentation, you're still pleased with your motivational material, your use of manipulative activities, and kids' level of interest, but now you feel that something was missing. But what?

Naturally, when students can't recall key concepts, all factors must be considered. The effectiveness of your presentation, the appropriateness of the activities, and kids' concentration levels affect whether they master a lesson. But if you are confident of those areas, then there is a fourth you should consider: Did you end the lesson with closure?

Closure helps fix learning, student by student, so it can be recalled and used the next day, the next week, or the next month. Closure helps learners know what they learned, why they learned it, and how this knowledge is useful.

The five most common methods of closure include lesson wrap-ups, homework assignments, quick quiz evaluations, extensions, and applications.

1. LESSON WRAP-UPS

Students need to be aware of the whats, hows, and whys of what you're asking them to learn. Orient them at the beginning of lessons to what the class will be doing, what you think should be achieved, and why. It may sound obvious, but many kids can repeat what has been done, without knowing either why or what constitutes mastery. Active participation helps kids understand. Try these formats to encourage greater student involvement. In turn, kids will more likely internalize learning and be able to relate it to other experiences.

- Refer to individual students in wrap-up conversations. At first, kids may perceive your comments as criticism and feel threatened. But if you use the technique consistently and fairly with all students, you'll get past this problem and encourage kids to be more candid, too. Tell a few of them ahead of time that they will be asked to explain the key points of the lesson.

- Experiment with a variety of wrap-ups. You might close with a story and ask what it has to do with the lesson. Also, try asking for written evaluations of a lesson or listings of key words or concepts. Kids could also judge a lesson to be easy, moderate, or hard or rate it on a scale of one to ten, with one for least interest and understanding and ten for highest. Or use a key of S, M, or N ("I'm **S**ure I have it," "**M**aybe I have it," or "**N**o, I don't have it"). Usually answers will show candor.

- Occasionally, lighten up the wrap-up process with a game or a gimmick. For example, you might invest in an inexpensive applause meter: You make true or false statements and the kids applaud when statements are true.

2. HOMEWORK

Assigning homework is a familiar use of closure time. To make homework a better extension of what you've taught, make it as individualized as possible, and assign it only when needed for practice, review, application, and consolidation of material. Its purpose should be clear when children do it later. When kids understand the importance of the material they're studying, they're less likely to view homework as busy work.

These variations can make homework more effective as closure:

- Work your review into homework assignments: "What did we do today, Jason? Yes, we found the main idea in paragraphs. Please take home these sheets containing paragraphs and write the main idea under each one."
- Pair up students of equal ability. When there's no one at home to check papers, buddies can compare results by phone.
- Give alternative assignments to spark interest and stretch thinking. Your assignment might be: "Make a list of six tools, then see if you can write the scientific principle by which each operates. Or, invent a useful household item, make a model or drawing of it, and explain the scientific principle that makes it work."

3. QUICK QUIZ EVALUATIONS

Occasionally, you may want to make a quick quiz your method of closure. Make it simple enough so that, in the five to eight minutes you allot to closure, kids can take the test, self-correct it, and analyze their progress. Results will help you decide whether the class needs more work on a concept or whether just a few kids need remediation.

Try these techniques:

- Explore a variety of quiz formats, such as a prepared written quiz or reading aloud true/false or multiple-choice questions.
- Once in a while, ask the children to be the testers. Divide the class into two groups: One questions while the other answers. Try cross-subject testing. For example, test for closure in a math lesson on measurement by asking kids to make art projects that are five-by-six-inches, or check mastery of solar system facts by encouraging students to write a story about space travel.
- Swap mini-tests with colleagues on the same grade level. You'll save time and better prepare kids for standardized tests. Besides, the different formats you each choose and what you consider important may surprise you.

4. EXTENSIONS

Extending a lesson works best when basic concepts are internalized. Extensions build on those concepts to develop special talents and interests, and to demonstrate many ways of gaining information.

These extension activities reinforce learning and help kids discover new avenues for expression:

- Use wrap-up time to review how kids can find out more about the topic.
- Jot down queries that come up during a lesson, then use them for closure. For example, children may be curious about what caused certain inventions to be

created. Ask volunteers to find the answers and report back to class.

- Take advantage of spontaneous excitement. A book about juggling may tempt students to try learning the skill. A science unit may interest kids in finding samples of leaves and in setting up their own procedures for collecting, classifying, and mounting specimens.

5. APPLICATIONS

The ultimate closure is when kids apply new knowledge to a life situation. You'll need to wait until basic learnings are well in hand, then try to relate what you've taught to children's own experiences. Here are some helpful application strategies:

- Look for ordinary activities that can illustrate lessons. For example, popping corn in class can reinforce a lesson about the properties of heat and gases. Drinking through straws is good closure for a lesson on lungs and breathing.
- Encourage kids to experiment independently to test conclusions reached in class. For example, after doing a unit about taste with young students, send home an activity sheet asking parents to sample with their kids a variety of favorite family foods that are either sweet, sour, salty, or spicy.
- Involve children in projects that help others. A lesson about world hunger might end with kids collecting food to distribute to the needy either locally or abroad.

Application helps students to stretch and to combine talents, skills, and knowledge to better understand their world. And that's the whole point.

■ From *Instructor*, 62, no. 3 (October 1977), pp. 36-38. Reprinted by permission of Scholastic, Inc.

The Holy Spirit in Education

Jay E. Adams

*When does the communication of truth actually qualify to be called
"Christian education?" The views of this veteran educator call into
question some practices and presumptions currently taken for granted.*

Apart from the personal devotion of individual Christian teachers and administrators (and, I admit that God uses this—often powerfully), there's little
dependence on the Holy Spirit and His work for teaching and learning. The present
fundamental structure of education—borrowed as it is from a pagan, humanistic model
that has no place for God and sees no need for Him—allows for no way to change the
situation. And, in it, there is no concern for such change. Indeed, a few might even
consider talk about the Holy Spirit "unprofessional."

How has this strange divorce of the Holy Spirit and Christian education come
about? A major reason for the sort of professionalism that separates God's power from
education is the acceptance of the pagan academic model (which comes from Greek
thought, and emphasizes truth for truth's sake) which separates truth from life. Akin to
that tragic disjunction is a second: the separation of truth from wisdom (or, God's way
of viewing and living life). Modern humanistic educators think that truth can be known
(1) apart from God's perspective on life, and (2) apart from living life by the Holy
Spirit's power. Both of these errors, working hand in hand, have effectively eliminated
the Holy Spirit from the serious thinking and planning even of most Christian educators.

In the Scriptures, the Holy Spirit is called the "Spirit of truth" (John 16:13). It is He
who "guided" the apostles into all truth. Clearly, from these words, one can see that
His concern is educational; the Spirit is inextricably involved in the impartation of truth
(which is more than knowledge). How, then, can Christian educators, who purport to
be in the business of searching out and dispensing truth—and, as a matter of fact,
ought to be, as they study and seek to obey God's command to occupy and control—
fail to take into account the place and the work of the Holy Spirit in education? If truth
isn't a central concern of Christian education, then what is?

True Christian education, then, is education that is bound up with sanctification,
i.e., growth in one's spiritual life. It is a moral, life-altering experience, not an amoral
activity. This education is dependent on repentance and faith that leads to wisdom; it is
an education that, through the work of the Holy Spirit, spiritualizes all of life. That is to
say, Christian education depends on the Spirit's illumination and application of His
Book, the Bible, for the correct perception and relationship of every fact, and on His
energizing power for living according to biblical truth in all aspects of life.

What I have been leading up to is this: the Holy Spirit educates differently. He
does not educate as the humanists do, or even as Christians who follow humanists do.
His educational objective is not merely the acquisition of facts; it is not even the
acquisition of truth. He has more in mind: He is concerned about what is done with
that truth and what that truth does. His objective is changed lives.

This emphasis surfaces most clearly in that great educational passage, Matthew
28:18-20:

And Jesus went to them and said to them, "All authority in heaven and on earth has been given to Me. Go, therefore, and make disciples from all nations, baptizing them into the Name of the Father and of the Son and of the Holy Spirit, teaching them to observe all that I have commanded you; and remember, I will be with you always, to the close of the age."

Usually this passage is referred to as the Great Commission, and it is that, of course. But in making an emphasis on missions, the sturdy educational framework of the passage often has been ignored, or even distorted.

Because, by His death and resurrection, Jesus Christ had been given "all authority in heaven and on earth," He sent out His apostles to recruit students (disciples) from all nations. Those who were saved would be matriculated into His school by baptism, and would thereupon enter into a life-long course of education. It is the description of that educational curriculum with which we presently are concerned: "teaching them to observe all that I have commanded you." The words "teaching . . . to observe" say it all. Obedient observance of Christ's commandments is the objective of the Holy Spirit's education.

Much needs to be said (elsewhere) about the latter portion of that program ("all I have commanded you"); here our focus must rest strictly on the words "teaching them to observe." Always, biblical discipleship is twofold, in contrast to the more limited academic objective of modern education. Academic teaching today is teaching in the abstract. Facts are individually hung out on the clothesline to dry. They flap in the breeze, unrelated to one another and to life. Biblical (Spirit-energized) education, on the other hand, is education for life; it is teaching to be "observed" (i.e., put to use in daily living). Dewey spoke of learning by doing and was wrong. Christians must speak instead of learning for doing, if they are to be right. Truth, in the Scriptures, is never taught for its own sake; it is always taught for use. In introducing the letter to Titus, Paul said that God had chosen him to "promote the faith of God's chosen people and the full knowledge of the truth that brings about godliness" (Titus 1:1). Truth is for use. That is why one of the Bible's favorite phrases is "walking in the truth."

This biblical concept of truth for use means that the academic model ("Here are the facts; learn them and show us that you have on tests.") is inadequate. What should Christian educators wish to achieve? Godly living; that is what. All truth—yes, even about pigs, and business, and roads—ought to be so related to Jesus Christ that one is more godly because he has learned it. That will happen only when his learning is for doing. Every fact that he acquires must be (1) oriented properly into his Christian stance toward life, placing God's interpretation on it, and (2) turned into life and ministry.

■ Adapted from Jay E. Adams, *Back to the Blackboard: Design for a Biblical Christian School* (Presbyterian & Reformed Publishing Company, 1982). Used by permission.

The Spiritual Dynamic in Christian Education

Roy B. Zuck

The Holy Spirit empowers the gift of teaching and is called the one "who will lead us into all truth." But is there more? Yes! And this article articulates the powerful relationship of the Spirit to those who teach.

Christian education is unique because of its subject matter—the Bible, God's written revelation; because of its goals—spiritual transformation of lives; and because of its spiritual dynamics—the work of the Holy Spirit. To neglect the Spirit's ministry in teaching is to overlook a critical aspect of Christian education.

THE NEED OF THE HOLY SPIRIT IN EDUCATION

Why should the Holy Spirit be necessary in Christian education? Is it not enough to place the Bible in the hands of Christian teachers, encouraging them to follow proper pedagogical principles and use appropriate methods and materials? What can the Holy Spirit bring to the teaching/learning process in the Christian realm that is unique to Him? Why is the Holy Spirit necessary in the educational process?

REASONS FOR THE SPIRIT'S ROLE IN TEACHING

One reason the Holy Spirit is necessary in Christian education is that the Christian teacher needs divine enabling. Only by the Holy Spirit can teachers be guided and enabled to teach the Bible and related subjects effectively. A spiritual task—involving spiritual truths to meet spiritual needs—requires spiritual power. Effectiveness in service demands salvation and yieldedness to the Holy Spirit. Seeking to serve the Lord in one's own strength apart from dependence on the Holy Spirit avails little by way of lasting results.

Purity of life, stemming from submission to the Spirit's control, contributes to effective teaching. Conversely, failure to model the truth makes a teacher ineffective. Students are not drawn to truths taught by a teacher who "mouths" them without modeling them. Inconsistency between "lip" and life turns students off and turns them away.

Another reason the Holy Spirit's work is necessary in the teaching and learning process is that the Spirit makes the Word of God effectual in the students' lives. Bible knowledge and comprehension of spiritual truths, essential as they are, do not of themselves guarantee spiritual change and growth. Not all who hear the Word believe or respond (John 10:25; 12:47-48; Acts 7:57-59; 17:5, 32). As the Word of God regenerates (Psalm 19:7; Romans 10:17; James 1:18; 1 Peter 1:23), the Holy Spirit must be on hand to remove spiritual blindness and give eternal life (John 3:5-7; Titus 3:5).

Believers too must be open to the ministry of both the Word and the Spirit. The Word sanctifies (John 17:17-19; Acts 20:32; Ephesians 5:26; 1 Peter 2:2), and so does the Spirit (2 Thessalonians 2:13; 1 Peter 1:2). The Word enlightens (Psalm 119:105, 130; 2 Timothy 3:16), and so does the Spirit (John 14:26; 16:13; 1 Corinthians 2:10-15). The written Word, to be effective in the lives of unbelievers and believers, requires the ministry of the Holy Spirit. Changed lives require both the Word and the Spirit. And since Christian education focuses on bringing about spiritually transformed lives, the teaching/learning process requires both the Holy Scriptures and the Holy Spirit. One without the other is inadequate.

FALSE CONCEPTS OF THE SPIRIT'S ROLE IN TEACHING

Some educators, consciously or not, neglect the work of the Holy Spirit. Committed to high standards in educational theory, programs, and personnel, committed to the need for a proper learning environment, and to the importance of well-defined educational goals and learning objectives, some creative and well-meaning teachers tend to operate "on natural grounds without the aid of the Spirit."[1] This overlooks the frailties of man's fallen nature, and "elevates man's creativity and methods over God's and fails to realize that only the Spirit can accomplish the spiritual goals of Christian education."[2]

Teaching is more than "dispensing the truth." Helping students understand Bible facts falls short of the spiritual dimension of Christian education. The goal is to help students come to know God and love Him, not just know about Him. It involves helping them walk in accord with His will, growing in spiritual maturity and Christlikeness—and that requires the ministry of the Holy Spirit.

Others stress the work of the Holy Spirit to the neglect of human teachers. They suggest that education is the enemy of spirituality, that education is a work of the flesh and conflicts with and opposes the work of the Spirit. This view, however, overlooks the fact that in Bible times God used human teachers (Matthew 28:19-20; Acts 5:42; 15:35; 18:11, 25; 28:31; 2 Timothy 2:2), and that God has given the gift of teaching to some believers (Romans 12:6-7; 1 Corinthians 12:28; Ephesians 4:11). Human teachers, as instruments of the Holy Spirit, can stimulate and challenge students, guiding them into a proper understanding and application of God's Word.

Stressing the role of the Holy Spirit in the teaching process does not suggest that teachers need not study and prepare. Far from it! "Only the teacher who is well prepared can do the most efficient task while at the same time relying on the Holy Spirit to work through him and his students."[3] Since teaching is a divine-human process, a ministry involving the Holy Spirit and teachers jointly, preparation makes the teacher a better instrument, a sharper tool in God's hands. Depending on the Holy Spirit in one's teaching does not mean being unprepared and "simply letting the Holy Spirit speak through me," as if preparation competed with spirituality. Just the opposite is true.

Unpreparedness is not a sign of being "more spiritual." Sometimes, however, the Holy Spirit has seemed to use poorly prepared teaching efforts and has apparently accomplished much. How can we account for this fact? While it is true that the Spirit can and does override a teacher's bungling, lack of preparation is nowhere encouraged in the Bible.

Paul's words in I Corinthians 3:6, "I planted the seed, Apollos watered it, but God made it grow," make it clear that human effort is accompanied, not substituted, by the divine working of God Himself. Rather than an excuse for laziness or ignorance, the role of the Spirit in the educational process provides a challenge to excellence.

THE RELATIONSHIP OF THE HOLY SPIRIT TO THE TEACHERS

Christian education is a cooperative process, a venture involving both the human and the divine. Human teachers communicate and exemplify truth; the Holy Spirit seeks to provide guidance, power, illumination, and insight to the teachers.

Human teachers must depend on the Holy Spirit to work through them, to use them in reaching their students with the truth, and the Holy Spirit desires to fill and control the human instruments. In expounding the truth, teachers should help students see how the truth can be applied to their lives, and the Holy Spirit seeks to motivate and enable students to appropriate the truth.

Teachers are to encourage their students to understand the Word of God and to relate it to themselves, and the Holy Spirit seeks to encourage students to appropriate it personally. Without the work of the Holy Spirit in the teaching/learning process, the educational goal of spiritual transformation cannot be accomplished.

To be effective, human teachers must exemplify the truth they teach, being models of Christlikeness and growing in spiritual maturity. This requires obedience to the Word of God, dedication to the will of God, and submission to the Spirit of God.

The relationship of the human to the divine is clearly demonstrated in 1 Corinthians 2. Paul wrote that his message was not communicated with mere human eloquence, wisdom, or persuasion, but with inner spiritual power (vv. 1, 4). He was involved in giving a message of God's wisdom, but the Holy Spirit was involved in enabling him to understand God's wisdom (v. 12) and to have insight into God's ways (v. 16). Paul spoke (v. 13) what he had been taught by the Holy Spirit (v. 13). Teachers are also responsible to learn how God made people to learn, then to teach accordingly. Since teaching helps others learn, teachers must know the ways in which students of various ages best learn and teach accordingly. In doing so they are cooperating with the Holy Spirit.

Notes
    1. C. Fred Dickason, "The Holy Spirit in Teaching," in *Introduction to Biblical Christian Education*, ed. Werner C. Graendorf (Chicago: Moody Press, 1981), 112.
    2. Dickason, "The Holy Spirit," 112.
    3. Roy B. Zuck, *The Holy Spirit in Your Teaching*, rev. ed. (Wheaton, Ill: Victor Books, 1984), 75.

■ Adapted from Chapter 2, "The Role of the Holy Spirit in Christian Teaching," by Roy B. Zuck, in Kenneth O. Gangel and Howard Hendricks, eds., *The Christian Educator's Handbook on Teaching* (Victor Books, 1988), pp. 32-42. Used by permission.

Successful Assignments

Howard G. Hendricks

Many teachers give assignments out of habit, or to give students something to work on until the end of class. Here is a more mature way to approach this subject: benefits, characteristics, and examples.

et's think briefly about the value of assignments. I see three benefits:

1. **They precipitate thinking.** Assignments are the mental warmup. They preheat the mind so it's working before class time begins.
2. **They provide a background, a foundation on which to build.** The student is aware of problems and issues concerning the passage and how it relates to his life. Questions have surfaced. Curiosity is rising.
3. **They develop habits of independent study.** This is the most important benefit of good assignments. They encourage people to be not simply under God's Word, but in it for themselves. And just watch what happens when they are!

Remember, your goal as a teacher is to develop lifelong learners. Your teaching time is to be a stimulus, not a substitute. And the only way you'll get people personally excited about the word of God is to motivate them to get in touch with this reality firsthand. What are the characteristics of good assignments?

First, they must be creative, not simply busy work. That means you need a clear objective for the assignments; they must be designed with a purpose. This takes a lot of preparation time, because creative assignments don't just fall out of the air.

Second, they must be thought-provoking. They should question more answers rather than answer more questions. Stretch the learners' minds. I know thinking is painful, but it can also be profitable when the Spirit of God is directing it.

Third, assignments must be "doable." Don't heap on an unrealistic load.

But if you've done your best to give assignments that are creative, thought-provoking, and doable, what do you do in class if—for whatever reason—the students haven't done them? A simple solution: Do an assignment in class, right then and there. Write a thought-provoking question on the board, then have them read through a selected passage that sheds light on it. (Be sure to follow that order—raise the question first, the read the passage—so they know what they're searching for.)

Another approach: Tap their experiences. Ask what problems they're facing now at home, on the job, at school. I tried this in a couples class about which I had been warned, "These people won't talk in class, and they won't do assignments." Won't, won't, won't.

"Thanks for the information," I said. Then I took a stack of three-by-five cards to the first class I taught, passed them out and said, "You know, I have a lot of confidence in you people. I know you come from a variety of backgrounds, you're involved in a number of businesses and activities and so on. So I want you to take one of these cards—but don't put your name on it—and write down your answer to this question: If you knew you could get answers for any concern in your life right now, no matter what, which three would you most want answers for? What three things are really kicking the slats out of your life?"

They spent a few minutes writing, then passed the cards up front and I began reading some. Pretty soon someone said, "That's the kind of thing we ought to be talking about in here." Before long I had a hard time shutting down the discussion. After all, if people can't talk about these things in your Sunday school class and your Bible study group, then where in the world can they talk about them?

Studies have shown, interestingly enough, that there's a direct correlation between predictability and impact. The higher your predictability, the lower your impact. Conversely, the lower your predictability, the higher your impact. (Please note that this has to do with methodology, not morals.)

The classic illustration is the life of Jesus Christ. They could never figure him out. One day the Herodians and the Pharisees got together—men who never got together over anything. They wouldn't be caught on the same side of the street, except when they had a common enemy. But because of this troublemaker Jesus, they convened and said, "Let's hit him with the problem of taxation. After all, Herodians are pro-Rome and Pharisees are anti-Rome. So we'll ask him about it. If he says he's for taxation, we nail him. If he says he's against it, you nail him. Let's go."

They found Jesus and said, "Teacher, should a man pay taxes or not?"

"Got a coin?" Jesus said.

"A coin? Sure, right here." And they passed him a coin.

"Whose inscription is this on it?"

"Ahhh . . . Caesar's."

"Then render to Caesar the things that are Caesar's, and to God the things that are God's."

Stunned, they left him and quietly regrouped on the sidelines. Finally someone spoke: "Who thought up that dumb question anyway?"

Jesus was far too unpredictable to ever be boring.

It's so painful to go into many of our churches and Sunday school classes and Bible study groups—they're so predictable you can fall asleep, wake up ten minutes later, and find them exactly where you expected them to be.

It's like what the bishop from England said: "You know, wherever the apostle Paul went, they had a riot or a revival. Wherever I go, they serve tea."

And what do they do where you go? Construct assignments on the "predictability" rule: the less predictable, the greater the impact.

■ From *Teaching to Change Lives* by Howard G. Hendricks, © 1987 by Multnomah Press. Published by Multnomah Press, Portland, Oregon 97266. Used by permission.

Retention

LAW FOUR

TOPICAL SURVEY

The Art of Memorizing Scripture

Charles R. Swindoll

Is the memorization of Scripture really so important, especially for those who teach it frequently anyway? This well-known pastor thinks so, and offers seven tips for successful memorization and retention.

I know of no other single practice in the Christian life more rewarding, practically speaking, than memorizing Scripture. That's right. No other single discipline is more useful and rewarding than this. No other single exercise pays greater spiritual dividends! Your prayer life will be strengthened. Your witnessing will be sharper and more effective. Your counseling will be in demand. Your attitudes and outlook will begin to change. Your mind will become alert and observant. Your confidence and assurance will be enhanced. Your faith will be solidified.

Now, I know you've been challenged to do this before. But is it happening? Perhaps you have procrastinated because you have mental blocks against it. Maybe you tried, but you either did not see the value or could not get beyond the method that was demanded by some memory program—little cards, booklets, check-up techniques, hearers, etc. Perhaps that seemed elementary and insulted your intelligence. I understand.

Here are seven things I have found helpful:

1. Choose a time when your mind is free from outside distractions . . . perhaps soon after getting up in the morning.
2. Learn the reference by repeating it every time you say the verse(s). Numbers are more difficult to remember than words.
3. Read each verse through several times—both in a whisper and aloud. Hearing yourself say the words helps cement them into your mind.
4. Break the passage into its natural phrases. Learn the reference and then the first phrase. Then repeat the reference and first phrase as you go to the second phrase. Continue adding phrases one by one.
5. Learn a little bit *perfectly* rather than a great deal poorly. Do not go on to the next verse until you can say the previous one(s) perfectly.
6. Review the verse(s) immediately. Twenty to thirty minutes later, repeat what you've memorized. Before the day has ended, firmly fix the verse(s) in your mind by going over it fifteen to twenty times. (You can do this as you drive or do your job).
7. Use the verse(s) orally as soon as possible. After all, the purpose of Scripture memory is a practical one, not academic. Use the verses in conversation, in correspondence, in teaching, in counseling, in everyday opportunities. Relate what you've learned to your daily situation. You'll be thrilled with the results.

How to Memorize Large Sections of Scripture

Ray Crawford

As with many Christians, your Scripture memory may consist primarily of isolated, single verses dealing with specific topics. Take the challenge of learning to memorize chapters—even whole books! You can do it!

First, if Scripture memory hasn't been a significant part of your life in the past, don't try to dive right into memorizing whole books of the Bible. Start by memorizing a hundred or so individual verses on various topics. That will give you a well-rounded understanding of the Bible as a foundation for life, and will help you establish the discipline in your life before you take on the bigger challenge.

Second, don't take up Scripture memory to impress others. Your pride will show through, and the passages you memorize will have little effect on your life. If you tend to be proud, memorize and meditate on ten or twenty verses about pride, humility, and arrogance as part of your personal preparation for Scripture memory.

IN THE BEGINNING

As you begin this process of memorizing large sections of Scripture, pay special attention to three prerequisites: *intention, initiative, and interest.*

Cultivate the *intention* to remember passages forever, not just temporarily. You must take the *initiative* to do this kind of Scripture memory. One reason people never complete a project like this is that they never begin.

Select a book or passage in which you have strong personal *interest.* If you're not interested in the passage of Scripture, the chances of your memorizing it are slim.

PROCEDURES AND PRACTICES

1. Get An Overview

A. *Read the book several times per day,* or at least once each day, for the first few weeks after you decide to memorize it.

B. *Read the book aloud* during some of your reading sessions.

C. *Listen to the book on a tape that you record.* It helps to hear it in your own voice more than in someone else's. You'll discover that the verses you memorize after listening to the book fifty to one hundred times are easier to memorize than the ones you memorized earlier in the project.

D. *Use Bible study techniques.* Divide the book into natural divisions. Do an inductive study of each division until, after several weeks or longer, you have carefully studied the entire book. This way you'll pick up the overall flow of the author's thought, and that flow will often help you remember what comes next when you're memorizing the book.

2. Memorize a Skeleton

Identify key verses and memorize them early in the project. If any other verses are special favorites of yours, memorize them. Or memorize verses that begin new paragraphs or chapters. Be sure to learn the references for these verses. Visualizing the locations of your key verses on the pages of your Bible can also help you keep the units in proper sequence. You might photocopy the pages from your Bible and mark the location of the verses on the pages.

3. Fill in the Remainder

Consider each of the natural divisions that you studied in the overview phase as an individual unit, and memorize it as such. The skeleton that you memorized will help you keep the parts of the book in order. Make a list of all the verse reference numbers in the book. As you memorize them, mark them off your list. Not only will this help you know what's left to be done, but also it will be a great encouragement as you see the number of marked verses growing and the number of unmarked verses getting smaller.

4. Don't Rush

Your goal is to appreciate, understand, and practice the wonderful Word of God. That means taking time.

5. Avoid a One-Track Mind

While memorizing a book of the Bible, keep up with other forms of Bible study and reading. Don't just memorize the book; read it, examine it, analyze it, and meditate on it. And pay attention to other portions of the Bible, too.

6. Aim At Word-Perfect Memorization

Passages of God's Word are infinitely rich in meaning and application. Knowing their exact wording will make us more receptive to all the ideas and applications we can get from them. Sometimes we'll go for years thinking that a particular passage has such-and-such a meaning. And then, one day, by noticing a certain turn of phrase or repetition of words in the passage, our understanding of it can be drastically changed. If we memorize the passages precisely as they stand in the Bible, we'll be prepared to notice that special detail that unlocks riches.

7. Use Periodic and Systematic Review

As you work your way through a book, review regularly what you've accomplished. Set aside individual days, at regular intervals, when you'll work only on review, not on memorizing new verses. When you've completed the book, wait for at least a few months before you begin another. During those few months, review the book every day, either in its entirety or in units. And after you've begun a new book, go back to the other one often to review it again. Reciting it aloud can be especially helpful in this phase of the project.

PROBLEMS AND PREDICAMENTS

You will undoubtedly encounter obstacles during this adventure in Scripture memory. The enemy wants to thwart your progress, but the Holy Spirit wants you to put more of the Sword of the Spirit into your mind and heart. What are some of the obstacles, and what can you do about them?

I'm Bored! It sounds almost sacrilegious to say that you will likely become bored with the book you're memorizing. But don't be surprised when it happens. Memorizing a book in the Bible can be such a lengthy process that the content occasionally seems to lose its appeal. Try pressing on anyway. Perhaps after several weeks of persevering through this obstacle, your interest will revive. The very boredom might have a positive effect: it might clear your mind of your preconceptions about the book and ready you for new insights. And when those new insights come, they can put new thrills into your memory work.

If your lack of interest continues, set this project aside for a few weeks and study something else. During these weeks it's still a good idea to read the book regularly, or listen to it on tape, so that you don't lose much of what you've already memorized. After these few weeks, go back to the book you're memorizing, and take up the work where you left off, being sure to check the accuracy of your memory of what's gone before and to correct it if need requires.

I Don't Understand This Part! You're bound to encounter, in any book of the Bible, some sections that you have trouble understanding. Memorize them anyway. Maybe you'll begin to understand them while you meditate on them. Or you might postpone memorizing them until you've memorized the rest of the book. Then your knowledge of the rest of the book will help you understand those difficult passages and make memorizing them easier. Or the passage may simply not make sense to you for years to come. Memorize it anyway: your chances of understanding it someday are much greater if you've memorized it than if you haven't.

Another thing you can do to increase your understanding of a passage is to pray for understanding. God gives us this advice through Solomon: "My son, if you accept my words and store up my commands within you, turning your ear to wisdom and applying your heart to understanding, and if you call out for insight and cry aloud for understanding, and if you look for it as for silver and search for it as for hidden treasure, then you will understand the fear of the LORD and find the knowledge of God. For the LORD gives wisdom, and from his mouth come knowledge and understanding" (Proverbs 2:1-6).

I Can't Do It! If you begin by telling yourself you can't do it, and if you continue saying that in your mind, you'll begin to believe it. But my own experience, and my observations of others, tells me that many people can memorize whole books of the Bible if they're willing to do the work necessary.

Instead of having the self-defeating attitude of the person who says, "I can't do it," adopt the attitude of the apostle Paul, who wrote, "I can do everything through him who gives me strength" (Philippians 4:13).

MEMORIZE THE WORD AND GROW

The phases of the memorization process I've suggested aren't distinct steps, each completed before moving on to the next. They blend and overlap. Sometimes you'll be doing one phase with one portion of Scripture and another phase with another portion. Be flexible and persistent, and it will work.

Memorizing large passages of Scripture, or entire books, can help in your own spiritual growth and in your ministry to others. Why not start now? Which book would you choose?

■ From *Discipleship Journal* 6, no. 3 (May 1986), pp. 39-41. Used by permission.

The Power of Memory

Harry Lorayne

How much do you know about the power of observation and memory?
We could remember multiplied amounts more than we do if we only knew
and practiced some simple techniques. Here's a brief introduction.

Don't look at your wrist watch, and answer this question: Is the number six on your watch dial the Arabic number 6, or is it the Roman number VI? Think this over for a moment, before you look at your watch. Decide on your answer as if it were really important that you answer correctly. You're on a quiz show, and there's a lot of money at stake!

All right, have you decided on your answer? Now, look at your watch and see if you were right. Were you? Or were you wrong in either case, because your watch doesn't have a six at all! The small dial that ticks off the seconds sometimes occupies that space on modern watches.

Did you answer this question correctly? Whether you did or did not, you had to look at your watch to check. Can you tell now the exact time on your watch? Probably not, and you just looked at it a second ago! You saw, but you didn't observe. Try this on your friends. Although people see their watches innumerable times every day, few of them can tell you about the numeral six.

I've taken the time and space to talk about observation because it is one of the things important to training your memory. The other, and more important thing, is association. We cannot possibly remember anything that we do not observe. After something is observed either by sight or hearing, it must, in order to be remembered, be associated in our minds with, or to, something we already know or remember.

Association, as pertaining to memory, simply means the connecting or tying up of two (or more) things to each other. Anything you manage to remember is only due to the fact that you have subconsciously associated it to something else.

"Every Good Boy Does Fine." Does that sentence mean anything to you? If it does, then you must have studied music as a youngster. Almost every child that studies music is taught to remember the lines of the music staff or treble clef by remembering, "**E**very **G**ood **B**oy **D**oes **F**ine."

I've already stressed the importance of association, and I want to prove to you that you have used definite conscious associations many times before, without even realizing it. The letters E, G, B, D, and F don't mean a thing. They are just letters, and difficult to remember. The sentence "Every Good Boy Does Fine" does have meaning, and is something you know and understand. The new thing, the thing you had to commit to memory, was associated with something you already knew.

It is probably many years since you learned the jingle, "Thirty days hath September, April, June, and November, all the rest have thirty-one, etc.," but how many times have you relied on it when it was necessary to know the number of days in a particular month?

I am sure that many times you have seen or heard something which made you snap your fingers, and say, "Oh, that reminds me. . . . " You were made to remember something by the thing you saw or heard, which usually had no obvious connection to the thing you remembered. However, in your mind, the two things were associated in some way. This was a subconscious association. Right now, I am pointing out a few examples of conscious associations at work; and they certainly do work. People who have forgotten many things that they learned in their early grades still remember the spaces and lines of the treble clef. If you have read this chapter so far, concentrating as you read, you should know them by now, even if you've never studied music.

One of the best examples I know is the one which was a great help to me in my early grade spelling classes. We were being taught that the word "believe" was spelled with the *e* following the *i*. In order to help us to commit this to memory, we were told to remember a short sentence, "Never believe a lie."

This is a perfect instance of a conscious association. I know for a fact that many adults still have trouble spelling "believe." They are never quite sure if the *i* is first, or if it is the *e*. The spelling of the word "believe" was the new thing to remember. The word "lie" is a word we all already knew how to spell. None of the students that heard that little sentence ever again misspelled the word "believe." Do you have trouble spelling the word "piece"? If you do, just remember the phrase "piece of pie." This phrase will always tell you how to spell "piece."

Can you draw anything that resembles the map of England, from memory? How about China, Japan, or Czechoslovakia? You probably can't draw any of these. If I had mentioned Italy, ninety percent of you would have immediately seen a picture of a boot in your mind's eye. Is that right? If you did, and if you draw a boot, you will have the approximate outline of the map of Italy.

Most of those who have learned the secret of mnemonics in memory have been amazed, not only at their own tremendous ability to remember, but also at the kudos they received from their families and friends. The question that people ask me most often is, "Isn't it confusing to remember too much?" My answer to that is, "No!" There is no limit to the capacity of the memory. Lucius Scopio was able to remember the names of all the people of Rome; Cyrus was able to call every soldier in his army by name; while Seneca could memorize and repeat two thousand words after hearing them once.

I believe that the more you remember, the more you can remember. The memory, in many ways, is like a muscle. A muscle must be exercised and developed in order to give proper service and use; so must a memory. The difference is that a muscle can be overtrained or become musclebound while the memory cannot. You can be taught to have a trained memory just as you can be taught anything else. As a matter of fact, it is much easier to attain a trained memory than, say, to learn to play a musical instrument.

Remember, please, that there is no such thing as a bad memory! This may come as a shock to those of you who have used your supposedly "bad" memories as an excuse for years. But, I repeat, there is no such thing as a bad memory. There are only trained or untrained memories.

Help Students Memorize!

Sally A. Middleton

Looking for some creative techniques for reviewing and retaining information? Let a seasoned teacher share from her grab-bag of effective and proven memorization, review, and retention tools.

The following four steps will help children see verses in God's Word, say them correctly, understand them, and seal them in their hearts.

Step 1: See it!

Write the words of a verse on a poster or chalkboard. Let a volunteer come and read the verse from your Bible while the rest of the class looks at the visual to see if it says exactly the same thing. Then take time to allow *each* child to see it in *his* Bible. If your students bring different versions to class do not say, "Does your Bible say something different?" Rather say, "Does your Bible say *the same thing* using other words?" In fact, another version can help you with the next step.

Step 2: Spell it out!

Not literally, of course. Explain it so the child knows exactly what the words mean. When children do not understand a verse, they are more likely to misquote it. A friend reported teaching John 14:2 to young children and hearing one child quote it back, "In my father's house are many mansions. If it were not *sold* I would have told you." Another child continued saying, "I go to *repair* a place for you." Prevent this by careful explanations. Use appropriate pictures. Show how the verse affects their lives. To check their understanding ask, "What does this verse mean to you?" Also ask, "Why is it important that we learn this verse?" Then, on to the next step to begin memorizing.

Step 3: Say it!

You need to have the children repeat the verse about ten times. This beneficial activity need not be one bit boring. Try one of the following methods each day in your class. Repeat the favorite the fifth day.

• *Crazy Stand-Ups:* After you read the verse together twice, say:

"All of you wearing something blue, stand up and say this verse."

"All of you who like ice cream, stand up and say this verse."

"All of you who ate breakfast this morning . . ."

"All who are fans of (name favorite ball team) . . ."

• *Add-A-Word:* Divide your class into two groups. Let group A say the first word in the verse. Ask group B to repeat what group A said and add one word. The method sounds like this:

Group A: All
Group B: All we
Group A: All we like
Group B: All we like sheep

To add activity, have the children sit when their group is silent, stand when their group is speaking.

• *Echo:* Divide your class into three groups. Tell the children to pretend they are a B-I-G canyon. You, the teacher, are standing at the edge of the canyon. What you shout, the canyon echoes back several times. The first echo is fairly loud, the second softer, the third a whisper. The teachers says part of the verse and the first group echoes those words loudly, the next softer, the last whispers. The teacher says the next part of the verse and the first group echoes those words loudly, the next softer, the last whispers. The teacher says the next part of the verse and the process is repeated. Change the parts the children play so each group gets to be the loud echo and each gets to whisper. Give them larger parts to remember each time. The last time, say the whole verse and let them echo it.

•*Take-Away:* Repeat the verse two to three times. Then choose one child to come up front and take away some words (erase them from the board, cover them on a poster, remove them from the flannelboard). Have the children say the verse with those words missing. Stand when they get to the place where the missing words are spoken. Repeat the process until the verse "disappears" from the visual but "appears" in their memory.

Using one of these methods, the class will seem to know a verse perfectly after ten repetitions. But, to cement it in their brain cells you must include the next step.

Step 4: Seal it!

If you fail to review, the truth taught is soon forgotten. Begin to review the same day the verse is introduced. Use it in the Bible lesson and see if they can quote it with you. Later say, "Before we have our treat let's repeat today's memory verse." (Before your treat, repeat!) Also say, "Before we sing this song, let's stand and quote our new verse."

Discuss with the children how they can use the verse that day as well as in the weeks to come. Deuteronomy 30:14 says, "But the word is very near you, in your mouth and in your heart, that you may do it." (NKJV). Send the child home with the verse written on a piece of paper. Children are more likely to hold on to that paper if you add an attractive, collectible sticker.

Review verses in future class sessions as well. For each verse taught, make a heart out of posterboard. On one side print the verse reference. On the other, print a key word from the verse. This gives you two ways to review: you can hold up the reference and see if the children can say the verse or you can show the key word and see if they can remember the verse and the reference.

For each child, use construction paper and make small hearts with identical information. With a brass fastener, attach the hearts together at the points and make a flower. Add a smile face for the center. Now the child can take this reminder home and review the verses.

For a special treat, maybe as a craft, glue colorful memory-verse hearts, with references showing, to both sides of large pieces of construction paper (12" x 18"). Cover both sides of the construction paper with clear plastic (or run it through a laminating machine) and the child will have a placemat he can use at home to remind him of his verses.

■From *Keys to Christian Education* 25, no. 3 (Spring 1987), pp. 14-15. Published by Standard Publishing Co. Used by permission.

Memory Joggers for Kids

Jack and Jody Green

In Scripture, God transformed important events in the present into memorials which would carry the impact of the event into the future. You can do the same! Here are five creative ways to build memorials.

Memorials, defined by Webster as "something that keeps remembrance alive," are exhorted by God throughout Scripture (Deuteronomy 8:18; Ecclesiastes 12:1; Luke 22:19). Not only are we commanded to remember what God has done, but also to keep that remembrance alive in the hearts of children (Psalm 78:2-4). What memorials will your children carry with them into the next generation?

Listed below are five ways you can begin to develop memorials for yourself, the children you teach, and the generation to come.

1. A MEMORIAL NOTEBOOK

In Israel's first battle subsequent to their bondage in Egypt (Exodus 17:8-14), God proved Himself faithful in protecting His people. Yet as the dust of the confrontation settled and the taste of victory was still being enjoyed, God gave Moses the imperative command, "And the Lord said unto Moses, 'Write this for a memorial in a book, and rehearse it in the ears of Joshua'" (Exodus 17:14).

God wanted the victory rehearsed to Joshua, the one to whom Moses' baton of leadership would be passed, to give him courage and faith for the battles ahead. Certainly children face a world in which faith and courage are needed. Write a memorial book of God's victories and faithfulness in your life and rehearse these to them for their own battles ahead.

2. OLD "WAR" STORIES

The picture of children sitting on grandpa's knee seems to be the scene of Deuteronomy 32. Children of all ages are gripped with fascination over stories of people in years past who experienced both triumph and tragedy. Sixteen times in the book of Deuteronomy the Israelites were challenged to "remember." "Remember the days of old, consider the years of many generations: ask thy father, and he will shew thee; thy elders [grandfathers], and they will tell thee" (Deuteronomy 32:7, KJV). Use story times, bedtimes, or other quiet moments to share with children the events, people, victories, and struggles that God has used to shape and mold you.

3. MEMORY VERSE COLLECTION

God's Word needs to be implanted in our lives if we are to effectively impress it into the hearts of children. Many times God has used special nuggets from His Word to direct us, comfort us and correct us personally. This storehouse of verses is a treasure that God has used in real life situations and should be kept as a collection of favorite (and perhaps life-saving) verses. Whether in the form of wall plaques, refrigerator displays, or in book form, these testimonies of God's faithfulness need to be displayed for all to see.

4. YEARLY CELEBRATIONS

God commanded the nation of Israel to remember His deliverance recorded in Exodus 12 through a yearly celebration known as Passover. Yearly celebrations can be used not only as remembrances but also as teaching tools.

Celebrate Spiritual Birthdays. Pick one day a year to celebrate the spiritual birthdays of your class or family. This will emphasize the joy of their salvation and also provide an opportunity to witness to the unsaved children. Spiritual birthday celebrations provide a wonderful atmosphere to again emphasize to all that they must simply, "believe on the Lord Jesus Christ, and thou shalt be saved" (Acts 16:31).

Spiritual Holidays. Use Easter and Christmas to teach the important truths of the deity, birth, life, death, and resurrection of our Lord Jesus Christ. Plan to do special projects with a spiritual emphasis which you don't do at any other time of the year—a drama, mural, devotional time, testimonies, etc.

Spiritual Victories. Stop the routine of life long enough to talk about the times when God brought you through particularly hard situations. How did God provide your new job after the layoff? What prayers have been answered that can be shared with others?

Christian Heritage Days. Use Memorial Day, Independence Day, and Thanksgiving to emphasize what our forefathers went through to bring Christianity to us. Invite a Christian war veteran to your children's group or to your home to share those events that preserved our Christian heritage.

5. MEMORIES FROM PAST VICTORIES

Collect rocks—stones, to be more exact. The Lord informed Joshua to collect twelve stones out of the midst of the Jordan River after the children of Israel had crossed the river bed on dry ground (Joshua 3:17). Joshua was told to set rocks in the midst of the camp at Gilgal. Talk about a vivid reminder! Each time a person had to go around, jump over, or stub his toe on this pile of stones, God was remembered.

There are a variety of ways to preserve God's heritage. Record some of God's timeless truths with your own practical insight on audio or video tapes; write a book on how God brought you through the hills and valleys of your life; write a letter to each member of your children's group or your family, sharing with them one special thing God has done. Continually put before children the praises of our God and His wonderful works.

What can be the result of such diligence? "That they [children] might set their hope in God, and not forget the works of God, but keep his commandments" (Psalm 78:7).

Yes, memorials are vital. Our nation recognizes this and sets forth monuments, statues, and holidays. And though we as Christian teachers and parents would agree a national heritage is important, we must strive with even greater diligence to preserve a spiritual heritage for the generation to come.

■ From "Memory Joggers for Kids," *Evangelizing Today's Child* 16, no. 3 (May–June 1989), pp. 16-17. Used by permission.

Teaching for Memorization

Kenneth O. Gangel

Teaching and memorization have been compartmentalized in modern education. In a biblical context, however, teaching was for memorization. Learn it and live it—forever! Here is a wholistic view of the subject.

All of us want to think that we are biblical in our teaching methodology since we recognize that the Word of God is not only the foundation for the content that we teach, but also our example for technique. Almost every book on teaching emphasizes the dialogue approach, which Jesus frequently used, and urges the participation method, based on His example. Such an emphasis is correct, but sometimes we forget the great heritage which the Old Testament Jewish faith provides for Christian education. The focus on the family, the centricity of Scripture in all learning, and the later commitment to quality learning in the synagogue schools are all worthy of our study. The one teaching methodology which reigned supreme throughout all of those Old Testament centuries was catechism, or memorization.

Memorization may be defined simply as the power, function, or act of reproducing and identifying what has been heard or experienced. It has been suggested that there are at least four steps in the memory process:

1. **Impression**—the original, conscious, meaningful experience itself.
2. **Retention**—the process by which the experience is retained in the mind.
3. **Recall**—the act of calling upon the mind for certain needed past experiences or ideas.
4. **Recognition**—the recalled memory as an experience which the individual has had previously.

Not all memorization is of the kind that we have come to call "rote." Rote memory describes the exact reproduction of past experiences, such as the memorization of a verse of Scripture which a student has learned. It is perfectly legitimate, however, to use memorization of general content and context of information as an approach to teaching. For example, one might memorize the general theme of each chapter in the Book of Acts although none of his reproduced content is exactly in the words of the text itself.

VALUES OF MEMORIZATION TEACHING

Memorization can be enjoyable for students. Too often we think of it only as a regular discipline which requires concentration and drill. But there is intrinsic motivation and instant reinforcement in the child's learning program when he realizes that he can accurately reproduce information which he has studied. Incidentally, one of the most popular types of adult classes in some Sunday schools recently is the Bible memory class.

Some educators would argue that the very process of discipline in memorization is a valid and important technique. It is mind training of the highest order and will develop proficiency which is applicable in the entire development of one's educational pattern.

God has promised us that there is an inherent spiritual value in memorization of Scripture. David once wrote, "Thy Word have I hid in mine heart, that I might not sin against Thee" (Psalm 119:11). Although later subconscious recall is certainly not the first aim of Scripture memorization, many young people and adults who were trained in the memorization of God's truth while children, later came to a real awakening of spiritual values because of that vital information hidden in their hearts.

PROBLEMS IN MEMORIZATION TEACHING

A constantly hovering cloud over memorization teaching is the possibility of substituting words for meaning. Sometimes children reciting memory verses seem too much like the trained seal who has been conditioned to bounce a rubber ball on his nose. They become performers whose striking ability is fascinating to the audience but has little inherent value or understanding to the performer.

Of course this does not have to be the case. Those of us who take a serious view of the inspiration and authority of the Bible will always be concerned that the experiences which a child has, teach him the *meaning* of God's truth, but also that meaning is inherent in the *words* of God's truth. However, the extraction of the meaning from the word is not always automatic. That is where the role of the teacher comes in.

Another problem with memorization teaching is that sometimes the process can become dull. I have already suggested that it does not have to be so, for memorization can be interesting, even exciting. But if we "sell" the technique as a hardship instead of a blessing, as a discipline instead of a delight, we build in negative attitudinal responses when we want precisely the reverse. Of course, the responses we get in any kind of teaching are determined largely by the way the presentation is made.

PRINCIPLES FOR EFFECTIVE MEMORIZATION

Try to follow these guidelines when employing this teaching technique:
- Remember that the memorization for general content can be as important and valuable a learning experience as rote memorization.
- Master all the memorization which you require of your students.
- Use helpful visual aids in teaching memory work. These will include pictures, flash cards, chalkboard, flannelgraph, and other media.
- Remember that review is the key to retention. Your students may memorize information and then forget it days or weeks later unless you subject them to frequent recall.
- Always emphasize understandings and meanings. Don't let students of any age memorize just for the sake of performance, but make sure they understand the significance the learning has in their own lives.

From Chapter 15 of Kenneth O. Gangel, *24 Ways to Improve Your Teaching* (Wheaton: Victor Books, 1974). Used by permission.

Secrets to Strengthen Your Memory

Robert P. Kendall

There are techniques and insights which make memorization more productive. Here is a short list of insights gleaned by one who has researched—and applied—this subject in the local church.

The learner should take time to determine if his memory is predominantly one of *sight* or *sound.* If the learner remembers what he sees quicker than what he hears, his memory is one predominantly of sight. If it is sight, he may want to *write the material* out in longhand.

The learner should strive to be *properly motivated,* free from compulsion and with a desire to remember. Proper motivation will come if the learner will focus on his material. When memorizing, seek to capture the meaning the author had in mind.

Proper motivation will aid in *concentrating.* Concentration is always necessary when memorizing. Seek to relive the scene and be one of the characters you are learning about. While concentrating, notice any *feelings evoked* by what you read. Try to *visualize* what you read. *Read the material aloud* to hear the material. *Listen* to yourself on a tape recorder. Utilize any *metrical patterns* found. Use the alliterations if the author has given them to you. Make up your own *artistic outline* if the material naturally allows for it. Note the *total arrangement* of the material, its mood, its purpose; the climaxes, contrasts, and continuity.

Use the *same written text* always. Notice its *structure* and *syntax.* Place *symbols* on the written text, especially where the material is difficult to remember. Note the *associations* which normally occur as you read and study the material. If a picture of your home town comes to the screen of your mind while reading about a town, use this association. Associate as much as possible. When material is hard to remember, use *extraordinary associations.* Something which is not normal imprints itself easily on the memory. An elephant wearing pink pajamas is hard *not* to visualize!

Use *body movements* and gestures in your memorizing. Feel free to "talk" with your body. *Associate lines with certain body gestures.* Imagine yourself playing charades. *Memorize in one-half hour periods.* Give the memory time to rest and assimilate the material. If at all possible separate these times of memorizing by *sleep.*

Above all: *PRACTICE!* You can never over-learn the material. You can review at any time and in any place. No one knows what you are thinking! If you have a hard time with remembering, return to the original text. Do not try to force memory. Give it help by looking at the text. But don't baby your memory! It is a servant. Memorize *difficult material* at times. Force it to work. But don't get discouraged!

Dr. Robert Kendall wrote a master's thesis on the subject of memorization, from which this article is taken (Dallas Theological Seminary, 1978). Used by permission.

Improve Your Memory in Seven Easy Steps

Morton Hunt

Here's how the pros do it. The following seven types of "memory-makers" are techniques employed by those who memorize things for a living. If it works for them, it will work for you!

Use the following "memory makers" to remember almost anything.

1. External Memory. This refers to all physical devises that help you remember: lists, memos, diaries, and alarm clocks. We forget to perform a chore because we felt we didn't need to jot it down.

2. Chucking. This means grouping several items of information into one piece that's as easy to remember as a single item. We recall an acronym like UNICEF as a single name, not as six letters. Can you think of others?

3. Mediation. This means attaching the item of a list to some easily remembered "mediating" device, such as the jingle most adults use to recall the lengths of the months: "Thirty days hath September . . . "

4. Associations. To remember names, think of a visual link between a person's name and some facial feature. For instance: You've just met a Mr. Clausen, who has bushy eyebrows. Think of a "keyword" (a soundalike) for his name—claws; then visualize a lobster claw tearing at his eyebrows. When you try to recall his name, you see his eyebrows, then remember the claw tearing at them and—aha!—Clausen!

5. Reliving the moment. Studies have shown that sensory impressions are associated in memory to what we're learning and later to help remind us of what we learned. So, if you're trying to recall a name or fact, picture the place in which you learned it, the people around you at the time, even the feeling of the seat you sat in; your chance of remembering it will be greatly increased.

6. Mnemonic pegboards. Memorize these ten "pegwords" (since they rhyme with the numbers one to ten, it's easy): one/*bun*; two/*shoe*; three/*tree*; four/*door*; five/*hive*; six/*sticks*; seven/*heaven*; eight/*gate*; nine/*line*; ten/*hen*.

Now make up a list of ten other words and number them. Link each one to the pegword with the same number by means of an image. Suppose your first word is *bowl*; picture a bun lying inside a bowl. If your second word is *desk*, picture a shoe parked on a desk. A minute should be enough for all 10.

7. Weaving it into the web. All the above methods are useful for recalling simple lists and names. But with more complicated information, you can't merely memorize; you have to connect it to the many related items you already know. That, according to psychologists, is the best way to retrieve it later.

How to Remember Names

Margaret Rickers

Perhaps your students aren't required to memorize everyone's names, but the teacher is! Here are tips to help you separate Ricky from Nicky from Dicky. The principles have even wider application than just names.

Names are too important to forget. Remembering people's names tells them they're valuable. Unique. Special. A gift. And names are so important to God that he calls each of us by name. "I have summoned you by name; you are mine" (Isaiah 43:1). God remembers everyone's name.

WHAT'S IN A NAME?

Names hold power. The ancient Hebrew people believed that once you knew a person's name you were in control of him or her. That's why they couldn't speak the name of "Yahweh" (God); they couldn't control God. Even today, Orthodox Jews don't even write the complete name of God.

Think about it. If you're in a crowded shopping mall and someone shouts your name—"Margaret!"—they do have some control over you. You look around until you find the person who hailed you.

Now, imagine the boost to a teenager's self-esteem when you actually say, "Hi Rob! How's it going?" instead of "Hi. How's it going?" You can make a young person's day by remembering his or her name.

TIPS FOR REMEMBERING NAMES

You meet lots of people. They remember your name. And they all expect you to remember their names. Several tricks help you remember people's names. But, you have to take time to use them. A few fun ways to remember names:

1. Use word-association

When you first meet a young person, notice something distinctive or unusual about him or her. Maybe a dimple on her chin or a cowlick in his hair. When you register that person's name in your mind, include this significant information too. For example: Susan—dimple, or John—cowlick. Believe me; it'll stick.

2. Interview the kids

When you're getting to know your group members, take time to ask the kids some significant (or even insignificant) questions. From my first youth group, I'll never forget that Sandy's favorite thing in the world is frozen strawberry yogurt. Now I don't ever walk by a yogurt stand without thinking of Sandy. And I never forget her name because I remember that little bit of trivia about her.

3. Association: places and events

Getting to know kids in their own environment helps you associate their names with an activity, hobby, another family member or some other significant thing in their lives. The association helps you connect a name and face with an item or event. For example, you might remember that Chad loves to skateboard and he collects posters of people skateboarding. You'll connect the posters and Chad's name.

4. Learn the meanings of names

The Bible contains many references to the actual meanings of people's names. Isaac was "the laughing one." Miriam means "bitter." Abraham, "father of many nations." Joshua and Jesus mean "he shall save his people." You'll remember the stories of these Bible people easier if you remember what their names mean.

Learn the meanings of kids' names. You'll be surprised how many times the meanings will correspond to kid's actual characteristics.

Some names have interesting stories behind them. Ask kids: Who were you named after? Why did your parents choose your name? Does your name have a unique spelling? What do you like about your name? Not like?

5. Listen

Although my friend Hillary was quite patient each time I confused her name with her sister's, I could've eliminated the problem if I'd listened carefully when I first met the duo. Too often we greet people and don't even hear what they're saying. We hear the name, but it doesn't stick in our minds. Repeating people's names as they're being introduced imprints the names in our minds.

6. Name Games

It's important for you to remember kids' names. And it's important for kids to remember each other's names. Some fun name games you can play in your group to make names unforgettable:

• *Name tags*. Have kids write their name on a card and use each letter of the name to make an acrostic with words that describe them. An example: **A**rty, **N**oisy, **N**ervous, **E**nergetic

• *Alphabetical order*. Have kids form a circle in alphabetical order. Although this may sound juvenile at first, the kids have fun finding their places in the circle— especially if the group is large. It's a bigger task than it sounds like. First there's Andy, then Anne, Bill, Christa, two Jasons, two Jennifers, Jessica, Jim, and three Johns. Then we skip to Mike (two of those, too) and the list goes on. Turn this community-building activity into a game by timing the group. Repeat the activity for two or three weeks and see if kids can improve their time. As you're playing the game, be sure to make a mental picture of the order the kids are standing in.

• *Picture poster*. Take a Polaroid picture of each kid in your group and make a poster with the names and pictures of all the kids. Feature one kid each week and let the group interview him or her for five minutes. They'll find out something new about even the youth group veterans.

Names are important to us. They give us identity and set us apart from every other Tom, Dick, and Harry. So work at remembering names. Kids appreciate an honest effort.

■ Reprinted by permission from *Group Magazine* (September 1987), pp. 74-77. © 1987, Group Publishing Inc., Box 481, Loveland, Colorado 80539.

Why Do Students Fail Tests?

John Hatten

Have students failed our tests because we failed to tell them what they needed to know? That's only one correctable reason students fail. Here's a whole list to challenge you, and help your students pass—with "As"!

There is simply too much material to retain. A common perception in education is "more is better." Course content is sacrosanct, and completion of the class outline is of paramount concern. We equate *telling* with *teaching.* To teach more, we tell more.

2. **The important material receives no greater emphasis than other material.** The learner has no idea which facts or thoughts to retain and which to simply review. Following one of my more long-winded lectures, a student asked, "What of all that is important for us to remember?" I answered, "All of it." My answer was smug, cute . . . and stupid.

3. **The presentation of the material lacks general organization and clarity.**

4. **The material is presented with such a lack of vigor that the student is not captivated.** I have no desire to turn the classroom into a circus or a comedy routine, but I do believe that the teacher has a responsibility to make the content come alive for the student.

5. **The exam is too long.** Too many questions confront the student, which results in panic and inability to recall information. When confronted with an impossible task, some people simply give up and face the consequences of poor performance. Others get frantic and respond in a shotgun or helter-skelter way

6. **The questions are ambiguous.** The student is left to guess what the test developer is seeking. When tests become guessing games—when the learner is more interested in knowing what was meant by a *question* than in understanding the *information*—learning suffers.

7. **Teachers teach one way but test another.** The questions do not reflect the tone or level of specificity of the lecture or the way the text was covered in the class.

8. **Teachers do not clearly spell out their expectations.** Because we all develop our own grading practices, it is a common student survival skill to learn what each of us expects. It's sad to think that many students need to know us and our idiosyncrasies more than the content of the class.

9. **The questions are too long and too complicated.** A student once showed me a true/false question with four negatives. It appeared to me that the test developer had become confused over whether he was testing for content or the ability to read complex and awkwardly worded text.

■ From *The Teaching Professor* 3, no. 6 (June–July 1989), pp. 1-2. Published by Magna Publications, Inc., 2718 Dryden Dr., Madison, Wisconsin 53704; 800-433-0444.

How to Use Memory Systems

Joan Minninger

A memory expert clearly presents some of the most widely used—and ancient—mnemonic devices. They really work, and will help your students gain untold confidence as they learn—and remember!

Memory systems can seem overwhelming at first, but many people who approach them in a sufficiently playful manner discover that they can be invaluable tools for remembering. "The advantage," says Dr. K. Anders Ericsson of Carnegie-Mellon University, "is that it (mnemonics) relieves the burden on short-term memory because recall can be achieved through a single association with an already existing code in long-term memory." Mnemonics simply means memory aids. A mnemonic can be simple or intricate, logical or silly.

Of course, a short, snappy, and exact mnemonic is best. The ones we remember are usually funny, or intriguing and have a rhyming structure. You probably remember "i before e, except after c or when sounded like a, as in neighbor or weigh." A few of you may even have learned the sequel of exceptions: "neither leisured foreigner seized the weird heights."

NUMBERING THINGS

Numbering or counting things can be an aid to learning. There are several counting systems that let you relate two visual images, one for the number and one for the object. If you tend to be verbal, try this one that uses rhyming words.

A Verbal Counting System

one/*bun*	six/*sticks*
two/*shoe*	seven/*heaven*
three/*tree*	eight/*gate*
four/*door*	nine/*vine*
five/*hive*	ten/*hen*

Having committed all those pens or hens to memory, you then match them to the new things you want to remember. For instance, you want to remember to do the following ten errands. You would list them mentally, matching them to either the rhyme number of the picture number.

1/bun. Buy stamps. (A sticky cinnamon bun has stamps stuck all over it.)

2/shoe. Buy tape at the hardware store. (Your shoe is wrapped tightly with tape so that it is hard to walk.)

3/tree. Buy washers at the hardware store. (A Christmas tree is hung with rubber washers, like ornaments.)

4/door. At the market you need bread. (A door won't shut because a big loaf of bread is in the way; it is getting crushed and scattering crumbs.)

5/hive. . . . and pickles. (The bees have turned green as they tote pickle juice instead of nectar to their hive.

6/sticks. . . . and lightbulbs. (Smash burned-out light bulbs with a big stick as you anticipate your new ones.)

7/heaven. Go to the bank. (Imagine golden streets, angelic wings on the tellers as they run their hands through the coins in their drawers.)

8/gate. Pick up your dry cleaning. (The plastic garment bags are draped over a gate . . . don't open it too fast or your best suit will fall in the mud.)

9/vine. Buy a newspaper. (Your paper is sprouting tendrils.)

10/hen. Get goldfish food at the pet store. (Your goldfish is so hungry it could eat a hen. See her chasing one around her bowl.)

ABBREVIATIONS

Abbreviations are a quick way to say something complex, and they can also be a memory aid, furnishing the skeleton of the whole.

You may not be sure what the initials stand for in TNT (trinitrotoluene) or UNICEF (United Nations International Children's Emergency Fund), but you probably know what they mean. See how many of the following you can identify:

U.S.A., I.B.M., S.P.C.A., J.F.K., E.O.E., M.I.T., Y.M.C.A., E.T. (Answers: United States of America, Society for the Prevention of Cruelty to Animals, Equal Opportunity Employer, Young Men's Christian Association, International Business Machines, John Fitzgerald Kennedy, Massachusetts Institute of Technology, Extra Terrestrial.)

Here are some other abbreviated or acrostic memory aids:

- **E**very **G**ood **B**oy **D**oes **F**ine. (The musical notes on the lines of the staff.)
- **PEWSAGL** (**P**ride, **E**nvy, **W**rath, **S**loth, **A**nger, **G**luttony, and **L**ust (The Seven Deadly Sins).
- **K**ings **P**lay **C**ards **O**n **F**airly **G**ood **S**oft **V**elvet (**K**ingdom, **P**hylum, **C**lass, **O**rder, **F**amily, **G**enus, **S**pecies, **V**ariety (biology classifications).
- **P. COHN'S CAFE** (**P**hosphorus, **C**arbon, **O**xygen, **H**ydrogen, **N**itrogen, **S**ulfur, **C**alcium (Ca), and **I**ron (Fe) (the chemical shorthand for the elements most common in the human body.)

USE LOCATION TO HELP REMEMBER

The Greeks used the structure of something they already knew, their homes, to arrange and remember lists of things such as the main points they wanted to make in a speech. They called this system *lochi* meaning rooms, and the Greek word has given us the English word, location. *Lochi* is a "peg system" that uses a structure you know to arrange what you want to remember. You can use the rooms of your home, your body, the streets between your home and office, any series of objects that is firmly fixed in your mind. Now project the new items onto this structure. Exaggerate them. Make them ludicrous, bizarre, so the picture will stand out. The crazier the image, the more likely you will be to remember it.

IT'S OKAY NOT TO LOVE SYSTEMS

If you've made a sporting try and you still feel frustrated and baffled by memory systems, that's okay. They work magnificently for some people and not at all for others. If you're one of the latter, you probably have many unconscious mental systems of your own that just don't mesh with outside ones. Try to keep a relaxed, open-minded, and playful attitude toward these external memory structures, and they may come in handy some day.

Need

LAW FIVE

TOPICAL SURVEY

Spiritual Needs in America

George Barna

In assessing needs, you feel that because you know your class, you've got it covered. But do you know your country and culture, and the church at large? You must in order to meet individual needs of students.

We have begun to witness a decline in the religious attentiveness of adults. In 1987, nearly six out of ten adults said that religion was very important in their everyday lives. That proportion has consistently dropped since then. Similarly, whereas almost three out of four adults described themselves as "religious" in 1986, just three out of five adults make the same claim today. The indications are that the window of opportunity for evangelism, wide open during the early and mid-80's, is rapidly closing.

WE "SAY, AND DO NOT"

There is an interesting contradiction between what most of us say we believe and what we do (or don't do) in response to those beliefs. The vast majority of Americans have orthodox Christian beliefs: they acknowledge the virgin birth, the death and resurrection of Jesus, the power of prayer, the reality of miracles by God, the importance of the Church, the reality of Satan and hell and the life of the Holy Spirit in believers. More than nine out of ten adults own a Bible, and a majority of them even believe that it is God's written word, totally accurate in its teaching. Perhaps surprisingly, a majority of American adults—about three out of five—claim that they have made a personal commitment to Jesus Christ that is still important in their lives today.

But our actions indicate that our beliefs are not held to be significant enough to share them with others. In the past seven years, the proportion of adults who have accepted Jesus Christ as their personal Savior (thirty-four percent) has not increased. Church attendance remains steady, although lower than three decades ago (less than half of all adults attend church on any given Sunday.) Loyalty to the Church, as an institution in which we have a personal investment and which we care about, is dropping. Attendance in adult Sunday School classes is diminishing. Membership in Christian churches is waning. Involvement in small group Bible studies has not increased in several years. Willingness to assume a leadership role in the congregation is declining. Time spent in Bible reading and Bible study has remained constant—and at a minimal level—for the past seven years.

The place of the Bible in America is worth further evaluation. It is revered as "the good book," and is found in most homes across the country. Yet, less than half of America will open that book during the week. Those who do read it during the week do not make the Bible a priority; they spend more time on almost every activity in which they engage than they do reading the Scriptures. Studies show that we have become a nation of biblical illiterates, lacking both knowledge and application of what is in the Bible.

AMERICA BY THE YEAR 2000

We are in for a rough ride in the decade ahead. The trends suggest that the importance of religion in people's lives will continue its slow decline. By 2000, less than half of our adult population will say that religion is very important in their daily lives.

For millions of Americans, religion will simply refer to a series of Sunday morning rituals that a shrinking number of traditionalists play. Less than forty percent of the population will even associate themselves with a Protestant denomination. Barely one out of three adults will include church attendance on their list of things to do on Sundays.

This situation is all the more disturbing because, by all rights, 2000 should provide a reasonably optimistic picture for the Christian faith. Baby-boomers will have matured to ages at which people generally become more stable, more serious and more interested in spiritual matters. We know that the Boomers, even more than most generations, have searched intensely for years in an attempt to understand their purpose in life. As most of them are still seeking answers to their fundamental questions of purpose and meaning, the Church should arise as a reasonable solution to their dilemma. Yet, this is not likely to be the case.

On the other hand, research consistently shows that people are most likely to accept Christ as their Savior before they reach the age of eighteen. Currently, about two-thirds of all decisions for Christ happen by that age. The demographic curves, however, point out that we will have a declining pool of young people to reach as the decade unfolds.

WHAT WE LIKELY WON'T DO

Why won't Christianity transform Americans in the '90s? Realize that Americans most readily accept institutions, philosophies, programs or individuals that respond to our felt needs through highly personalized and relevant messages. We are looking for that which is fresh and exciting, but credible and substantive. We are interested in that which is solid but flexible. The Christian faith, as promoted in our churches today, offers few of these traits.

The '80s were a decade in which millions of young adults gave the Church another chance. But relatively few found much that was of perceived value, and the majority have again turned their backs on the Church, perhaps permanently.

The Church will continue to emphasize aspects which are of little importance or meaning to the common person. For instance, some church leaders will recognize that congregations that grow are those in which a significant worship time is provided each Sunday. There will be a rush to imitate those churches, in the belief that pushing worship is the key to growth.

The fact is that most young adults have no concept of worship. One study showed that Boomers who are lay leaders in their churches have only a vague notion of what real worship is about, and that what their churches do in the realm of worship has little to do with their commitment to a church.

More generally, adults will also find the call to sacrifice, obedience and selflessness to be out of line with their own direction in life. The commands of Jesus will seem like an appeal to asceticism to most Americans, an unappealing prospect at best. In an era in which we are seeking to build our self-esteem and to feel good about ourselves through conscious, overt acts of generosity and kindness, the hardline requirements of Christianity will simply be too much for millions of people to accept. They may not vociferously challenge or oppose the Christian lifestyle and belief structure, but they will dismiss our faith as impractical and unreasonable for today's world.

WHAT MANY HAD RATHER BELIEVE

Left to their own devices, adults will be less impressed by, and less accepting of, Christianity's most basic and important beliefs. Instead, as adults continue their search for truth and purpose, they will become syncretistic. Syncretism was a form of religion developed many centuries ago, in which people took the best facets of each religion they encountered and formed a new, blended faith. As elements of Eastern religions become more prolific, the most appealing aspects of Christianity (which will be the lifestyle elements, rather than the central spiritual tenets) will be wed to the exotic and fascinating attributes of eastern faiths. The result will be a people who honestly believe that they have improved Christianity, and who would even consider themselves to be Christian, despite their creative restructuring of the faith.

This synthetic religion will coincide with the philosophic bent of the nation. By 2000, Americans will be even less interested in absolutes, preferring those perspectives which allow for relative values to gain credence. Casting issues in a black-and-white mode will disgust many people, since they will cling to the notion that there is no absolute truth, no absolute reality and no absolute force. Even our understanding of God is in the process of being reshaped due to this acceptance of conditional truth.

A decade from now, increasing numbers of Americans will think of God not as the singular, all-powerful Being who created and rules in the universe, but as a general and impersonal power. In 2000, most Americans will no longer assume that your God is my God, and that the God of the Christian Church is the only God in existence. Those who feared the takeover of communism railed against the dangers of America becoming a godless nation. They need not fear; we will become just the opposite, a nation filled with many gods.

CHALLENGE AND OPPORTUNITIES TO THE CHURCH

The first challenge we must rise to meet is the need to awaken the Christian community to America's spiritual crisis. Incredibly, most Christians do not perceive the Church to be in the midst of the most severe struggle it has faced in centuries. Perhaps we have simply become accustomed to hearing gloom and doom preaching, or reading books about the impending decline of civilization. Just as the general public have been anesthetized to the gospel, maybe we have been inoculated against cries alerting us to the present danger.

The encouraging realization is that Americans characteristically respond to a good fight. In the '90s, as we seek adventure and excitement, if the Church positions the nature of our crisis properly, and works intelligently toward arming the people for the battles ahead, this could be an exciting decade of response to the threat of the Enemy.

DON'T DOWNPLAY DISCIPLESHIP

One of the glaring weaknesses of the Church has been in the area of discipling and accountability. If we are to make inroads during these next ten years, we must support each other in deeper, more personal ways. While we may feel threatened by the vulnerability of confession, learning, and sharing needs, there seems to be little chance that the Body of Christ can be strengthened sufficiently to progress without the discipline of discipleship.

We will be tempted to downplay the importance of commitment and obedience. We will be tempted to soften the truth so that a hardened generation will give us a fair hearing. There is a fine line between clever marketing and compromised spirituality.

Does this mean we should not attempt to repackage the gospel in ways that may be more attractive to nonbelievers? No! We *must* do so if we hope to get our message to emerge from the flood of commercial messages that are directed at us each day. Our goal, however, must be to describe the faith in ways which are clearly relevant to today's circumstances and tensions, but without minimizing the hard truths that Jesus taught and demands of us. In a society that does not recognize absolutes, we must make absolutes seem not only relevant but natural and appealing.

EXPLAIN THE BASICS—RELEVANTLY

In approaching the public, let's not base our words and actions on unfounded assumptions. We tend to think that everyone knows the basics, that they understand how the Christian faith works and why they ought to accept Christ. All that's needed, we reason, is a push in the right direction. Unfortunately, the research shows that while people may have some "head knowledge" related to the faith, they have insufficient context to comprehend what the beliefs they have learned have to do with day-to-day reality. Even on matters which, from our perspective, are clearly explained in the Bible, there is much misunderstanding and ignorance about basic scriptural principles.

Thus, we cannot assume that when we urge people to pray, they know what that means. Similarly, when we encourage people to engage in meaningful worship or Bible study we cannot afford to let our assumptions dictate our actions and expectations. Even on matters of knowledge, the research indicates that while people may use concepts such as "sin" or "the Trinity" in polite conversation, they have little idea how those concepts fit into a deeper spiritual perspective.

STRATEGIC USE OF WORD AND WORKS

The way we use the Bible must be reexamined to achieve maximum impact. The Word can become more accessible to people, and therefore more likely to be incorporated into people's lives. Preaching based upon the Bible can use people's felt needs as the hook to grab their attention. Generally speaking, sermons which expound on Scripture without a clear relationship to people's felt needs will fall upon deaf ears. The main interest of people who attend churches is in practical applications of the faith to their lives. Thus, we have to enable people to use the Bible more effectively toward developing solutions to everyday problems.

From *The Frog in the Kettle* by George Barna, © 1990 Regal Books, Ventura, California 93003. Used by permission.

Twelve Ways to Motivate— Not Manipulate

Fred Smith

If you had to, could you differentiate between motivation (legitimate) and manipulation (illegitimate)? If not, how do you know when you're teaching legitimately? After reading this article, you'll know.

What are some motivational means? How can we bring out the best in people without resorting to manipulative tactics?

1. Establish a psychically friendly atmosphere. This is especially true with co-workers, whether volunteer or paid. In the corporate world, for instance, I'm very straightforward when hiring: I prefer "my kind of people"— people I can motivate. I can't motivate everybody. It's easier to manipulate than motivate. For long-term, day-to-day relationships, however, I need people I can motivate with integrity. I have never been able to fully motivate somebody I didn't like. But when I've genuinely motivated someone, I can look him or her in the eye and know we have an honest, friendly relationship between us.

2. Enjoy people's uniqueness. Being friends is beneficial; having the same tastes is not necessary. One young woman worked for me matching colors of ink. She could get tears in her eyes over certain shades of blue. "Isn't this a beautiful match?" she'd ask. I never could figure what went on in her head to make matching blue such a remarkable occurrence. But all I needed to do to keep her motivated was to share her excitement and appreciate her work.

3. Know a person's capabilities. With this employee, the most unkind thing I could have done would have been to say, "Don't you ever think of anything more important than shades of blue?" The truth of the matter was, more often than not, she didn't. Nor would my criticism have made her a better person. She was helping the company by doing what she enjoyed.

My color matcher didn't have extensive capabilities, and to motivate her above her capacity would have been cruel. If a musician has limited talent, it's a sin to talk about the joys of being a Mozart. When you're with a woman who is single at age fifty-five, you don't overdo motherhood. In motivation, desire must be matched with ability. You focus on the advantages of being who you are and not what somebody else is. The greatest demotivator is to say, "Do you ever think about what you could have been?" How cruel! Motivation always looks to the future.

4. Know how much responsibility a person can take. Some people can take sizable responsibility but not sole responsibility. They may have great abilities, but something in their psyche says, *I don't want the whole load. I want somebody to lean on, to report to.* Some people work best with assignments rather than responsibility. Assignments mean you explain what you want, when you want it, and how you want it done. Responsibility means the person takes initiative and gets the job done effectively by whatever means he or she develops.

5. Look for ways both of you can benefit. A certain honesty is required in motivation. It admits that unless there is a mutual interest, perhaps we shouldn't get involved in this thing together. If a person does have potential, a good question to ask is: "You have a lot more talent than you've been able to put to use. How much effort are you willing to exert if we give you the opportunity to develop that talent?"

6. Be honest about your goals. A young minister came to see me not long ago. He wanted to know how he could build his small church into a big church.

"What's your primary motivation?" I asked.

"Frankly, the size church I have can't pay me enough to live on," he said.

For him to begin an evangelism program, he would have to manipulate people. He couldn't be honest about it. His church was big enough to support a pastor if he could convince them to tithe, but he'd rather go into a church expansion program than try to teach people to tithe.

7. Use people as positive illustrations. In my speaking, I've told how certain people excelled at something, perhaps a Christian virtue, and they seemed to love being mentioned that way—and began to exhibit even more of those positive traits. This becomes manipulation only if what you're saying is untrue or slanted—or if you threaten to use a person as a bad illustration.

One of the ways I motivate people to think is to always carry some blank cards in my pocket, and when anyone says something worth writing down, I do so. For years I tried to remember memorable lines until I was alone and could jot myself a note. Then I overheard someone say, "I didn't know it was that good, but he wrote it down!" I realized people love to be quoted. And quoting them motivates them to think better.

8. Give a person a reputation to uphold. One of my bosses had a way of saying nice things about his workers that got back to them. True things but nice things. We appreciated it, and we couldn't keep from trying to do more things he could tell. People will work hard to uphold a good reputation.

9. Ask, *What is special about this person?* For example, some people rarely say anything negative. That's a beautiful reputation to start giving them. "Here's a person who looks for the best in his people." Of course, you can't be dishonest and say that about a cynic.

I have consciously augmented my wife's reputation as a creative listener. She is. I did it basically to comfort her because she'd always say after a social occasion, "I didn't have anything to say. All I did was listen," and yet, she does that better than anyone I know. Mary Alice has the ability to listen dynamically, to make people feel they're smart. And often they live up to it!

10. Compliment with credibility. I learned a secret of complimenting from Sarah Jarman, a gracious, intelligent, impeccable woman. Hers were never general compliments, rather they were always specific. "That tie and that suit are exactly right for each other." From then on, I'd wear that tie with that suit.

It was obvious her observations were well thought out, believable, and correct. She never tried to compliment you on something outside her field of expertise. She understood social graces, and the thing she knew best she would compliment you on. She was believable. Compliments mean the most when you know what you're talking about.

11. Show people you enjoy your work. I learned from my former boss, Maxey Jarman, that it is fun to work. One time, half complaining and fishing for praise, I said, "I sure am working hard."

Maxey replied, "What would you rather be doing?"

"Nothing," I had to admit.

"Then," said Maxey matter-of-factly, "you shouldn't complain about doing what you'd rather do."

By observing him and seeing how grateful he was for his responsibility, I realized I liked to work. That's when I had the most fun and satisfaction.

A friend once said, "I was a sophomore at Princeton before I realized it was fun to learn. Then school became exciting." He was fortunate. That doesn't happen to a lot of students until it's too late.

I don't have a higher education, but one of the blessings is that I never learned to study for grades. My friends in higher education have confirmed that those who learned to study for grades are often delayed as thinkers. They say the B students in seminary will often be the best pastors.

Then, tongue in cheek, they say the A students come back as professors and administrators and they usually wind up calling on the C students for money, because they've become the money makers.

12. Find thirsty people. If the difference between motivation and manipulation is the quenching of thirst, then the key for a leader is to look for thirsty people.

People, however, have different thirsts, and motivating them means knowing what they are thirsty for. Viktor Frankl has taught us that almost everyone has a basic thirst for meaning in life. There are other thirsts: worthwhile accomplishment, utilization of talents, approval by God. One of the greatest for those in Christian work is a thirst to belong, a desire for community in the kingdom of God.

One of the secrets of identifying a person's thirst is to see what has motivated him or her in the past. People rarely outlive their basic thirst. If they get a thirst early in life, they seldom lose it. If they have a thirst for recognition, these people never seem to get quite enough fame. If they thirst for intellectual growth, they never get quite smart enough. If they want money, I rarely see them get to the point where they don't want more.

Then, once we've identified where people are dry, effective motivators ask themselves, *What kind of water do I have to satisfy that kind of thirst?*

When we are able to honestly and openly offer water to parched people, we are not manipulating. We are motivating.

■ From *Leadership* 6, no. 4 (Fall 1985), pp. 110-117. Used by permission.

How to Successfully Motivate Students

Paul Tatham

Set philosophy aside for a moment—it's time to get practical in the classroom! Here are twenty-two proven ways to drive boredom from your teaching, and your students. These motivators work!

Our desire is to produce a student who is intrinsically motivated, in the purest sense of the word. He reads that book to expand his horizons, not for the prize he will receive; he accomplishes a task more for the joy of achievement than for the grade. He mows a neighbor's lawn because it is the biblical thing to do, not so that his neighbor will feel indebted to him. Such a state of perfection, ideal as it may be, is our ultimate goal.

Extrinsic motivation, on the other hand, is necessary for the bulk of our students. They learn in order to get an A, earn a prize, receive recognition, win the use of the car for the weekend, or get off probation.

Our challenge is clear. The progression is to lift students with little or no motivation up to the level of intrinsic motivation, using extrinsic motivation as the means. Consider the following list of extrinsic motivators:

1. Get students physically involved. Teachers forget how demanding sitting all day long can be, until they themselves have to endure an all-day seminar. When they become the student, rather than the teacher, they begin to understand how motivating increased blood circulation can be.

2. "Brag on 'em." When a teacher "brags" about certain students to outsiders, within earshot of those students, it will rejuvenate their desire to perform. They will strive all the more to please their teacher. A compliment behind a student's back often returns to that student.

3. "Student footnoting." This means giving credit to students who might otherwise be overlooked: "Stephanie told me something just before class that I would like to share with you."

4. Let them taste success. In most schools, the average kid is rarely mentioned. To motivate the middle-of-the-road student, the teacher needs to let him/her occasionally partake of the spoils of success. This entails paying heed when he simply improves, albeit from a D+ to a C-, or perhaps directing questions his way that he is likely to answer correctly.

5. Give them responsibility. A student may be responsible for something rather insignificant, such as cleaning the chalk erasers, or something important, such as presenting a lesson. The point is that they be given a sense of ownership.

6. Show enthusiasm. Student motivation is closely linked to teacher enthusiasm. The teacher who triumphantly shares something new which he has learned while browsing in the library, may inspire a student to visit the public library for himself. When a teacher shows his photographs that he entered in a photo contest, he may find students bringing photos of their own to share the next day.

7. Use group pressure. Although basically a negative motivator, group pressure can be effective. Teachers are well aware of the power of peer pressure and can use it to their own advantage. Group pressure does not have to be a negative motivator. When students are assigned to work in cooperative teams, it may prove a refreshing change to the usual every-man-for-himself competitive approach. Teams can be designed so that members are helping each other reach a common goal.

8. Get physical. Although parents are becoming touchy about touching in this era of child abuse, it would be a shame to outright ban the physical side of motivation. A hug or pat on the shoulder might work wonders for some students. The personal "touch" is often just that.

9. Mix it up. Anything that is different will usually stimulate. For instance, a steady diet of the same teaching technique, though perhaps excellent in itself, will soon translate into boredom. Try something new—maybe a question-and-answer approach, discussion, drama, hands-on, research, debate, whatever. In some Christian schools, workbooks have become the teachers. School has become a dreary, fill-in-the-blank routine.

10. Build school pride. If a student is proud of his school, he is motivated to continue the tradition. Everyone has a need to identify with a successful group. Teachers and administrators who recognize this do all they can to see that their school, as a whole, succeeds in the community.

11. Keep them challenged. Challenge, in itself, is motivating. The horse reaching for the dangling carrot will trot faster. Most people work best when under pressure. Wise teachers know how to insert a little anxiety ("Don't forget Friday's test!") from time to time. They seem to know just when and where to squeeze.

12. Bite your tongue. What a teacher says, and how she says it, may be all the motivation a child needs. Unfortunately, research tells us that the typical student is exposed to three times as many negative statements, from teachers and peers, as positive statements (*Educators' Newsletter,* 1988).

13. Watch classroom arrangement. Physical aspects of the classroom can affect student motivation. Windows with a view of the playground, for example, may decrease motivation by distracting students. So do bright wall colors. If a classroom is too rectangular, students tend to feel detached, unless they are clustered more toward one end.

14. Build rapport. The teacher who has succeeded in building rapport with her class has reached the zenith of motivation. She is at the point where her students truly want to please her. Having children who want to please you may be motivation in its highest form.

15. Expect success. In some classrooms, motivation may be nothing more than an attitude. If a teacher expects his class to be winners, he will treat them as such. Soon they will start fulfilling his expectations.

16. Give them feedback. Most kids, even adults, think that only what is inspected is important. If a paper is returned ungraded, it is deemed unimportant by the student. If a teacher makes no remark about a student's extra credit assignment, then the implication is that the teacher thinks little of it. If a teacher shows no response to the class's comments, then why add to the discussion? Teachers seeking to motivate give their students ongoing feedback that alerts them as to how they are doing.

17. Use announced rewards. Although announced rewards are an excellent form of motivation, unannounced rewards are occasionally better. To surprise students, now and then, creates an air of eagerness and excitement.

18. Use noncompetitive rewards. Not all rewards should be competitive in nature because some students never win. They are, therefore, unmotivated by the rewards. Noncompetitive rewards, on the other hand, are given equally. An example would be the reward of no homework on a student's birthday.

19. Show relevance. Studies show that students are far more motivated when they understand the application, or usefulness, of what they are learning. Some teachers are like the salesman peddling a product for which no one sees the need.

20. Know them individually. When a teacher knows students individually, and their particular needs, approaches to motivation can be tailored more specifically. A boy may be motivated by surfing or customized automobiles, while a girl may be motivated by fashions. The teacher who is able to key in on specific motivations might be able to adjust his or her teaching accordingly.

21. Make them feel important. Every student wears an invisible "make me feel important" button. The wise teacher realizes that all students, elementary and secondary, must feel good about themselves before they will be motivated to look beyond themselves. A healthy self-image is basic to all higher levels of motivation. There are a variety of ways in which teachers can make students feel worthwhile:

- Have the principal write the student's parents a letter of commendation for a job well done.
- Draw the student aside, look her in the eyes, and tell her that you sincerely appreciate her. The student may squirm awkwardly, but she still needs it. She may even respond negatively, but that may be because she has been complimented so rarely that she is shocked.
- Learn original ways to say, "Good for you!"
- Give every student a title that advertises their forte: "Mr. Math," "Miss Manners," or "Mr. Baseball" might be appropriate. These students are called upon as resident "experts" in their field. Some teachers even print business cards for them.

22. Don't forget to pray. The teacher who truly believes that "prayer changes things" will petition heaven on behalf of her students. She will pray for insight into certain individuals, seeking God for ways to motivate them. With His help, she will produce students who are excited about school.

■ Excerpted from *Excel Magazine* 3, no. 32 (Spring 1990), pp. 6-11. Used by permission.

Children: Need-Based Teaching

Robert J. Choun, Jr.

When you were recruited to teach a class of four- to six-year-olds, were you given a chart of their physical, mental, social, and emotional-spiritual characteristics and needs? Not to worry; here it is! Plus more!

Ministry to children demands an understanding of age-level characteristics and needs. How did God design the child? What are our children like? Luke 2:52 reveals that Jesus grew in wisdom (intellectually); and stature (physically); and in favor with God (spiritually); and with man (socially and emotionally). The following chart describes early childhood (birth to five years) and childhood (grades one through six). Remember that these represent typical characteristics and needs. Children develop at different rates in different areas and must always be treated as individuals.

BIRTH, ONE-, TWO-, AND THREE-YEAR-OLDS [1]

	CHARACTERISTICS	NEEDS
PHYSICAL	1. Continually active.	1. Opportunity and space for activity.
	2. Hungry senses.	2. Use materials which child can see, hear, touch, smell, taste.
	3. Spontaneous, impulsive reaction.	3. Interest centers. Use all five senses.
	4. Sensitive nervous system.	4. Avoid all causes of hurry and strain—calm and unhurried program.
	5. Health frail, endurance limited.	5. Good health conditions, period of rest and refreshments.
	6. Difference in maturation.	6. Program geared to individuals.
	7. Small muscles not coordinated.	7. Utilize large muscles—crayons, paper, etc.
	8. Shorter legs in proportion to body—about two feet tall.	8. Size chairs, play toys, etc., within reach.
MENTAL	1. Love for repetition and routine.	1. Use the familiar.
	2. Imaginative and suggestible.	2. Use stories, suggest ways and means.
	3. Narrow experience, concrete conceptions, literal-minded.	3. Broaden experience, avoid abstractions and symbolism.
	4. Limited knowledge and vocabulary.	4. Use objects, pictures frequently, use child's adopted vocabulary.
	5. Undeveloped musical ability.	5. Program of music.

156

CHARACTERISTICS	**NEEDS**
6. Short attention span (two-and-a-half to three minutes).	6. Varied program of activities.
7. Unreliable memory.	7. Repeat essentials often—simple statements of directions.
8. Curiosity.	8. Provide materials to arouse.
9. Asks innumerable questions.	9. Answer questions simply—avoid detailed explanations.

SOCIAL

CHARACTERISTICS	**NEEDS**
1. Individualistic and self-centered.	1. Give individual care, provide time for free play, develop social consciousness.
2. Dependent and demand attention.	2. Child needs constant watching, recognition of fact that child is not responsible.
3. Imitative.	3. Proper examples of conduct, importance of attitude, consistency of life and word.
4. Negativistic, eager to please; "no" learned first.	4. Positive, acceptance of his activity, some conformity, recognition of contribution. (Don't ask — but TELL!)
5. Strong play interests.	5. Furnish room with equipment for meaningful play.

EMOTIONAL AND SPIRITUAL

CHARACTERISTICS	**NEEDS**
1. Timid and emotionally sensitive.	1. Create permissive and secure atmosphere.
2. Affectionate.	2. Direct to the Lord, develop a consciousness of God and His love for them.
3. Awakening spiritually, natural trust.	3. Individual feeling, place trust in a person.
4. Capable of worship.	4. Direct to the Lord, never underestimate ability.
5. Filled with awe and wonder.	5. Arouse the sensory experiences, appreciate color and beauty, develop prayer habits.
6. Fearful.	6. Counteract with concept of the protecting God; stories of children who have overcome fear.
7. Sensitivity to spiritual atmosphere.	7. Calm, Christlike atmosphere, sensitivity to their needs and responses.
8. Plastic, impressionable, teachable.	8. Tell truth, teach nothing which has to be unlearned.
9. Growing sense of right and wrong.	9. Distinguish between right and wrong, reward right, standards set by God.

FOUR-, FIVE-, AND SIX-YEAR-OLDS

CHARACTERISTICS	NEEDS

PHYSICAL

CHARACTERISTICS	NEEDS
1. Rapid growth, extreme activity.	1. Constant change, alternate program of activity and rest.
2. Small muscles, motor skills incompletely developed.	2. Provide large, sturdy, creative materials, paints, crayons, clay, etc. Sufficient room.
3. Learning health habits, growing responsibility for self.	3. Challenge with Christian responsibility. Don't baby, assist.
4. Health delicate, fatigued easily, eyes and ears easily strained, susceptible to disease.	4. No strain or overstimulation. Sanitary conditions. Precautions: isolate by inspection. Explain health standards to mothers.
5. Active sensory processes.	5. Large, durable pictures. Firsthand experiences. Opportunity to learn by seeing and doing.
6. Spontaneous motor reactions.	6. Direct activity; do not repress it.

MENTAL

CHARACTERISTICS	NEEDS
1. Short interest span (five to ten minutes).	1. Keep in mind when planning games, stories, programs, etc.
2. Mental immaturity, wants to do more than is capable of, vocabulary small but rapidly increasing.	2. Furnish things to do that they are able to understand. Explain slowly and clearly. Clarify understanding. Simple, clear routine. Limited choices.
3. Inquisitive, asks countless questions for information, initial thinking challenged.	3. Answer all questions honestly. Seek reasons behind questions. Encourage them to think for themselves.
4. Limited concepts of space and time. "Eternal now."	4. Refrain from referring to history or chronology. Emphasize present. Explain in terms of known. Increase their experience.
5. Thinking is concrete and literal. Makes mental pictures of things.	5. Use concrete terms. Avoid symbolism.
6. Highly imaginative.	6. Encourage imagination as essential. Distinguish between fact and fantasy.

SOCIAL

CHARACTERISTICS	NEEDS
1. Individualistic, negativistic.	1. Teach obedience and the joy of doing right. Accept necessary limits and restraints.
2. Imitative: language, manners, habits, etc. Conformist: what teacher is like is very influential.	2. Be a consistent example to them. Learn acceptable behavior. Guidance and a proper pattern of behavior to follow.
3. Group awareness, extremely	3. Promote opportunities for group

CHARACTERISTICS	NEEDS
social: want to be and do things with people.	activities. Teach give-and-take responsibilities. Circle games, not relays. Cooperative play.
4. Learning to lead in activities and adjust to others. Increasing independence. Widening scope.	4. Allow and encourage leadership activities. Tactful guidance. Service projects.
5. Thoughtful, mothering instinct.	5. Lessons on Christian virtues. Provide dolls and animals to play with. Illustrate Bible stories with stuffed toys.
6. Strong play interests.	6. Provide variety of cooperative games.
7. Strong desire to please. Wants adult approval.	7. Mediate to them God's approval.
8. Conversationalist.	8. Give opportunity to talk (learning activities). Allow place for his thinking (test teaching). Use as teaching clues.

SOCIAL

CHARACTERISTICS	NEEDS
1. Intense, but transient emotions.	1. Avoid arousing negative emotions, approve positive emotional expression.
2. Strong desire for love.	2. Stress God's love and care for them. Security of love and affection from parents.
3. Credulous.	3. Teach the truth. Teach nothing that must be unlearned. Encourage trust in the Lord.
4. Full of wonder.	4. Stimulate their desire to worship. Build reverence for prayer, Bible, the house of the Lord, etc.
5. Eagerness to be taught and learn.	5. Watchful of readiness of learners to receive spiritual truth. Requires time, patience, understanding and genuine interest of adult leaders.

EMOTIONAL AND SPIRITUAL

PRIMARY GRADES 1-3
AGES 6-8 YEARS

CHARACTERISTICS	NEEDS
1. Growth slower, small hand muscles not completely coordinated, but improving.	1. Use large muscles. Assign simple tasks, easily completed. Use regular crayons.

CHARACTERISTICS	NEEDS

PHYSICAL

2. Energy and vitality fluctuate. Tend to overdo.

2. Guard against overdoing. Balanced program. Opportunity for excess energy and restlessness to find an outlet.

3. Susceptible to disease, resistance greater, period of contagious disease.

3. Protect, observe, and exclude suspicious cases at the door. Avoid overcrowding.

4. Activity level high, restlessness.

4. Program providing ample opportunity for varied activities. Exploration methods.

5. Keen senses.

5. Provide objects to see and handle which teach. Firsthand acquaintance.

MENTAL

1. Wide range of reading ability, varied interests.

1. Graded materials. Divided classes. Teach to read the Bible. Supply good reading materials. Enjoy songs, rhythms, nature and true stories, comics, radio, movies, etc. Employ varied teaching techniques.

2. Widening experience, increasing ability and accuracy, developing reasoning power.

2. Furnish varied experience, confront and grapple with issues, exercise reasoning power in solving their own problems.

3. Concrete and literal thinking, beginning concept of abstract thought.

3. Avoid symbolism which is beyond their understanding. Multiply illustrations.

4. Learning greater self-control, employing more self-evaluation.

4. Teach joy of self-control (fruit of the Holy Spirit), and to rely on the Spirit. Establish standards; minimize interference.

5. Attention span increasing (seven to fifteen minutes).

5. Challenge thinking; do not tax it.

6. Memory improving, though unreliable. Growth from interest in present and immediate reality to interest in the past.

6. Meaningful memory program. Understanding what and why they memorize. Acceptance at their own level of development with understanding of nature and interests. Teach from past experiences.

7. Extremely conversational and increasingly communicative.

7. Promote self-expression and conversational opportunities.

8. Eager (more enthusiasm than wisdom) and curious. Desirous of learning.

8. Learns best through active, direct participation and concrete learning situations. Respond with eagerness and enthusiasm.

CHARACTERISTICS	NEEDS

SOCIAL

CHARACTERISTICS	NEEDS
1. Continuing growth from dependence to independence. Assuming greater responsibilities.	1. Give opportunity for responsibility through supervised group work. Encourage proper combination of independence and dependence.
2. Imitative and inventive. Enjoy dramatic play.	2. Play situations. Imitate great Bible characters and their characteristics. Write own words and music for songs. Set Scripture to music.
3. Make friends quite easily. Concerned about group status.	3. Encourage Christian fellowships. Learn to work out group plans and to cooperate with members of a group.
4. Sympathy easily aroused. Highly sensitive, emergence of class and race prejudice.	4. Be careful about expressing opinions. Direct sympathy in scriptural channels.
5. Desire to please and do well. Sensitive to adult feeling. Resent being told what to do.	5. Help in gradual development of acceptable manners and habits. Wants and needs adult approval. Encouragement, ample praise, warmth, and patience from adults.
6. Emotional immaturity, egotistic, individualistic.	6. Do not teach beyond their ability to respond. Foster group ideas. Centrality of the Lord in all of life.
7. Friendly and cooperative. Whole-hearted approach.	7. Encourage their working together. Contagious enthusiasm.
8. Strong sense of fairness. Demands own turn and rights. Highly competitive.	8. Equity and justice in all decisions. Encourage them to make their own rules.

EMOTIONAL AND SPIRITUAL

CHARACTERISTICS	NEEDS
1. Emotions easily aroused and played on.	1. Train emotions to love and hate appropriate things. Employ discrimination.
2. Concerned about right and wrong. Differences are black and white.	2. Apply the Bible to real-life situations to aid decision-making. Faithfulness in exposing error. Reward the right. Firmness with wrong.
3. Credulous and yet uncertain due to conflicting voices.	3. Direct belief to the Lord. Walk and rely on the Lord, the constant Friend and Confidant. Basis of authority.
4. Salvation-conscious because sin-conscious.	4. Present Christ for individual response. "After class" approach.
5. Fascinated with heaven and God.	5. Teach spiritual truth in the reality of their own experience.
6. Appreciation of supernatural.	6. Stress strange things that really happened. Miracles.

CHARACTERISTICS	NEEDS
7. Growing desire for love and security.	7. Teach God's care and love for them.

JUNIOR GRADES 4-6
AGES 9-11 YEARS

CHARACTERISTICS	NEEDS

PHYSICAL

CHARACTERISTICS	NEEDS
1. Abounding energy, rapid growth, loves to do things, acts first and thinks afterward.	1. Provide a variety of constructive things to do: crafts, shop work, active and dramatic play; encourage to think about consequences of their actions.
2. Strong and healthy	2. Expect regular attendance. Let him do "difficult" jobs; develop good health habits. Urge plenty of rest and good food at regular intervals.
3. Noisy, loves to fight.	3. Arrive before he does. Give something to do; encourage poise and calm by providing quiet activities and atmosphere.
4. Loves the out-of-doors.	4. Take on hikes, camping, nature walks, tours.
5. Appreciates doing the difficult and competitive, manifesting individual differences and abilities.	5. Challenge ability with projects. Bible learning activities in which they can compete and excel, training in game skills.
6. Interested in babies, somewhat curious about sex.	6. Considerate answers to questions concerning the coming of physiological changes. Wholesome sex education on an appropriate level.

MENTAL

CHARACTERISTICS	NEEDS
1. Strong geographical and historical sense, factual (not fantasy) studies.	1. Teach chronology and geography in the Bible. Trace journeys, make and use maps, time lines, models.
2. Collector.	2. Interest in a worthwhile hobby. Collections related to missions, stamps, coins, curios.
3. Inquisitive, varied interest, daydreaming common.	3. Help answer questions. Encourage interest in varied areas, confront with reality.

CHARACTERISTICS	NEEDS

MENTAL (con't)

4. Likes to read, write, and talk. Varying ability.

4. Provide good reading material (biographies recommended). Use Bible studies that require some writing.

5. Critical, especially of adults.

5. Set example of thoughtfulness and kindness. Listen to and talk with them.

6. Logical reasoning power developing. Increasingly aware of other ideas and beliefs.

6. Reasonable explanations, provide opportunities to make behavior choices, various teaching approaches, evaluation of different viewpoints.

7. Rote memory at its best.

7. Promote memorization of Scripture.

8. Literal-minded, symbolism difficult to understand.

8. Avoid using object lessons which confuse rather than clarify thinking.

9. Desires to do well but loses interest if discouraged or pressured.

9. Encourage attempt at new activities as well as finish ones already started. Challenge and praise constantly.

SOCIAL

1. Can accept responsibility.

1. Organize classes with officers who have special duties and specific responsibilities, committee, and group planning.

2. Does not like authority over him, strong sense of justice and honor, will argue over fairness in clubs and play, patriotic.

2. No threats or ultimatums. Be a guide, not a dictator. Opportunities to discuss respect for property and others, consistency in life and discipline, Christian citizenship and loyalty.

3. Strong "gang" instinct, clubs, teams.

3. Let class be a club, give sense of belonging and personal attention.

4. Scornful of opposite sex, close friendships with same sex.

4. Separate classes for boys and girls.

5. Hero worshiper, impressionable.

5. Be an example, present Christ as his Hero.

6. Undisciplined, unwise in spending.

6. Develop disciplined habits, provide an opportunity to earn and manage an allowance, teach to assume responsibility for personal dress and grooming.

1. Has few fears, but many problems.

1. Teach what to fear and what not to. Learn how they feel about things, personal counseling.

	CHARACTERISTICS	NEEDS
EMOTIONAL AND SPIRITUAL	2. Quick-tempered, self-centered.	2. Avoid causes of flare-ups, life to be centered on Christ.
	3. Dislikes outward display of affection, distaste for sentimentality in religion.	3. Avoid such display, private counseling on spiritual matters.
	4. Keen sense of humor, much noise and giggling.	4. Challenge and channel humor. Teach evaluation of what is, and what is not funny.
	5. Recognizes sin as sin.	5. Teach Christ as Savior from penalty and power of sin. Praise good work and commendable behavior.
	6. Has questions about Christianity.	6. Answer truthfully, help them find the answers in their own Bibles.
	7. Emotions feature little in religion.	7. Avoid emotional stories and appeals.
	8. Sets high standards for himself but his ideals are not fixed.	8. Meet high standards in your life. Set biblical standards.
	9. Intensely practical, needs encouragement and spiritual motivation.	9. Doer, not a hearer. How does Christianity work? Correlation of teaching and everyday life, activities in which he will develop spiritually, provide devotional helps.
	10. May express concerns about home life, especially when separation or divorce takes place or in his relationships with stepparents.	10. Be sensitive to and understanding of the child's situation. Do not ridicule or be judgmental. Show God's unconditional love. Support each child as a special person.

Notes

1. Age-Group Characteristics and Needs Chart adapted from unpublished materials developed by Scripture Press Ministries, Wheaton, Illinois.

■ Taken from Chapter 7, "Teaching Children," by Dr. Robert Choun in Kenneth O. Gangel and Howard G. Hendricks, eds., *The Christian Educator's Handbook on Teaching* (Wheaton: Victor Books, 1988). Used by permission.

Needs of Youth: Grades 7–12

Robert J. Choun, Jr.

Ever tried describing the universe? That's a cinch compared to painting a picture of the "average" Jr. or Sr. Higher. This is an awesome article, dudes, and will make you bodacious rather than bogus—like, you know?

Characteristics of a Junior Higher—Grades 7–9

PHYSICAL

1. He is growing rapidly.
2. Girls grow more rapidly than boys.
3. He is undergoing many internal bodily changes.
4. He is usually awkward.
5. He has boundless energy alternated with periods of fatigue.

MENTAL

1. He has a keen memory.
2. He is interested in adventure and discovery.
3. He is capable of real thinking (moving toward the abstract).
4. He often will question authority.
5. He will make quick judgments.
6. He has an active imagination.
7. He has a strong sense of humor.

SOCIAL

1. He wants to be an adult.
2. He desires to be independent of adults.
3. He wants to belong to a "group."
4. He has a strong sense of loyalty.
5. He is usually self-conscious.
6. His social problems reflect his sexual development.
7. He is looking for a model—a hero.

EMOTIONAL

1. He often feels misunderstood by adults and peers.
2. His emotions fluctuate—extreme joy to sadness.
3. He lacks self-control of emotions.
4. His emotions are very intense.

SPIRITUAL

1. He wants a faith that is practical—here and now.
2. His spirit is ripe for the gospel message.
3. He has a vision for service—"needs to be needed" to serve.
4. He can have many doubts about Christianity.
5. He is looking for the ideal (in thoughts and in people's actions).

CHARACTERISTICS OF A SENIOR HIGHER—GRADES 10–12

PHYSICAL
1. He is outgrowing his awkwardness.
2. He has an attractive, grown-up appearance.
3. His appetite is usually great.
4. His physical habits are being formed.
5. He is usually concerned about his sexual nature.

MENTAL
1. His reasoning powers are reaching new heights.
2. He likes argument and debate.
3. He is very creative and idealistic.
4. His judgment is improving.
5. His imagination is usually under the control of reason and judgment.

SOCIAL
1. He belongs to a clique or exclusive social group.
2. He is attracted to the opposite sex (though not always).
3. He is very much interested in personal traits and outward appearance.
4. He wants social approval.
5. He is trying to find his place in society.
6. He usually has an increasing desire to help others.

EMOTIONAL
1. His emotions are still intense.
2. He now has more of an ability to control his emotions.
3. He may be moody.
4. He wants security.
5. He likes excitement and entertainment.

SPIRITUAL
1. His religion is personal.
2. His religion is one of action.
3. His religion is emotional.
4. His doubts may increase about his faith.
5. He can now appreciate the abstract and the atmosphere of worship.

From Chapter 8, "Teaching Youth," by Dr. Robert Choun in Kenneth O. Gangel and Howard G. Hendricks, eds., *The Christian Educator's Handbook on Teaching* (Wheaton: Victor Books, 1988). Used by permission.

The Needs of Adults

Kenneth O. Gangel

The teacher who thinks an adult class is an adult class is an adult class is, well, wrong! There are significantly different needs among adults in our churches, and classes should be planned—and lessons taught—accordingly.

UNDERSTANDING ADULT AGE-GROUPINGS

Young Adults: Eighteen to Thirty-five. Essentially almost any church contains five groups of young adults who call for attention. There are those we refer to as the college and career group, post-high school adults over the age of eighteen who have had no relationship to marriage and may not for many years. The second group we'll just call young couples—newly marrieds—usually in their twenties, most likely still involved with education or career, but separate from the first group because they are married.

The third group we can label new parents, a term which speaks for itself. Here again the new parents might still be in college or graduate school, certainly one of them (if not both) is involved with a career, but they differ from the first two groups because they have one or more children. The fourth group almost automatically takes us up the chronological age ladder as we identify parents of teens. This group would actually overlap into the middle adulthood area, but many folks under the age of thirty-five find themselves parents of teens and so the category must be included here. Finally, the very popular category of singles which we'll deal with in a later section of this chapter is a special need group.

How can we understand these people? Robert J. Havighurst, famous for his work on developmental tasks, suggests eight such tasks for early adulthood to which I have added two which seem particularly relevant to Christian adults:[1]

1. Selecting a mate.
2. Learning to live with a marriage partner and achieving a fusing of two lives into one.
3. Starting a family; having the first child successfully.
4. Raising children with accompanying adjustment to the expanding family, the whole new life of a family, and the psychological problems involved.
5. Managing a home.
6. Getting started on an occupation.
7. Taking on civic responsibilities.
8. Finding a congenial social group.
9. Accepting one's place in the local church.
10. Learning to assume Christian leadership and discipline with respect to oneself, one's family, and others.

Middle Adults: Thirty-five to Sixty. Daniel Levinson has identified five major transitions occurring about ages twenty, thirty, forty, fifty, and sixty.[2] The "mid-life transition" of the early forties brings middle adults (particularly men) face-to-face with mid-life crisis forcing appraisal of the past and preparation for a seemingly uncertain future. It may be helpful to list some of the development tasks of middle adulthood as we did for young adults:

1. Learning advanced job skills.
2. Changing careers.
3. Planning for retirement.
4. Returning to careers (women).
5. Adjusting to aging parents.
6. Relating to one's spouse as a person.
7. Finding new interests.
8. Keeping out of a rut.
9. Compensating for physiological changes.
10. Developing a realistic time perspective on life.

Senior Adults: Sixty and Over. Senior adulthood offers a challenge in our day and will continue as a major target for church ministry as well into the next century. One million baby-boomers will reach the age of one hundred and after the year 2000, there will be more "old people" than "young people" in the United States for the first time in the history of the country. The church must affirm senior citizenry because we live in a society that puts a premium on youth. We tend to look at retired people in the light of what they have been or have accomplished rather than what they are or perhaps still will accomplish. The result to the older person is a feeling of having been shelved, and the body of Christ should provide a balanced view.

The church can respond to senior adult ministry by developing both intellectual and interpersonal relationships. It is foolish to believe that adults can no longer learn; learning ability does not wear out. The rate of learning may decline but the capacity remains constant. We must all cultivate this capacity and encourage our senior adults to recognize that they need to exercise their minds. Like an atrophied muscle, the ability to learn tends to weaken only because it has not been used.

One more time, a list of developmental tasks, here adapted from the work of Malcolm Knowles:[3]

1. Adjusting to retirement.
2. Find new ways to be useful.
3. Understanding Social Security, Medicare, and other retirement programs.
4. Adjusting to reduced income.
5. Learning to live alone.
6. Relating to grandchildren.
7. Understanding the aging process.
8. Keeping morale high.
9. Keeping up personal appearance.
10. Preparing for death.

Rather than shunting off our senior citizens, or in some way belittling their contribution to the church's task, we should help them make uncommon demands on the church. In a very real sense, the opportunity to have a voice and role in the church's ministry has been *earned*. Our culture shames itself by catering to teenagers who have no idea what the church ought to be doing (encouraging their participation and seeking their advice), while bypassing people in whom the Spirit of God has been working for fifty years or more.

UNDERSTANDING SPECIAL NEED GROUPS AMONG ADULTS

Multiple "special need groups" surface among adults in almost any church. We will look at just four and even those ever so briefly.

Singles. Consider four types of singles: those who have never been married (either by choice or by circumstances); those who have been married and whose spouse still lives (representing either divorce or separation); those who have been widowed; and those who might be called "spiritual singles," Christians whose partners do not know the Lord. What do our singles need?

They need acceptance. Only as lonely people recognize their acceptance by the Heavenly Father—and by His people—can they move on to seek and receive acceptance from others outside the body, and especially acceptance of themselves.

Singles also need a strong sense of self-worth. The church, the place for Christian fellowship and encouragement, sometimes seems to alienate the single person because of its emphasis on marriage and the Christian family.

Singles need a sense of belonging. Loneliness and insecurity are dispelled not only by a sense of belonging but also by the genuine reality of belonging both in attitude and act.

Single Parents. One major need here is freedom from stress. Most of the things we have talked about in relation to the loneliness of singles can become elements of psychological and emotional stress of much greater dimension for single parents. These are complicated by what might be called domestic stress. Family pressures build, especially in the home of single parents, because their children struggle with adjusting in school and peer relations. Financial stress also comes about because of limited income and the necessity to work full time, sometimes during afternoon or evening hours, which makes effective parenting most difficult. Social stress creates problems as single parents ask themselves whether they ought to be dating, remarrying, or even spending so much time with their married friends. To these stressful, needy people, the body of Christ must bring a sense of security and peace; we must deal with the practical issues of their lives in real and helping ways.

Divorced. Without arguing different views on or about the rightness or wrongness of divorce, let us confine ourselves here to how we minster to adults who find themselves in this situation. Certainly, forgiveness figures prominently. Assuming repentance and a willingness to follow the will of God, the body of Christ dare not be judgmental nor condemning. Divorced people must be restored to fellowship in the body, though some congregations may have specific restrictions with respect to certain offices.

The pastor particularly should make himself available to divorced people, representing the symbolic response of the body in a somewhat official way (Galatians 6:1-5). Finally, some kind of care group needs to be established, most likely made up of divorced people themselves. Relationships, group dependency, and prayer support can all come out of this kind of ministry.

Families. Sunday school classes and other church educational experiences must focus on the real issues parents and children face in the late twentieth century. They must be aware of studies like those conducted by Yankelovich in which parents themselves enumerate the kinds of study groups which would interest them:

1. Parenting and handling the attendant problems, 34 percent.
2. Teaching children about sex, 31 percent.
3. Handling problems of discipline, 36 percent.
4. Dealing with drug use among children, 49 percent.

5. Convincing children not to smoke, 37 percent.

6. Understanding new classroom teaching methods, 42 percent.

7. Teaching children about religion, 32 percent.[4]

Is the ministry of teaching adults in the church anachronistic—a leftover dream from an earlier day? Or is it a newborn baby wishing to be nurtured more effectively? According to a Church Data Service survey conducted by Denver Seminary, only 78 percent of the adults who attend church also attend Sunday school at least every other week.

Adult education faces an exciting future. But only if educational leaders are willing to make it an area of significant concentration in their ministries. That kind of focus is not an option; it is a necessity. As Westing argues, "Your church can still have a growing adult Sunday school if its leaders are willing to adjust to our changing society."[5]

Notes

1. Robert J. Havighurst, *Developmental Tasks and Education.* New York: Longmans, Green & Co., 1948, pp. 72-98

2. Daniel Levinson, *The Secrets of a Man's Life.* New York: Knopf, 1978.

3. Malcolm Knowles, *The Adult Learner: A Neglected Species.* Houston: Gulf, 1973.

4. Daniel Yankelovich, et al. *Raising Children in a Changing Society.* Minneapolis: General Mills, 1977.

5. Harold Westing, "Comeback in the Classroom," *Moody Monthly* (July-August, 1987), p. 26.

■ From Chapter 9, "Teaching Adults in the Church," by Kenneth O. Gangel in Kenneth O. Gangel and Howard G. Hendricks, eds., *The Christian Educator's Handbook on Teaching* (Wheaton: Victor Books, 1988). Used by permission.

Teaching to Meet the Needs of Adults

Jerry Martin

Quick: in thirty seconds list the three basic age groupings of adults and what they perceive to be their major responsibilities in each of these stages of life. (Reason? They want your teaching to help them fulfill their responsibilities.

At the current divorce rate in America, half of all American marriages begun in the early 1980s will end in divorce. The number of unmarried couples living together is three times that of 1970. One out of four children does not live with both parents. Child abuse, including sexual abuse, stands at an all time high.

In 57 percent of American households, both parents work to make ends meet. In many places wages are stagnant, house prices have escalated beyond reach, while medical expenses and tuition costs have skyrocketed. The American dream that many young adults looked forward to has turned into a nightmare. The idealism of the 75 million baby boomers (those born between 1946 and 1964) has turned to realism as they face midlife and the challenges of careers, family, and growing older.

George Barna of Barna Research predicts that we have a whole new breed of church attenders. The key will not be loyalty to the church but, "How will the church satisfy my need?" Small group ministries will be critical to growth. Barna indicates that children's programs will be the flagship of growing churches.

STAGES OF ADULTHOOD

Many psychological studies have described various stages or phases through which adults pass. The following represent generally accepted categories.

Young Adulthood (age 24-34) Responsibilities:
1. Career development.
2. Selecting a mate.
3. Learning to live with a marriage partner.
4. Starting a family.
5. Rearing children.
6. Managing a home.

Middle Adulthood (age 35-60) Responsibilities:
1. Civic responsibilities.
2. Establishing and maintaining economic stability.
3. Building teenagers to adulthood.
4. Husband/wife relationships.
5. Accepting and adjusting to physical changes.
6. Adjusting to one's own parents.

Older Adulthood (age 61 +) Responsibilities:
1. Physical adjustments.
2. Economic adjustment and retirement.
3. Adjustment to loss of loved ones.
4. Becoming a part of the older adult society.[1]

MEETING NEEDS OF ADULTS

Young Adults. For the most part they are urban and mobile and very independent as they search for something new. They react against the impersonalism of being lost in a crowd and hesitate to take what they are told at face value, especially if it comes from institutions. Dr. Clifford Anderson has suggested that young adults can be classified by three words: liberated, skeptical, and searching.

Middle Adults. Teach the Bible so that it makes a difference in individual lives. They have questions about such things as teenagers, communication in the home, and stewardship of time and money. They need to adjust to changes and problems of middle age, questions of death, illness, loneliness, loss of employment, the empty home, marriage of children, and menopause (male and female). Channel abilities and experience into meaningful service.

Older Adults. The ministry should be planned *with*, not *for*, these people. We can help older adults find spiritual fulfillment. Feelings of uselessness, loneliness, depression, and insecurity can be eliminated. Attempt to meet the physical and emotional needs of older adults. Provide facilities with good lighting, easy access, adequate heating, a good sound system and hearing aid adapters.

The education of children and adults differs in many ways. Pedagogy (education of children) is, for the most part, teacher-centered and teacher-directed. But andragogy (education of adults) should focus more on learning experiences that are primarily self-directed. Adult education must take into consideration all the varying backgrounds, experiences, needs, attitudes, community distinctives, family distinctives, and age characteristics.

Adults tend to present themselves to learning experiences that provide immediate application. They will assess learning by asking, "How can I use this now?" Often real needs must be converted to "felt" needs before an adult will actively participate in a given learning experience.

Because adults have so many more life-related experiences than children, they have more to add to a teaching session. Adults learn best through a variety of methods which help them discover principles from God's Word that relate to their daily lives.

An adult is motivated to learn when he/she senses a felt need to be met, a problem to be solved, a curiosity to be satisfied or a frustration to be relieved. If we ignore these areas of adult motivation we will become ineffective in our teaching ministry to adults.

In order to be continually on the "cutting edge" of a vital teaching ministry to adults, we must continually be aware of their needs, and restructure our Christian Education programs to meet them.

Notes

1. Robert J. Havighurst, *Human Development and Education* (New York: David McKay Company, Inc., 1953), pp. 257-83.

■ From *Christian Education Today* (Fall 1990), pp. 6-8. Used by permission.

How Kids Learn

Kathleen A. Butler

The teacher who only lectures is missing the primary avenue of learning for the majority of her students. How many learning styles are there? As much as possible, students need to be taught the way they learn best!

Anthony F. Gregorc (*An Adult's Guide to Style*, Gabriel Systems, Inc., 1986) has found that mannerisms and outward behavior provide clues to how people approach the world, and how they approach thinking in particular. He observes that in any given situation, people can perceive either concretely or abstractly, and that they organize their thoughts either sequentially or randomly. Based on ways of combining these four approaches to learning, Gregorc has identified four predominant learning types, or "mindstyles."

The *concrete sequential* learner is structured, practical, predictable, and thorough. The *abstract sequential* learner is logical, analytical, conceptual, and studious. The *abstract random* learner is sensitive, sociable, imaginative, and expressive. The *concrete random* learner is intuitive, original, investigative, and able to solve problems.

When teachers consistently provide learning situations and strategies that match these four styles of learning, Gregorc found, students thrive academically, develop positive self-images, and learn to respect others' differences. Just as important, teachers can help students flex their thinking when their learning style doesn't match the requirements of the task at hand.

A LEARNING-STYLES FRAMEWORK

First, it gives teachers a framework for examining their own learning and teaching styles—for asking: How do I learn? Have I developed or masked my own strengths? Do I enrich the child who thinks like me? Do I frustrate or harm the child who learns differently from me? How can I be flexible enough to meet the needs of learners with styles different from mine?

Second, by understanding how and why people learn as they do, teachers can understand the child as a person as well as a learner. They have definable ways to ask themselves: What motivates this child? What brings out his creative energy?

Third, with this approach, teachers learn to value their own learning styles and then expand their teaching repertoire by asking questions, offering choices, and honoring divergence. Teachers retain the decision-making power; the approach does not dictate it.

Fourth, when teachers have many ways to organize for style differences, they can create appropriate lessons with greater ease, more purpose, and wider flexibility.

A FLEXIBLE CLASSROOM

The secret to success with learning styles lies within you as you integrate your experience as a teacher with your knowledge of how each of your students approaches learning. The following suggestions are starting points for considering learning styles in the classroom.

Gain personal understanding of learning styles. Give yourself time to learn about style differences. Start slowly to build a knowledge base. Become more versatile and open to students' style differences, but don't abandon your own teaching style for a generic approach.

Team with others. Join forces with a teacher who complements your strengths, and plan together. Find ways to observe and learn from teachers who teach differently than you do.

Observe your students. Step back from everyday demands and look at your students through a "styles lens."

Build on strengths. When you reinforce your students' strengths, rather than continually pointing out mistakes caused by their weaknesses, you give them confidence. Looking at it another way, encourage individual learning styles, rather than first telling students their way was a mistake.

Ask your students to think about their own thinking. Tell them about the learning-style demands of an assignment or activity and ask them to think in advance about how they'll handle the task. Discuss the value of many ways of approaching it. When they're finished ask them what they'd do differently the next time.

Help your students vary their own styles of learning. Many times you need to require all students to do the same activity in the same way—a spelling test, for example. Some learners may have trouble with this sequential task. Bridge the gap by showing them how to use association, humor, or visual connections.

Ask your students their opinions through open-ended questions. A brainstorming session at the beginning of a unit can give you a good idea of what your students already know. Plan some activities and projects around their ideas.

Offer choices. Provide for various learning styles within your lessons, perhaps in homework assignments. For example, allow many ways to do a book report. Provide for different learning styles and include visual, auditory, and kinesthetic/tactile approaches. End a unit with individual project choices. But be sure that activities for each style truly meet your objectives.

Examine your curriculum. Choose programs that provide for different learning styles. Analyze teacher's guides to textbooks. Activities that would intrigue learners who don't fit the usual verbal, logical school mold are often hidden in the enrichment section.

TEACHING THE WHOLE CHILD

Expecting children to continually learn in ways that go against their natural inclinations can have serious consequences. This is especially true for at-risk students, who have little energy to deal with school at all. Some children, caught in a frustrating learning-style mismatch, escape through rebellion or illness; some through apathy or conformity. But such escape routes deny children access to their own potential. Understanding learning-style differences can open the way to teaching the whole child—mind and heart, body and spirit.

The Need for . . . Suspense!

Dave Gibson

Did you know that in this article is a description of the missing ingredient in most teaching? That element which transforms eye-closing lectures into eye-popping experiences is . . . well, read for yourself!

The same tragic story replays thousands of times in Sunday-morning America. A teacher pours his heart into a quality Bible lesson. It has sound Bible content, ample illustration, relevant applications. He then teaches that lesson with sincerity, while the minds of students wander aimlessly through football games and dress rehearsals, business proposals and turkey dinners. Most of the biblical truth never reaches the back door on Sunday, let alone the market place or the playground on Monday.

WHAT'S MISSING?

Why do sincere and mature believers pay little or no attention to ideas which they claim to cherish? Why so much window-staring and daydreaming? Why all that energy invested with so little return? The answer is simply the "missing link" in modern teaching and preaching.

Perhaps the answer can best be illustrated with this story. When I lived in a remote area of Alaska we would have scores of all the day's sports activities on the 6:00 P.M. news. Then, at 11:00, the station would broadcast a tape-delayed game for which I already knew the score. I usually ignored those games because I already knew how it turned out. There was no suspense involved.

The missing link in most teaching is intrigue, suspense, or tension. Suspense, the teacher's hook, traps the mind. It blocks the escape routes to the playgrounds. But suspense is not "innate" to a lesson or sermon as it is to a game or contest.

Most preachers and teachers give us no reason to stay with them. They pose no problem, create no tension, stir no suspense. They simply tell us what they are going to tell us and what we should do, then close with what they told us. The average mind is too lazy to concentrate on these faded presentations. As soon as we know what they are telling us we dismiss ourselves mentally and travel to more intriguing places. Minds must be hooked—forced to stay by the sheer curiosity of how tension will be resolved.

If a teacher or preacher will learn the nature of suspense, its benefits and how to do it, he can captivate his listeners. Fans never leave before the end of a "barn burner" in sports. The following discussion is a guide to instill that same element of suspense in messages or lessons.

SUSPENSE IN COMMUNICATION

Suspense is central to quality communication—the kind that changes people. Haddon Robinson maintains that "the preaching introduction must turn voluntary attention into involuntary attention." At the beginning of the lesson or sermon listeners give us their attention out of curiosity. But, we only have twenty seconds to two minutes in which to hook their curiosity further.

Nathan's parable to King David is one of the classic uses of suspense in communication (2 Samuel 12:1-14). Nathan confronts David's sin against God, Uriah, and Bathsheba by telling him the story of a rich man stealing a pet lamb from a poor man. King David becomes anxiety personified as he waits for the identity of the heartless culprit. Of course, the culprit turns out to be David, himself. (Nathan was a master communicator in that he not only hooked David's attention with suspense, he also hammered home the lesson with an unexpected and shocking ending.)

Jesus continually used suspense in communication. His conversation with Nicodemus (John 3:1-21) demonstrates the superb use of suspense. Jesus hooked Nicodemus completely. "How can a man be born when he is old? He cannot enter a second time into his mother's womb and be born, can he?" (v. 3). Paul mastered suspense also. On Mars Hill at Athens, Paul said to his listeners, "I'll tell you who the unknown God is!" (Acts 17:16-34).

WHY USE SUSPENSE IN COMMUNICATION?

Captivation. Suspense traps the listeners' attention—forcing them to "stay" in order to see how the tension is resolved.

Concentration. Suspense increases learning because of heightened interest and thus increased involvement and interaction. When we follow to see the final outcome our concentration is tremendously elevated. The more we are hooked the more we concentrate; the more we concentrate the more we learn.

Entertainment. Suspense clearly enhances enjoyment. We are allowed to enjoy learning. Entertainment is not the goal of communication nor is it the primary goal of suspense. But when a student experiences joy in learning, two good things result. First, he or she is more likely to try it again. And second, Bible teachers can compete against the manifold entertainment diversions available in modern America.

Excitement. The thrill of suspense excites learners. It thus motivates the listener to interact, tell the principle to others and act upon the lesson. Haddon Robinson nailed this truth by saying, "The fact that we are happy to be right about something doesn't give us the right to be boring about it" (*Focal Point*, July/September 1989).

Induction. Suspense is the backbone of the inductive method of communication. In the inductive method the communicator explores with the audience the "bits of data" which relate to the problem. In the end, he or she draws a conclusion or principle from the accumulated data. (The introduction and the transitions must be clear in order to show the audience where you are going—to keep them in the flow of thought.) Perhaps the easiest way to understand the inductive method is to think of Perry Mason examining all the pieces of evidence and coming to a final conclusion— which is supported by each piece of the puzzle. In Bible lessons we explore all the particulars for the Scripture text and come to one final principle or truth supported by each particular of the passage. We can bring the learner along in this process through the use of suspense.

HOW DO WE USE SUSPENSE IN COMMUNICATION?

The teacher may choose from several methods to build suspense into a lesson or message. One of the best plans is to begin immediately with a "life related" tension, suspense, or intrigue. (Do not create a "phoney" or "artificial" tension unrelated to the lesson or to life.) In the introduction the teacher simply poses a problem or need which the lesson will answer—eventually. These problems can be "life related," such as loneliness, fear, anxiety, temptation, laziness. (An example of tension might be, "What can we do to overcome loneliness?") Conflict also breeds suspense. We can start with a conflict between people or between ideas or within ourselves. Suspense can also be hatched with a striking statement or quote or with a mysterious happening.

When the suspense has been introduced the teacher proceeds to resolve the tension slowly—in the course of the lesson. We want to give students the answer in small chunks and not fully resolve it until we are ready for them to stop listening. Often the conclusion of the lesson will contain the final resolution and a powerful statement of the biblical principle. (Remember that TV episodes are never resolved until the producer is willing for the audience to leave!)

There are other ways to create tension. One option is to use "chain tension" throughout the lesson. In other words, the teacher raises a problem and then teaches the material needed to solve that problem. But he immediately introduces another tension or problem. Then the student must listen again and again throughout the teaching time. I have used this technique in a message on Christian values in which I introduce each section with a question. (Does God care if we make a lot of money? How does God feel about physical attractiveness? What is God's definition of success?) I answer each question in turn, but immediately introduce another point of suspense.

One of the best ways to create suspense is through the use of a story. Everyone loves a story and the elements of suspense involved. (I once taught a junior high Sunday school class which was transformed each time I would read Christian fiction.) As a teacher you can draw from a wealth of powerful Christian fiction or just write your own short story which deals directly with the students' needs.

Finally, humor is actually a useful form of suspense. Something is funny because it positions two things or people or ideas side by side which we do not commonly think of together. The suspense in waiting for the "punch line" is really the curiosity about what two incompatible items will be set together. Humor will only be successful if it is tasteful, really funny, and makes a point.

CONCLUSION

Suspense must be one of the most ignored, most useful and most powerful elements of Bible teaching. The constant and varied use of suspense is invaluable. It can be a revolutionary tool, a surprise weapon, in effective communication. Build it into your next lesson or message. Don't make a big fuss over the method—don't even tell the class what you are doing. Just create a sense of suspense related to one of their heart-felt needs. Then give them the Bible's answer—slowly. Don't fully resolve the tension until you are willing for them to run off to the mental playgrounds.

Adapted from *Christian Education Today* 42, no. 4 (Winter 1990), pp. 24-27. Used by permission.

Are You An Effective Listener?

Carol Reinberger

If you missed the "Techniques of Listening" course in college (it probably wasn't even offered!), here's a little checklist on listening skills to determine whether you are a listener or a "hearer only."

Listening means more than hearing the words. Being an effective listener takes lots of special skills and qualities. See for yourself. Complete the following self-evaluation and determine whether you're listening effectively. Circle the appropriate response:

1. Do you give young people your undivided attention when they're talking to you?
   Yes   No   Sometimes

2. While listening, do you maintain good eye contact?
   Yes   No   Sometimes

3. Do you make sure you have enough time to listen when young people approach you with a problem?
   Yes   No   Sometimes

4. Do you clear your mind of all distractions so you can be fully present to each person?
   Yes   No   Sometimes

5. As you listen, do you empathize with young people and try to understand what they mean?
   Yes   No   Sometimes

6. Do you let young people finish what they're saying before you give input?
   Yes   No   Sometimes

7. As a listener, do you convey acceptance of young people regardless of their manner of speaking or choice of words—even if you don't agree with them?
   Yes   No   Sometimes

8. Do you resist the temptation to stop listening when you can anticipate what they're about to say?
   Yes   No   Sometimes

9. As a listener, do you remain non-judgmental?
   Yes   No   Sometimes

10. Do you make sure young people know you're listening by smiling, nodding your head, or giving other acknowledgments?
    Yes   No   Sometimes

11. When appropriate, do you give feedback or reflect what they're feeling so they know you understand?
    Yes   No   Sometimes

12. Do you remain separate from the problem, trusting young people are their own best problem-solvers?
    Yes   No   Sometimes

13. Do you genuinely want to help young people?

Yes   No   Sometimes

14. As you listen, do you suspend your own thoughts and feelings in order to "be there" for young people?

Yes   No   Sometimes

HOW DO YOU RATE AS AN EFFECTIVE LISTENER?

12-14 yeses—Good work! Teach others to do the same.

7-11 yeses—Hang in there. And keep practicing.

0-6 yeses—Take a class on listening soon. (Maybe from someone who got 12-14 yeses!)

CHARACTERISTICS OF A GOOD LISTENER

Empathy. This happens when listeners feel what the other person is feeling. Empathy means vicariously experiencing what the other person is going through.

Acceptance. Exhibiting this trait lets young people be exactly who they are at the moment. Acceptance doesn't demand people to be different.

Genuineness. With this characteristic the listener is required to reveal his or her own internal experience. In other words, effective listening involves transparency, honesty, and the willingness to reveal oneself.

HELPING SKILLS NEEDED FOR EFFECTIVE LISTENING

Physical posture. To really "be there" for someone the listener must be in physical attendance to the other person, make level eye contact, and maintain an open body posture while listening.

Silence. Remaining silent puts pressure on the other person to say more. Silence omits the need for the listener to probe or question. Use this passive listening technique when you sense it's appropriate; it can be powerful especially if the person is experiencing sadness.

Brief acknowledgments. Non-evaluative responses let young people know you've heard what they've said. For example, "Oh," "Really," and "I see" let young people know you're with them. Keep the door open for additional communication by adding little phrases like, "I'd like to hear what you think about that," "Would you like to talk about it?" or "Could you say more about that?" All these statements offer an open-ended invitation for them to say more if they want to.

Active "caring" listening. Listen actively by feeding back the person's message in your own words. For example: Tina enters your office in tears and cries, "I just broke up with my boyfriend and I don't know what to do!" By combining clues from words, tone of voice and body language, caring listeners reflect back what they heard. "Tina, it sounds like you're really upset," or, "I get the feeling that you're angry with your boyfriend."

Prayer. Pray for guidance before starting to listen. And after the sharing time, pray again. It's important for your young people to know you pray for them and care enough to listen to their hearts' innermost feelings.

The Art of Listening

H. Norman Wright

When this author suggests listening is an art, he implies that it becomes a thing of grace and beauty. If you've never thought of the listening half of communication that way, then this article will open a new vista for you.

Would you like to improve your listening skills? Let me share a few general hints on how to polish them.

1. Listen in an active manner. Be alive when you listen: no one wants to talk to a corpse. Pay attention to the other person's language. Notice how he talks. If he asks questions or gives feedback in an abbreviated form, do the same. If he gives detail and elaborates with descriptive words, do the same.

When you actively listen, you do three things: paraphrase, clarify, and give feedback. Paraphrasing means stating in your own words what you believe the other person said. This helps you understand what he means. It also lets him correct you if you are mistaken. Clarifying often accompanies paraphrasing. It is very simple: you just ask questions until you fully understand what the other person means. Feedback is sharing your own thoughts and feelings in a nonjudgmental way.

2. Listen with empathy. This means both caring and seeing the situation from the other person's perspective. You may not like or agree with what is being said, but as you listen, you realize that if you were experiencing what he is experiencing, if you were standing where he is standing, you would probably feel the same way. Romans 12:15 tells us to weep with those who weep and rejoice with those who rejoice. That is what empathy is all about.

3. Listen with openness. Selective listening, defensive listening, and filtered listening are not open listening. Listening with openness means discovering how the other person's point of view makes sense to you. How do you do this? Someone has suggested that you listen as though you were an anthropologist and the other person were from another planet. His customs, beliefs, and way of thinking are different from yours, and you are trying to understand them.

4. Listen with awareness. Be aware of what the other person says and how it compares with the facts. Be aware of whether or not the message of the other person is consistent. If you have listened actively, empathetically, and openly and still don't understand the other person's point of view, you don't have to attack. One of the best ways to respond is by asking a question so you can gather more information from which to evaluate what was said. "Could you tell me a bit more?" or "Could you give me a specific example?"

Or you might say, "Thank you for letting me know your perspective. I'll think about it." Or, "That's interesting. I hadn't considered it in that light." Or, "What you're saying may have some truth to it. Tell me more."

The art of listening is a skill *you* can develop with practice!

■ From H. Norman Wright, "The Art of Listening," in Howard and Jeanne Hendricks, eds., *Husbands and Wives* (Wheaton: Victor Books, 1988). Used by permission.

Getting Close to Kids

Mary Eason

*Thinking back about your own teachers, did you have one who seemed
really to be friends with the students? Really liked to be around them?
He or she had probably internalized the principles given here.*

Are we friends to the children in our classes? Proverbs 18:24 says, "A man that hath friends must show himself friendly."
The following questions may help you discover how close you are to boys and girls in your sphere of influence.

1. Do I plan time in my class or club to get to know the children as individuals?
2. Do I ask about their interests and remember what they have shared about themselves?
3. Do children stay behind after class time seemingly just to be near me?
4. Do I occasionally hug a child who is talking to me, or touch an arm affectionately?
5. Do I cut a child off in midsentence when an adult approaches me?
6. Am I verbally supportive of each child or do I regularly leave some out?
7. Do I use the pre-session only to teach while they listen, or do I sometimes gather the children around me for a conversation time, and listen attentively?

LOOKING FOR CLUES

How do children show that they want you to get close to them? Younger children will pull on your arm or snuggle into your side. Older ones may come to you after class, offering to carry your materials to the car. They may even mess up those materials to get your full attention! They'll tell loudly, with sound effects, about the horror film on TV last night, or how they beat up someone in the school yard who "started it." They'll stand around posing until you comment on a great new cowboy buckle, a terrific new dress, or pair of boots. Or, like Susan, some will come regularly when class is over and stand nearby, fiddling with objects in the missions display, not even really looking at you.

Children show us in many ways that they want closeness. Some ways they choose are extreme and unsettling, but let's not make the mistake of thinking these actions only mean they are spoiled, neglected, or mischievous. They need closeness with their teacher and this need can be met.

Children need to know you know who they are. Tags with names in bold, black print pinned to collars act as cue-cards so that names may be used often, even if only to say, "John, I'm glad you're here today!"

Children need to know they can do good things. They know this when you choose them to hold song cards or pass out fliers and you act pleased to have such a reliable person for the job.

Children need to know they are valuable. A child feels valuable when you give an out-of-your-way hug and remind him that God made him a very special person. Try this on your worst child, and see what happens.

There are times when children overstep boundaries and need immediate, firm discipline. Occasionally, however, a teacher will be so frustrated with a mischievous child that temper comes into play, even sarcasm. One morning I "lost the battle" before my entire group of juniors. I accused Danny of kindergarten behavior, trying to shame him before his friends. There was dead silence. I was shocked at myself. I went on with the program, but could sense the Lord guiding.

"Let's stop for a minute," I said. "Danny, I need to publicly apologize to you. I embarrassed you in front of your friends, when I could have walked back to your chair and spoken to you in a low voice or a whisper."

Everyone turned to stare at Danny. With a shy smile on his face, he said, "Hey, no sweat, Mrs. Eason!"

We've been super close ever since that day and Danny has done his utmost to be everything a Christian should be. I was amazed at the attitude of warmth and affection that came from the other children. It was one of the really great mornings in children's church.

In the private world of children's morals, being unfair is the worst of crimes. Being fair can bring a lovely quality of closeness that couldn't come any other way.

Children also need time to talk to you when you have planned absolutely nothing else but to listen.

PLANNED CONVERSATION

A planned conversation period for your group will bring surprising results. You could choose fifteen minutes before or after class. Invitations could be mailed to all, describing the talk-time. You might select one or two conversation starters from this list to get things going:

1. What do you like to do . . . with your family, with a group of friends, with your best friend, alone in your room, up in a tree, at the beach, or in the kitchen after school?

2. What do you do when you are afraid . . . because of a nightmare, when someone tells on you, when you have a fight, when you forget your homework, have a bad report card, when you go to the doctor, or when someone yells at you?

3. What do you do when there's nothing to do . . . at home, at school, when you're camping with the family, cooped up in the car on a long trip, at Grandma's house or at the babysitter's?

4. Who would you be if you could be anyone? What would you do? Where would you go?

We are challenged as week by week we watch some of our children react to our program with blank stares, shuffling feet, giggling in pairs, and loud yawns. Many of us have for years been attacking this problem by making the program more interesting and using effective forms of discipline. But we also see that something more is needed. Cultivating children's love and convincing them of our love, not only nourishes their hearts (and ours) but brings about better behavior and better learning.

ONE-ON-ONE COMMUNICATION

Love is not something to keep hidden. Plan to work on it during the week and keep it strong and expressive. Look for opportunities to talk with children individually. Prayerfully vow to keep these visits a friendship time, not a lesson time. Keep the communication warmly comfortable; reserve lengthy advice for another time.

These few tips might help you talk with a child:

• Sit with him as informally as the circumstances permit.

- Ask him what he thinks about his own questions before you answer.
- Keep your answers brief, compassionate, and nonjudgemental.
- Express sadness and sympathy when a child tells of his wrongdoing.
- Be as respectful of a child's opinions and problems as you would be of an adult's.
- Listen attentively, even if you aren't as interested as he is in *Star Trek*, snakes, or baseball scores.
- Assist the child in further explaining his feelings by using monosyllabic "nudging"—"Hmmm!" "Oh?" "Oh!" "Aah!" "Yes?" and a few conversation movers like: "Then what happened?" or "How did you feel about that?" or "You feel that was unfair, don't you?"
- Continue to verbally assure him of your love.
- Keep confidences. Resist the urge to chat with the child's parents or your friends about some of his cute sayings. Children know real friends aren't tattle-tales.

Part of our calling from the Lord as children's workers is to love them. We do love them; that's why we teach a Good News Club or Sunday school class. We rejoice as children demonstrate their growing love for Christ. We pray regularly for them and for their families and are sad when we observe any of them behaving poorly. But do we act out this love?

A song reminds us, "Love isn't love until you give it away." Plans to give love must be made and carried out with imagination. Feed and water the love growing between yourself and the children. In that closeness, you can be most effective in ministering Christ to them.

From *Evangelizing Today's Child* (January-February 1983), p. 6ff. Used by permission.

Keeping Kids in School

Learning Magazine

In the midst of a small, economically depressed community, one teacher caught a vision for helping students create, and reach, higher goals for their future. She made an impact—and so can you. Catch <u>her</u> vision!

All teachers want their students to graduate and go on in school. But what happens when that dream clashes with reality? In Diana Stender's community of one thousand, reality is unemployment and woeful educational funding. But instead of giving up, Diana summoned all her creativity and resourcefulness and took aim at two major stumbling blocks to her students' success; a high dropout rate and a lack of career awareness.

Diana had known about her county's dropout problem, but she didn't fully realize her students' dearth of career information until she surveyed them. Only 50 percent could identify a specific career they wanted to pursue, and 22 percent had no plans for further education after high school. Even more troubling, 12 percent said they didn't plan to finish high school. So Diana embarked on a yearlong career study project to help them figure out their futures. "Forget about getting these kinds into Harvard. We just want them to graduate," she says.

The students took an interest survey and discussed the results with the school guidance counselor. Then they talked with the high school counselor about possible courses to take and about the kinds of jobs that would be available upon graduation. Diana also invited guest speakers to class and arranged for her students to work for a day at local businesses—like the bank, post office, pharmacy, supermarket, upholstery shop, bus garage, and so on. Afterward, the students gave oral presentations to classmates about what they'd learned. They also kept a journal of their activities, tracking their budding career goals throughout the year.

To determine the project's impact, Diana asked her students the same survey questions they'd answered earlier. The result? Nearly 90 percent identified a specific career they wished to pursue and 100 percent said they planned to finish high school and seek additional education. Diana's students presented their career study project at the state social studies fair, where it earned first place.

Despite her success, Diana hasn't given up fighting. Now, she's working to open the county vocational school to at-risk middle school students. Currently only high school kids may attend. "We have students who are almost sixteen, just waiting for their birthday so they can quit," she laments. But with Diana in their corner, they're sure to come out winners. Says she, "Every child's different, and we just have to find the road that's going to lead each one to success."

Helping the Depressed Child

Brenda Poinsett

It is so difficult for teachers to know precisely the cause of under-achievement in every student. This article presents a mini-course in learning to watch for one cause: childhood depression.

D epression is not easy to recognize in children. Adults will acknowledge, "I'm depressed," but a six-year-old will rarely say, "I'm feeling down in the dumps" or, "The future looks pretty hopeless." A child does not recognize such feelings. He may realize he feels bad but not have any idea why.

Certain symptoms should alert teachers to the presence of depression: feelings of sadness or hopelessness, lack of enthusiasm for anything, inability to play or have fun, complaints about feeling tired or bored, irritability, constant whining about physical ailments that can't be verified, constant fidgeting, references to death, and inability to concentrate. A depressed youngster frequently cannot focus sufficient interest and attention on his work or anything else worthwhile. Two other symptoms which may be more obvious to parents than to teachers are appetite changes and sleeping problems.

Often depressed children are quiet and passive; teachers may overlook them because they seem so well-behaved. However, about forty percent of depressed children exhibit aggressive behavior. They may mistreat younger siblings, have temper tantrums, lie, get into trouble, and generally misbehave. The aggressive behavior may be a defense against experiencing the painful feelings associated with depression. The Sunday school teacher can be God's light to the depressed child. Here's how:

1. Learn the causes. Stress sets off depression in children who have experienced rejection, depreciation, or personal loss. The stress of moving brings with it several losses—loss of familiarity, loss of friends, and loss of security.

Sometimes the loss is not so obvious. The loss could be a string of "failures" on the playground, demeaning comments by teachers, parents or peers, chronic depreciation by a parent, continually being overlooked, or family tensions that seem to be destroying his precious connections.

2. Get the child to communicate. Searching for apparent losses and identifying them with the child can help prevent and relieve depression. One Sunday school teacher recommends small group times for this. The prayer requests of the children, their writings, and art work may reveal what is bothering them. The child may talk or write spontaneously, or he may respond to questions and reveal that he feels hopeless, worthless, unattractive, unloved, and that suicidal ideas keep running through his mind.

In a non-threatening, supportive way, the teacher should seize opportunities to spend time with the child, to listen and to acknowledge the child's feelings. When youngsters are "down," it is important to accept the validity of their moods. Urging a disheartened person of any age to "cheer up, you'll get over it" usually only increases his depression.

3. Visit the child's home. Efforts to get the child to communicate individually or in small groups may still not tell the teacher why the child is depressed. A home visit might help. Has there been a divorce in the family? Job loss? A death? Is one of the parents depressed or had a problem with depression in the past?

4. Provide an atmosphere of love. When parents fail to express love, depressed children try to find some other adult (like a Sunday school teacher) who can fill the gap. To a child, love is like sunshine and water to a plant.

To provide this love, the teacher needs to be emotionally available. Regardless of how major or trivial a loss may seem, it is essential that the teacher be available to assist the child in sharing whatever he experiences. Using frequent eye contact and a gentle touch effectively communicates to the child that he is accepted and loved.

5. Enhance the child's self-esteem. During depression, self-esteem sinks to an all-time low. The Sunday school teacher needs to withhold criticisms that might create feelings of inadequacy or inferiority. Instead, she needs to provide the depressed child with opportunities to affirm his self-worth.

Betty was sensitive to this in working with Richard, a quiet, overlooked child who was depressed. She did not use Bible drills requiring speed and quick reflexes to answer since this made Richard feel insecure. Betty assigned him small responsibilities with a younger age group where he could learn to serve without the threat of peer pressure.

6. Use stories. Once Sunday school teachers understand the causes of depression and how it affects children, they can use stories of how others handled depression. The Bible has several good examples, e.g., Moses, Job, Elijah, and Jonah. In each case, God provided a solution for the depression.

7. Work with the parents. If the depression lingers, if it intensifies, or if the child indicates suicidal thoughts, the parents should be contacted. Any one of these three indicates severe depression and professional help may be needed.

At this point, the teacher may want to consult with the pastor and together they can approach the parents. Whether alone or together, contacting the parents should never be put off. In one newspaper account an eleven-year-old boy who committed suicide had bragged to his classmates how he was going to smother himself with a plastic bag. The night he died his teacher was grading a composition in which he revealed his plans to smother himself. Noting the unusual content, the teacher called the principal. They decided that tomorrow they would contact the boy's parents. Tomorrow was too late.

While a very small percentage of depressed children commit suicide, this incident is a reminder that depression can have serious consequences. Professional help may be needed to avoid drastic ends. The earlier the diagnosis, the better the chances for effective treatment.

Six to ten percent of this nation's children are depressed. By knowing the causes of depression, by getting the child to communicate, by visiting in the home, by providing an atmosphere of love, by enhancing self-esteem, by using stories that show solutions, and by working with parents, teachers can play a valuable role in helping depressed children. They can be God's light to children in darkness.

■ From *Christian Education Today* (Spring 1989), pp. 16-18. Used by permission.

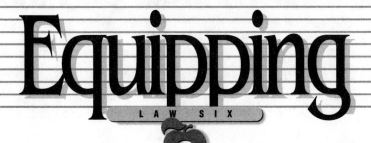

Equipping

LAW SIX

TOPICAL SURVEY

Dr. James Dobson's Mentors

Rolf Zettersten

Most people wonder how leaders arrive at their positions of influence. It is rarely done "on their own." Rather, other leaders have directed their path. Here's a look behind the scenes at one such process.

While James Dobson's parents instilled in him a sense of moral character and heart for God, four men he met in college were particularly significant forces in shaping his professional life. Their influence helped Jim integrate his Christian principles with his education and ultimately directed him into his career.

AN UNRELENTING ENGLISH PROFESSOR

During his freshman year in college, James Dobson studied under two of the four mentors who would so dramatically affect his future. The first was Dr. Eddie Harwood, professor of English who taught creative writing for the more talented students. Jim had not intended to take the notoriously tough class, but he was assigned to it because he had scored high marks on an entrance exam. When he learned of Dr. Harwood's reputation as a tough disciplinarian, Jim approached him and asked for a transfer. "I don't think I am capable of doing the work in your class," he told Dr. Harwood.

The professor had heard every excuse through the years, and he wasn't going to buy this one. "I will not approve your transfer," he told the freshman. "You'll see that you *will* be able to do the work, and I will want you in my class."

Indeed, the freshman composition course turned out to be the most profitable academic experience of Jim's undergraduate training. It is true that he worked much harder than he had intended, and there were times when he thought he would not survive. Dr. Harwood was as tough as nails and twice as sharp.

"I can't teach you how to write," he told the class. "But I can sure teach you how *not* to write. You try it, and I'll tell you what you've done wrong."

The professor gave the students assignments designed to draw out corny colloquialisms and syrupy sentimentality. He then massacred their compositions, spreading red ink everywhere, and topping them off prominently with D's and F's. It was a grueling experience, but slowly the principles of sentence structure and good writing began to come alive. The students were learning how to write, but more importantly, they were learning how to *think*.

Not only did Jim survive that experience, but he thrived on it. He earned an A that semester and proceeded to take three more classes from Dr. Harwood. The last one was entitled "Advanced Exposition" and was designed specifically for Dobson and three other talented students. Today, he credits Dr. Harwood not only with teaching him how to use the English language, but with transforming him from a high school pupil to a college student in that one freshman class.

A MAJOR PROFESSOR AND MENTOR

The writing skills Dobson learned in his college composition classes applied to his other academic courses as well. They were particularly helpful in his psychology classes, where he encountered another intellectual "giant," Dr. Paul Culbertson, who became his major professor and mentor for years to come. Dr. Culbertson recalls a seventy-page report Dobson wrote comparing various theories of neuroses. "When I read that paper I knew this young man had a future in psychology," he said.

During his first year in college, Dobson was relatively certain he wanted to be a psychologist. Culbertson's teaching had opened his mind to the fascinating studies of human behavior. By his third year in college, he was on track headed toward a Ph.D. and a career in the field of mental health. From that moment on, he never wavered his course. Jim was something of a guided missile. Once he knew his target, he was totally committed to the pursuit of it.

A PIONEERING PSYCHOLOGIST

His plans at this point in life also called for getting married, having children, and buying a home. But then he had an encounter with a third influential educator whose advice helped him zero in on the goal he had established for himself. His aunt, Lela London, had heard a Christian psychologist named Clyde Narramore speak one day, and he offered to spend an afternoon with any promising student who wanted to enter the field of mental health.

"We need Christians in this work," he said, "and I'll help those who are interested." Dr. Narramore was a pioneer in Christian psychology. Prior to his time, behavioral studies had been widely regarded by evangelicals as a field for practicing atheists. From his aunt, Jim learned of the open invitation and decided to take advantage of it.

"I called Dr. Narramore a few days later, and he graciously agreed to see me," Dobson recalls. "This busy man gave me two hours of time in the living room of his home. Thirty years later I still remember his words. Among other things, he warned me not to get married too quickly if I wanted to earn a doctorate and become a practicing psychologist.

"He said, 'A baby will come along before you know it, and you will find yourself under financial pressure. That will make you want to quit. You'll sit up at nights caring for a sick child and then spend maybe $300 in routine medical bills. Your wife will be frustrated, and you will be tempted to abandon your dreams.'"

As a result of that counsel, Dobson postponed marriage until he was twenty-four years old, and he and Shirley waited years beyond that to have their first child. While it is typical today for couples to start families at a later stage in life, in the 1960s it was highly unusual. This late start explains why Dobson was, in his words, "the oldest living father of a teenager."

Jim's decision to follow Dr. Narramore's advice caused some external stress, but it was that singleness of purpose that made such an impression on Dr. Narramore. One day in 1988 he visited Focus on the Family to see his protegé, and he told me, "I can vividly recall the day that Jim came to see me. He made such an impression on me that I can even remember what he was wearing that day! He was different from many other students seeking my career counsel because he was so sincere. I knew he'd go far."

AN ANGEL-LIKE ADVISOR AND FRIEND

Earlier in his college career, Jim had intended to pursue his graduate studies at the University of Texas. This was a natural choice since he had grown up in that state and it would bring him closer to his parents and family.

But one afternoon he had a conversation with Dr. Ken Hopkins, the fourth mentor who left his mark on Jim Dobson. Dr. Hopkins had graduated from Pasadena

College three years earlier and had just earned his Ph.D. from the University of Southern California. Jim had called him about a research project, and near the end of their conversation, Hopkins asked Jim about his plans for graduate studies.

"Why don't you consider USC?" Hopkins asked. "Come on down here and let me show you around."

Jim accepted his offer and eventually decided to enroll at the university, which was located near downtown Los Angeles. The decision was life changing because a move to Texas would have taken him away from Shirley at a crucial time in their relationship.

On the night of enrollment at USC, Jim wasn't sure he had made the right decision. He was apprehensive about being on the huge campus. He felt lost among the twenty thousand students registering for classes, and he wondered if his faith would be respected in that university. Suddenly a familiar face appeared. In that mass of humanity, Dr. Hopkins found him and put his arm around his shoulder. He invited Jim up to his office and told him he believed in him and then offered to serve as his major professor.

"He was like an angel the Lord put in my path at a precise moment," Dr. Dobson recalls. "He understood and shared my faith, and he guided me through the next five years. He was my advisor on research. He told me which classes to take and which to avoid. I will always be grateful to God for placing Dr. Ken Hopkins there at such an important time in my life."

With this guidance, Jim was able to graduate with precisely the number of units needed for his degree. On April 3, 1967, he received a Ph.D. in Child Development and a minor in Research Design. In five years of graduate study, he had earned straight A's, with the exception of three B's, giving him a graduate GPA of 3.91. The guided missile had found its target.

Many years have passed since those early days of training and career development, but Dobson has not forgotten the roles those four men played in shaping him. Their influence was incalculable; without it, he would be a much different person today.

Reflecting today on Dobson's relationships with these four compassionate professionals, one theme emerges—the value of older, more established men and women who are willing to give their time and energy to impressionable members of the younger generation. Dr. Narramore devoted only two short hours to a promising student one afternoon, and yet that investment reverberates down to this day. Focusing our energies on a leader of tomorrow might be the most important thing we'll do in a lifetime. Doctors Eddie Harwood, Paul Culbertson, Clyde Narramore, and Ken Hopkins are to be commended. They were there when it counted.

■ Taken from Rolf Zettersten, *Dr. Dobson: Turning Hearts Toward Home* (Dallas: Word Books, 1989). Used by permission.

What Is a Spiritual Gift?

Charles C. Ryrie

A master at "mastering the minimum," this renowned Bible scholar and teacher gives us the short course in spiritual gifts. Read and digest this article before moving on to deeper levels of understanding.

THE DEFINITION OF SPIRITUAL GIFTS
The word for spiritual gifts (*charisma*), obviously related to the word for grace, means something that is due to the grace of God. The use of the word in the New Testament ranges from the gift of salvation (Romans 6:23), to the gift of God's providential care (2 Corinthians 1:11), to the most frequent use in relation to gifts of grace to the believer. When used in this latter relationship I suggest that a spiritual gift is a God-given ability for service.

In this proposed definition the synonym for gift is ability. A spiritual gift is an ability. "God-given" reminds us that Christ and the Spirit are the givers of gifts, and "for service" seeks to capture the emphasis in the central passages that gifts are to be used in serving the body of Christ. Though there exists a close analogy between spiritual gifts and talents (certainly both are God-given, 1 Corinthians 4:7), talents may or may not be used for serving the body. Let's notice some further contrasts between spiritual gifts and natural talents.

NATURAL TALENTS	SPIRITUAL TALENTS
•Given by God through parents	•Given by God independent of parents
•Given at birth	•Evidently given at conversion
•To benefit mankind generally	•To benefit the body particularly

Thus a spiritual gift is a God-given ability to serve the body of Christ wherever and however He may direct.

THE DISTRIBUTION OF SPIRITUAL GIFTS
They are distributed by the risen, ascended Christ (Ephesians 4:11). The fact that the Head of the body gives gifts to His body raises the use of gifts to a high and holy level. These are His gifts, entrusted to us because He needs us to use them in order to build up His body. What dignity this gives even to what may seem to be the lowliest kind of service.

They are distributed by the Holy Spirit at will (1 Corinthians 12:11, 18). Why does He give a believer a specific gift? Because He knows best what is needed by the body and what best fits each believer for service. If we would believe that it would keep us from complaining that we are not like someone else, and it ought to motivate us to use to the fullest what God has given us.

When does the Spirit give us our gifts? Most likely at conversion. If these are gifts of the Spirit, and if we do not possess the Spirit until conversion, then it seems that His gifts would be given at that time. We may not discover all the gifts given at salvation, but I am inclined to believe that we have them all at that time.

They are distributed to all believers. No believer is without at least one spiritual gift. Peter makes it clear that all have at least one (1 Peter 4:10). Every believer is either single or married, and both states are said to be spiritual gifts (1 Corinthians 7:7). Possibly many believers also have the gift of helps or serving.

But no believer has all the gifts. If so, then the metaphor in 1 Corinthians 12:12-27 would be meaningless. If any believer possessed all the gifts then he or she would have no need for other believers. He would be the hand and foot and eye and ear—the whole body, which is impossible. Believers need other believers simply because no believer possesses all the gifts.

They are distributed to the body of Christ as a whole. By this I mean to emphasize that not every congregation need expect that it will have all the gifts represented in it. The state of growth and maturity may not require this. God knows what each group needs and will see that it is supplied accordingly.

Additionally, I mean that not every generation may necessarily expect to have all the gifts. A gift given once is a gift given to the whole body of Christ. God gave the foundation gifts of apostles and prophets at the beginning (Ephesians 2:20). After the foundation was laid by those who used those gifts, other gifts were needed. But in the twentieth century we are still benefiting from and building on those foundational gifts. They were given in the first century to the whole body in all centuries. No generation has been slighted. The Spirit endows the church as He wills, and He knows exactly what each believer, each congregation, and each generation needs. [One of the most balanced and concise treatments of this entire doctrine is William J. McRae, *The Dynamics of Spiritual Gifts* (Grand Rapids: Zondervan, 1976).]

THE DISCOVERY AND DEVELOPMENT OF SPIRITUAL GIFTS

The "peril of the pendulum" operates in relation to spiritual gifts. On the one swing of the pendulum is the idea that spiritual gifts are essentially irrelevant to Christian service today because the gifts were given to the early church only and the important matter today is maturity, not gifts. On the opposite swing is the emphasis that you cannot even begin to serve unless you are sure of your spiritual gift(s). If spiritual gifts were given to the early church only or are irrelevant to service today, then why do they appear in New Testament books written to the second generation of believers and to those who lived throughout the Roman Empire? (Ephesians and 1 Peter.) Furthermore, since gifts are necessary for the proper functioning of the body of Christ, how could they not be given today and yet maintain that proper functioning?

On the other hand, if a believer must know his or her spiritual gift(s) before serving, then why are there no commands to discover one's spiritual gifts? We are all commanded to use our gift (1 Peter 4:10—"employ it"). No text says we must know what gift we have before we can be expected to serve. Yet I have risked using the word *discovery* in this heading in order to encourage the reader to use his or her gifts.

1. Inform yourself about the total package of gifts in your life. There exist three categories of gifts in every Christian's life.

- *Natural abilities.* God-given at birth, they include things like I.Q., a measure of health and strength, musical talents, linguistic abilities, mechanical aptitudes, etc.
- *Acquired abilities.* These include things like cooking, sewing, driving a car, learning a language, learning to play an instrument, etc. While we may tend to take such skills for granted, remember that many people in the world have few opportunities to acquire skills in these areas.

• *Spiritual gifts.* A believer should inform himself or herself of the total package of these various abilities which God has placed in his life. In other words, he should take inventory to know what stock he has available for the Lord's use. Just going through the process of taking inventory periodically may help the believer ascertain what areas of service he ought to explore.

2. Prepare yourself by taking every opportunity available. This principle applies to all three categories of abilities. Sharpen talents, acquire skills, and work on the development of spiritual gifts. If one thinks he may have the gift of teaching, then it will be necessary to study. The ability to communicate may be more directly given (though even that skill can be sharpened by education), but certainly the content must be learned.

If one suspects he has the gift of giving, then he will work on being a good steward in all areas of life (1 Corinthians 4:2). The ability to be generous requires discipline in financial affairs.

The gift of evangelism in the early church not only involved the preaching of the Good News but also itinerating with the message. To be able to do this may involve paying special attention to one's health in order to have the stamina to travel in spreading the gospel.

If one has the gift of exhortation, it certainly should be based on biblical knowledge. The only valid and worthwhile exhortation must be rooted in biblical truths. And, of course, to have biblical knowledge requires study.

3. Be active in the Lord's work. Gifts are both discovered and developed by activity. Practice brings perception of one's total package of abilities, and practice develops those abilities. If you are seeking to discover your gifts(s), then do not turn down opportunities to serve, even if you think they do not fall within the range of your abilities. God may be trying to tell you that you have abilities you do not recognize.

If you are active in doing what you can, then other opportunities may arise which will bring to light additional spiritual gifts. For example, when we first meet Philip in the Book of Acts we see him helping distribute the relief money to needy (and bickering) widows (6:5). It is doubtful that before he undertook this ministry he sat down to decide whether or not he had that spiritual gift! Here was an opportunity to serve and he took it. He proved faithful in performing this menial task. The Lord then entrusted him with another ministry, that of evangelizing the Samaritans (8:5), and later, the Ethiopian eunuch. As he used that gift he became known as Philip the evangelist (21:8). But first he was Philip the helper of widows.

The same principle was true in Stephen's life. He first served along with Philip in ministering to the widows. But he also was full of faith (6:5), and was a great witness (7:1-53). Faithfulness in one opportunity leads to other opportunities.

■ From Charles C. Ryrie, *Basic Theology* (Wheaton: Victor Books, 1986), pp. 367-372. Used by permission.

Unwrapping Spiritual Gifts

Kenneth O. Gangel and Stanley D. Toussaint

If we are going to equip our students for service, it makes both common and biblical sense to equip them in areas of their strengths and giftedness. This presumes an understanding of spiritual gifts by teachers!

The following discussion on the nature and use of spiritual gifts originated as a radio interview of Dr. Kenneth Gangel, noted author, educator, and student of Scripture. He was interviewed by Dr. Stanley Toussaint, professor of Bible Exposition at Dallas Theological Seminary.

Toussaint: We commonly use the term "charismatic" to describe churches which emphasize spiritual gifts. What's the derivation of the word "charismatic"?

Gangel: It has a very interesting derivation, but it's unfortunate that the term sometimes gets locked in to a particular denomination, group of churches, or a type of Christian. The word *charisma*, or *charismaton* in the New Testament Greek text, basically means "spiritual gift," and appears some seventeen times. As I sort these out, three different elements of usage appear to flow to the surface. Sometimes the word refers to God's gift of salvation. Sometimes it refers to a general gift of grace or love. But the most frequent usage is the one which we talk about commonly today, and that is, "a *charisma* or *charismaton* is a special endowment of spiritual ability to serve the Lord."

Toussaint: If we refer to certain churches or groups of people by the term "charismatic," are you saying we're not using the term properly?

Gangel: I think it has become too narrow. Although charismatic churches are highly interested in spiritual gifts, many churches interested in spiritual gifts are not charismatic in the way that we use the term. But they are charismatic in the New Testament sense.

Toussaint: Do you think that every Christian has a spiritual gift?

Gangel: I happen to believe that's true. In fact, I think that some Christians may have more than one. The key passage on the subject of spiritual gifts is 1 Corinthians 12. In verse 7 you have the wording, "Now to each one the manifestation of the Spirit is given for the common good," and at the end of that same paragraph in verse 11, "All these are the work of one and the same spirit, and He gives them to each man just as He determines." These verses and others indicate that every Christian has at least one gift.

Toussaint: Why did God give spiritual gifts to the church?

Gangel: The purpose certainly is not just to identify any special ability of a person or a small group of people, because the concept of service is very evident. The Greek lexicographer Thayer defines spiritual gifts as "extraordinary powers enabling people to serve the church of Christ." The concept of putting these things into practice for the good and the advancement of the body of Christ is the basic New Testament focus.

Toussaint: How many gifts do you think the Bible identifies?

Gangel: I think that we can identify at least nineteen or twenty gifts. In my book *Unwrap Your Spiritual Gifts* I identify twenty by name. In the reprint I have added to my original list because in my first handling of the text I rejected a couple of words that, after further study, I decided to include. So altogether there are about twenty gifts identified in the New Testament.

Toussaint: The four major passages—Romans 12, 1 Corinthians 12, Ephesians 4, and 1 Peter 4—contain different lists. Is any of these lists complete?

Gangel: I don't think that any one of the lists of gifts is complete in itself. An examination of all the passages and the seventeen uses of *charismaton* in the context of the whole New Testament will provide a complete list. It was not necessary for Paul or Peter to give a comprehensive list. I would also add that many people believe that the list is still open and that new spiritual gifts are being added even today. The only thing I would fight for, so to speak, is that revelatory gifts or anything having to do with new revelation is not possible today. I happen to think that the list of gifts is closed, but I offer that only as my personal opinion.

Toussaint: Do you see any difference between natural, human talents or abilities and spiritual gifts?

Gangel: I think there is a great deal of difference, and it has to do with how one operates in the natural realm. For example, a person who is a total pagan has strong natural abilities. He may be able to do all kinds of exciting things, but that has nothing to do with the spiritual realm because the gift or ability does not have a spiritual source and is not used for a spiritual purpose. Spiritual gifts cover both of those; that is, they come not just from training or skills, but from the power of the Holy Spirit in the life of the believer. They are intended not just to bless people in general as in a stage performance but rather for the edification of the church in a spiritual context.

Toussaint: Let's suppose that a person has a natural ability in the area of administration and then he becomes a Christian. Will his spiritual gift be basically the same as his ability?

Gangel: Not necessarily, because the sovereignty of God comes into play here. If the Spirit of God chooses to do so, He may do that, but I don't think that He is under any biblical obligation to do so, because we are talking about two totally different realms. I don't think there is anything in Scripture that requires that abilities before salvation automatically become gifts after salvation. The question of importance for the church, however, is really crucial. Paul begins the twelfth chapter of 1 Corinthians by saying, "About spiritual gifts, brothers, I don't want you to be ignorant." The more we know about spiritual gifts the more we will be able to find and exercise our own, and the more we will be able to find the kind of unity in the body of which Paul speaks in this important chapter.

Toussaint: How can a Christian determine what his spiritual gift really is?

Gangel: That is the question so often asked not only by students but also by people in the local church. There are several questions we can ask ourselves to arrive at the answer to that all-important issue. First of all, what do I enjoy doing in the service of the Lord? God wants us to be, as the hymn says, happy in the service of the King. Christian service ought not to be a neurotic compulsion to duty, but a real joy in serving the Lord. A second question is, What has God been blessing? Do I see fruit in my teaching? Are people really trusting Christ as a result of my evangelism efforts? It has been my exciting privilege for over two decades to watch college and seminary students discover their spiritual gifts through active involvement in ministry, that is, through discovering their gifts in the process of service for the Lord. There's a third question we can ask and that has to do with how others are encouraging us. Are people saying to me, "Yes, I really think that God has given you this gift or that gift." Now, I think that it's not just a matter of opinion. I think it's a question of exhortation and help because in the final analysis the real question is, How is the Spirit of God witnessing with my spirit? What is the inner witness of the Spirit regarding my spiritual gift?

Toussaint: When are spiritual gifts given?

Gangel: Evangelical scholars are fairly well agreed on this point, and it is at the time of salvation. Because unsaved people do not have spiritual gifts, it is at the time of salvation that spiritual gifts are bestowed. Now, they may not be noticed or discovered for many years. It's very interesting to talk to people who have been believers for ten or fifteen years and who have very recently discovered their spiritual gifts. They are now beginning to get on track for service for the Lord and to zero in on the ministry that God has designed for them.

Toussaint: How can a Christian be satisfied with his own spiritual gift?

Gangel: Once he has identified his gift or cluster of gifts, he begins to enter a recognition of the concept of grace, not only in salvation but also in service, because the whole idea of *charisma* or *charismaton* is built on the idea of grace. God gives this to us in an undeserving way. He gives it out of His grace. He gives it for the purpose of the advancement of his church. When we recognize that, rather than saying, "Oh, I don't want that gift; I wish I could have that one over there," we will say, "Thank you, Lord, for what I have; now help me use, develop, and practice this gift in the body for the glory of God and the advancement of the church of Jesus Christ."

Toussaint: I have seen spiritual gift inventory tests, which you take to help you identify your spiritual gifts. What do you think about these?

Gangel: I think they're helpful, as long as we recognize that they are not authoritative. They're only intended to be a useful device in looking over spiritual gifts and responding to some probing questions regarding what gifts we might have. We used to use one of those forms in our church in Miami quite consistently, but we always used it with the constant reminder that it is not the proof or the final formula, but just a means to help us think through spiritual gifts and to try to identify the ones we might have.

Toussaint: Ken, you've been in teaching for twenty or twenty-five years. Obviously, you feel your spiritual gift is teaching. How did you discover that?

Gangel: It was in conjunction with some of the questions that we've been asking. What do you enjoy doing? What have others indicated as really being profitable to them? What has the Lord blessed? On occasion I have thought about a number of spiritual gifts and tried to see myself fit into those patterns and then backed away simply saying, "That is not what God has for me." Many times various forms of Christian ministry have been suggested. Why don't you do this? Or why don't you do that? And upon reflection, it seems that God has not gifted me to go into those areas. This is one of the values of identifying your spiritual gift. It's of great help in trying to ascertain the kinds of ministries that you can do and the kinds that perhaps you should not do.

■ From the transcript of "Dallas Today," the radio ministry of Dallas Theological Seminary, 3909 Swiss Avenue, Dallas, Texas 75204. All rights reserved. Used by permission.

Disciplemaking:
A Life-on-Life Approach

Roger Fleming

If you've ever wondered what it was like to have been a disciple of Jesus, then read and make this article your own. It reflects the timeless, biblical truths of life-on-life learning, where truth is more caught than taught.

eaching facts is simple. But shaping the heart is what Christianity is all about. It requires intimate relationships.

JESUS MADE DISCIPLES BY HIS LIFE

One does not teach faith and love with words alone. Disciples' hearts cannot be set on fire by theories. Fire kindles fire; iron sharpens iron; faith calls forth faith; life begets life.

The Bible studiously avoids our Western concept of education in matters of true discipleship. God schools His people in the context of ordinary, and sometimes extraordinary, circumstances of life.

Jesus radically transformed concepts held by the Twelve about God, about Himself, about His Kingdom, about His message. He drew them after Him in a fast-paced, demanding work where they could watch Him deal with nature and demons, and with people from every station in life. He gave them jobs to do and problems to solve. He pushed them to the limits of their endurance (Mark 6:30-56) and drew them aside for periods of reflection and rest (Mark 7:24). He led them into deepest sorrow (John 16:20-22) and then, at last, they shared an incomparable joy together in the upper room. They learned their lessons in open air classrooms surrounded by filthy beggars, mutilated lepers, thronging multitudes, and malicious officials. Always they fastened their attention on Jesus to see what He would do. Later their own lives reflected His.

MAKING DISCIPLES JESUS' WAY

My own growth in discipleship is marked by people whose lives spoke to me of Jesus Christ. I don't know all that shaped them but I know how close association with them served to mold me into the person I am today.

One person who had such an impact on my life was Ken, whom I met for the first time when we were both freshmen in college. Often, when I wanted to compliment someone's character, I would say he reminded me of Ken. For several years I observed Ken from a distance. He stood for every fine quality I longed to possess myself and thought every person should have. But it was not until our senior year living together in the fraternity that the secret of Ken's life became evident to me. His presence affected all of us in the house. He was the only person I knew who openly professed Christ. He was the living picture of what I thought a Christian should be, before I surrendered my heart to Christ.

When Ken spoke to me of a daily devotional life, of prayer, of Bible study, it made perfect sense, because he lived what he encouraged me to do. He did not tell me I ought to witness. It was obvious just from watching him that Christians share their faith quietly, sensitively, prayerfully. His integrity and goodness, his values and choices, owed their quality to a carefully disciplined walk of faith.

Several months later we graduated and parted company. While other Christians encouraged me along the way, it was over two years later before God gave me another model like Ken.

Cecil Davidson, a Navigator staff member, opened his home to me and other servicemen like me. He was God's choice to be my new mentor, model, and guide into a life of discipling others.

TEACHING SERVANTHOOD BY EXAMPLE

I spent most of my off-duty weekends for two years in Cecil's home learning—learning what a Christian marriage looks like, how a Christian father trains his children, what values are truly important, how to manage finances. I learned from him what it meant to give myself to others in love, how important each person is, of God's sovereign power, of forgiveness and loyalty, of standards of excellence, of sensitivity to others, of patience, of the importance of inner conviction, of practical help instead of strong challenge. And what I learned came not so much from Cec's words as from watching him live what I learned.

Once we arrived a few minutes early for a meeting at the church and found the room in disarray from previous users. Cec set to work arranging chairs, placing song books, and setting up the podium area. It would have been embarrassing to have stood and watched, so I joined in. When the crowd arrived along with those in charge, Cec's work permitted the meeting to begin without confusion or delay. Yet no one knew that an alert and willing leader had set the stage for a successful meeting. I soon discovered this was typical of the man. I cannot imagine how the spirit of a servant could be taught in a classroom, yet Jesus prized that above most qualities we could name. Our Lord came among us as a servant and insisted His followers exhibit the humility of servanthood in all their relationships (Luke 22:24-27). But Cec was a true servant of God, and his life showed me what servanthood is.

However imperfectly I responded, Cec left an indelible mark on me. A few days ago we hosted overnight guests from a visiting church group. As I stood at the window with my morning coffee, enjoying the brightening sky, I noticed the windows of their van were heavily fogged with morning dew. "Cec would clean those windows." The thought intruded into my quiet contemplation. It took only a few minutes, but enabled our company to go safely on their way with clean windows. It was over twenty years ago that Cec patiently coached me to become more alert to others' needs. There was ample opportunity, though: Cec hosted overnight guests every weekend.

How well I remember "serving" a young officer by making his bed—all the while grumbling about his thoughtlessness and pride. When he repeated the offense the following weekend I complained to Cec. He listened patiently and then calmly suggested I make his bed. That lesson stuck. But I could accept his counsel because I knew his life—he would have made that bed cheerfully with no comment as often as necessary.

Cec also granted me opportunities to learn from Navigator leaders who came to visit—by serving them. Rod Sargent came for a meeting with the Navy fleet chaplains to discuss Navigator work. Rod needed someone to handle the audio-visual equipment for his presentation and I was delighted to help out.

When Rod finished his overview he opened the floor for questions. Two senior chaplains were particularly uncomplimentary and acrimonious in their remarks. I was seething with indignation at their words. Someone needed to set them straight about our ministry! But Rod's soft, godly response left me chagrined at my own attitude. The way he handled their comments transformed the spirit of that meeting. Animosity gave way to appreciation and cooperation. God taught me the power of a soft answer by that experience.

LIFE-ON-LIFE IN THE FAMILY

Perhaps the most wonderful opportunity for life-on-life discipling is the family unit. We are disciples of our homes, for good or ill. A stable, godly couple who follows Jesus Christ is likely to produce succeeding generations of the same kind. God's final words to His people through Malachi called them to repent of their unfaithfulness in marriage so succeeding generations might be godly.

Of all the lessons I learned from Cec nothing compares with what I learned about being a Christian husband and father. Yet Cec never gave me one verbal lesson on the subject of the Christian home. Every day I spent in his home contained more lessons than I could grasp. For a young man whose parents had divorced and who grew up without a father Cec's modeling was invaluable to me.

I never knew meal times could be fun, enjoyable, and stimulating. While I was growing up I always came to the table after everyone else had begun, wolfed down my food, and left before anyone had finished. But Cec led us into stimulating conversations, had us tell about our day, shared jokes and riddles, and played mind games. I looked forward to meals for the fellowship which often continued right through the clean-up chores. And I regretted times when I had to miss them.

Years later guests in our home made an interesting comment about our meal time: "For you, food is incidental to the meal. You come together to enjoy fellowship." Now where did that come from?

One experience had a profound impact on me. The sweat rolled down my back and I fidgeted uneasily while under my breath I pleaded with Cec's son to give in. This was the fourth time Cec had brought him downstairs from the bedroom to apologize to his sister. He stubbornly refused. Back upstairs they went—seven times. My relief was unbounded when the boy at last apologized.

Cec wasn't angry or impatient. He was gentle and kind. But his kindness was married to a stern insistence that this young boy yield to his father's will. How different that was from the only discipline I remember receiving as a boy, inconsistently dealt out in angry shouts that couldn't bend my will.

The second thing I noticed was the change that came over Cec's son. He was a happier, more willing child after that. Today he's a grown man, a godly man, like his father. My own children are on their way to adulthood as they pass through their teen years. Much of the best of our home they have experienced lies in lessons Cecil Davidson never preached to me. He lived them to me, life on life.

■From *Discipleship Journal* 15, no. 6 (November 1985), pp. 21-23. Used by permission.

The Art of Mentoring

Bobb Biehl and Glen Urquhart

Mentoring is in many ways a modern translation of the biblical concept of discipleship. One more-learned helps a less-learned pilgrim along the path to maturity and success. There is a price, but the rewards are great!

Mentoring is making the mentor's personal strengths, resources, and network (friendships/contacts) available to help a protege reach his or her goals. The mentoring relationship begins when a person with experience asks (formally or informally) a less experienced person with high potential two simple questions:

1. What are your personal and professional goals?
2. How can I help you reach your goals?

Mentoring is not using a protégé to accomplish the mentor's goals. Mentoring is not helping you become another me! Rather, it is helping you become a fully developed you!

MENTOR CHECKLIST

Before you choose a mentor, check to see if he or she has these qualities:
- Will the mentor be an objective, lovingly honest, and balanced source of feedback for your questions?
- Will the mentor be open and transparent with his/her own struggles?
- Will the mentor model his/her teachings?
- Does the mentor know and believe in you . . . one of your chief cheerleaders, not your chief critic?
- Will the mentor teach as well as answer your questions?
- Is the mentor successful in your eyes?
- Will the mentor be open to two-way communication . . . learning from you on occasion as well as teaching you?
- Does the mentor want to see younger people succeed in developing their spiritual and leadership potential?

PROTEGÉ CHECKLIST

Before you choose a protogé, check to see if he or she has these qualities:
- Will you be able to believe 100 percent in the protogé?
- Do you naturally enjoy communicating with the protogé?
- Will you be able to give without reservation to the protogé?
- Will you love him or her as a brother or sister?
- Do you admire his or her potential as a leader?
- Is the protogé teachable . . . eager to learn from you and mature in his or her spiritual and leadership potential?
- Does the protogé admire you, as a mentor?
- Is the protogé self-motivated even though not always confident?
- Will the protogé be threatened by you or threatening to you?

QUESTIONS AND ANSWERS ABOUT MENTORING

What is the difference between modeling and mentoring?

The primary difference between modeling and mentoring is that a mentor is personally aware of the protogé and wants to use his/her resources to help the protogé succeed in maximizing his/her unique strengths. A person you have never met can be a model for you, or a model can work with you closely but sees you only as a helper and not one to be helped, as a mentor does. At the same time, modeling is a part of the mentoring process as you show your protogé your life values by the way you live.

Where does mentoring happen? Everywhere?

Most mentoring takes place in a very relaxed setting as it did centuries ago in fatherly apprenticeships . . . walking, sailing, golfing, driving . . . anywhere you are with your mentor or your protogé. Mentoring often happens ten minutes at a time . . . here and there as you move through life together. Don't see mentoring as all work. It often involves the joy of mutual sharing. Mentoring happens more in the context of a relationship than a formal class room. Mentoring is a life attitude as much as a formal structure. It can be even more enjoyable as you are doing things you enjoy together!

At what age do you want to begin mentoring someone?

At the age where protogés have clear goals they want to reach. This may begin around age sixteen or in some situations even a little earlier.

What difference does age play in the mentoring process?

Age is not as large a factor as experience and maturity. Sometimes the mentor is actually a few years younger than the protogé. However, if you were to take all of the mentors in the world, our guess is mentors would most typically be five to twenty years older than the protogé.

What happens when a protogé or mentor fails?

No protogé wants to fail, but sometimes a protogé needs a mentor's help to know how to succeed . . . and how to learn from failure. A wise mentor expects a protogé to be less than perfect, especially in the formative years. A protogé should have *no fear of being rejected* by the mentor. It is also helpful for the mentor and the protogé to discuss failure, including the freedom to fail and not be rejected, before the inevitable failure occurs. No mentor wants to fail. A wise protogé expects the mentor to be less than perfect. A mentor should have *no fear of being rejected* by the protogé.

Does a mentor have to be perfectly mature, an ideal model of the Christian faith and an extreme success, to be a mentor?

No . . . no mentor is perfect! Each mentor only needs to be stronger in some areas than the protogé in order to be a big help. At the same time if the mentor has a major problem, it is difficult to lead a protogé in this area. That is why, ideally, each mentor also has one or more mentors.

What effect does a protogé's motivation level have on a mentor?

The more eager a protogé is to learn . . . the more eager the mentor is to teach!

Can a man mentor a woman . . . or a woman mentor a man?

Most studies indicate that in business today many men mentor both men and women. At the same time, many women mentor both sexes.

In Scripture the primary references, as in Titus 2:4-5, are to older women helping younger women and, in 2 Timothy 2:2, to older men helping younger men. The relationship between the mentor and the protogé typically becomes emotionally intimate. Therefore, the protogé and mentor relationship between members of the opposite sex is *potentially* very dangerous to have outside of marriage. *This is not recommended!*

Is mentoring at a distance possible?

Mentoring *can* take place at a distance. The main question: "Do you really believe in this person and want to see him/her succeed?" If so, you can help in many ways even at a distance via mail, fax, computer, telephone, and occasional personal visits.

If the focus of mentoring is reaching the protogé's goals . . . when do I get to teach my values to my protogé?

In the process of helping your protogés reach their goals, frequently they will ask, "Is there anything else I should know or be aware of right now?" At these *teachable, mentoring moments*, gently share any other helpful perspective you may care to give. Point out areas where the protogé needs to grow personally: irritating habits, poor attitudes, appearance, and even personal hygiene. Soon you can also give godly/biblical perspective and counsel. Share anything your protogés need to understand in order to grow into spiritual maturity and to realize their full potential as a Christian leader.

What role does accountability play in the mentor protogé relationship?

The main reason for accountability is to help the protogé reach spiritual maturity and to develop his or her full leadership potential. The mentor must hold the protogé accountable, not on a daily or weekly basis, but as needed and agreed upon. The frequency and the level of accountability will vary greatly with each protogé.

Note: It is important to remember that all accountability is ultimately to God. Just because a mentor will let you get by with something does not mean that God will. Just because a mentor feels something is okay does not mean that God does. Just because you can successfully hide something from the mentor who is holding you accountable does not mean it is hidden from God.

Just so, a mentor is not to be held accountable for the protogé's success. The mentor can help the protogé succeed in reaching his or her goals . . . but the responsibility for reaching goals always remains clearly with the protogé.

What if the mentor is emotionally unbalanced and begins using the relationship in an inappropriate way?

If you feel that your mentor is beginning to take unfair advantage of you, we would suggest the following steps:

1. Pray about the situation; ask for God's wisdom.
2. Talk with your mentor; get your feelings into the open.
3. Talk with a close friend; ask for wisdom and perspective on your relationship.

A mentoring relationship should be constructive, not destructive. When you feel that your relationship may have become destructive, you need to redefine your relationship.

What are the emotional rewards of mentoring versus managing people?

Mentoring people results in a feeling of *satisfaction,* the feeling you get when you provide a quality product or service, and *significance,* the feeling you get when you make a difference that lasts over time.

Managing people to carry out your agenda, without mentoring, typically results in a feeling of *success,* the feeling that results from reaching one's goals, but frequently the feeling is hollow, somewhat less than satisfying, and insignificant.

How confident do most people feel about becoming mentors?

Most of the adults alive today feel somewhat intimidated by the word *mentoring.* However, most people do not realize how effective they could be when working with protogés. At the same time, most adults can quickly name three young people who could benefit from their support and encouragement. Most people say they would have benefited from such a supportive relationship in their life or, in fact, did while they were younger.

Whatever you do, don't let a little discomfort keep you from approaching one to three high-potential young people and offering your mentoring support. They need your experience, wisdom, and encouragement.

What difference does mentoring make over a lifetime?

Mentoring can make an extremely significant difference in a leader's lifetime achievements. Often one timely idea or a single word of encouragement influences a young leader to hang in there. One simple conversation over coffee at a critical time often shapes a young leader's entire life direction. Wisely shared perspective can build faith, sustain courage, and lead to visionary change and powerful accomplishments for God's kingdom.

Frequently, suicide notes imply, "When I needed help . . . no one seemed to care about me personally. . . . I was all alone. . . . No one cares if I live or die!" As rare as physical suicide may be, spiritual, career, and family suicides are unfortunately quite common. However, with a mentor in place who loves the protogé, this is rarely the case. In some situations, mentoring may actually be the critical link to life.

■ © 1990 Masterplanning Group International, Box 6128, Laguna Niguel, California 92677 (714-495-8850), publishers of *Mentoring Today* newsletter. Used by permission.

Mentoring:
The Strategy of the Master

Ron Lee Davis

One who has been mentor to many shares an abundance of examples on the "how-to" side of the equation. The challenges, costs, and results of equipping through mentoring are all on display in this motivating article.

THE JOB DESCRIPTION OF A MENTOR

The calling of mentor is high and noble. The role of a mentor is crucial. The life of a mentor is risky. The rewards of a mentor's work are profound, but intangible. The job description of a mentor is demanding.

1. I am willing to spend the time it takes to build an intensely bonded relationship with the learner.
2. I commit myself to believing in the potential and future of the learner; to telling the learner what kind of exciting future I see ahead for him or her; to visualizing and verbalizing the possibilities for his or her life.
3. I am willing to be vulnerable and transparent before the learner, willing to share not only my strengths and successes, but also my weaknesses, failures, brokenness, and sins.
4. I am willing to be honest yet affirming in confronting the learner's errors, faults, and areas of immaturity.
5. I am committed to standing by the learner through trials—even trials that are self-inflicted as a result of ignorance or error.
6. I am committed to helping the learner set goals for his or her spiritual life, career, or ministry, and to helping the learner dream his or her dream.
7. I am willing to objectively evaluate the learner's progress toward his or her goal.
8. Above all, I am committed to faithfully living out everything I teach.

THE SEVEN CARDINAL RULES OF TENDER-TOUGH MENTORING

Rule #1: When you confront, be honest and direct.

Tenderness is not a matter of being diplomatic or tactful, of using euphemistic language, of "beating around the bush" and "softening the blow." Rather, we should say what needs to be said in clear and unmistakable terms. An effective mentor lays everything squarely on the line. As David Augsburger says, "If you love, you level."

A word of caution: I've seen people use words like "love" and "honesty" to disguise a multitude of sins. I've seen people screamed at, chewed up, and verbally abused in the name of "love." I've seen people ventilate their own anger at someone else in the name of "honesty."

None of us is qualified to confront until we have carefully, honestly searched our own motivations for doing so—including, as much as humanly possible, those motivations that evade our conscious minds. As mentors, we should always confront with reluctance, never with eagerness. We should confront honestly, directly, yet gently, and always with a genuine desire to bring about God's best in the other person's life. It is far more Christlike to confront another person through tears or sorrow than with a voice raised in anger.

Rule #2: Confront only with unconditional love and acceptance.

Our tough honesty should be covered with tender caring, affirmation, and unconditional commitment both to the learner and to the mentoring relationship. Let's say you are a mentor to a young woman named Janice who works alongside you in the business you own. You notice she has a problem dealing with your customers. She doesn't mean to offend people, and she isn't even aware that she does so; yet there is an abruptness in her manner that puts people off. What would be the tender-tough approach to making Janice aware of the problem?

Just listen to this approach: "Janice, I've got something to tell you. I know this won't be easy for either of us, but I respect you enough to give it to you straight. I care about you, I'm committed to our relationship, and I want you to be the best you can be for Jesus Christ. Janice, the problem is there's something in your manner that sometimes puts people off. You tend to be a bit abrupt at times, and some folks interpret that as unfriendliness. I know you don't mean it that way, and that you're probably not even aware of it. That's why I felt I needed to bring it to your attention."

She knows it wasn't easy for you to confront her, but that you performed this act of loving toughness because you are committed to the relationship and to her growth. Most importantly, she knows she is accepted and loved, regardless of her faults and failings.

Rule #3: When you confront, be specific, never generalize.

In your confrontation of Janice it would be important to specify times when you noticed her abruptness. You wouldn't simply say, "You're always abrupt and unfriendly." Rather you would say, "You were abrupt with Mrs. Jones yesterday. She came up to me later and asked, 'Whatever did I say to offend Janice?' I had to tell her not to take it personally, that you are really a warm and friendly person, but that it doesn't always show."

When you generalize about a person's character, faults, or habits, they usually become defensive. And understandably so. Such generalizations sound and feel like an attack on who a person is instead of a constructive reproof on what a person does. Moreover, the vagueness of such generalizations doesn't give the learner a clue what he or she should do to grow and change. But if you refer to specific behaviors and events, the learner has something tangible to react to and work on.

Rule #4: When you confront, demonstrate empathy.

One of the most important characteristics of an effective mentor is the ability to put ourselves in the learner's place. As novelist John Erskine once observed, "We have not really budged a step until we've taken up residence in someone else's point of view."

Some time ago, I was called upon to confront a staff member about his work. So I went to his office—not merely as the senior pastor but as a mentor and friend—and I laid out the areas where he was failing to perform as he should. It was very hard for both of us, and we both became teary-eyed as we talked.

"I want you to know that I'm your advocate, not your adversary," I told him. "I just wish you knew how much I want you to become a success in this job."

"I know that," he said. "I really do. I just have a hard time processing criticism. I get caught up in a shame spiral, going back all the way to when I was a kid. I never felt valued in my family. I was always being criticized and told how useless and stupid I was. I guess I just give too much power to criticism."

Rule #5: Build on the learner's strengths, gifts, and character through positive encouragement.

Earn the right to confront. Make sure that you affirm the learner ninety-seven percent of the time, so that when it's time to be tough in the remaining three percent, your tender caring and affirmation will be credible. How will the learner know you're on his or her side if the only evaluation you ever pass on is a negative one?

Kemp Smeal, the music minister of our church, offers this reflection on our mentoring relationship: "Ron is a 'wind beneath my wings' mentor—the kind of friend and encourager who lifts you up and teaches you to fly solo. He builds you up publicly. He spends time with you privately, cementing the friendship, making you feel valued. Then, in those times when he has to objectively evaluate or criticize your performance, he does so with grace, with a genuine concern for the individual."

Rule #6: Affirm in public, correct in private.

The goal of mentoring is to build up, not to tear down. If you rebuke a person in public, you bring humiliation, embarrassment, and shame on him or her. You destroy self-esteem. You set the mentoring process back.

But when you affirm in public, you build self-esteem, confidence, and incentive. Of course, that affirmation should be realistic and honest, not just empty words of praise. By affirming sincerely and publicly, you plant the seeds of greatness in the learner.

"Ron confronts me when I need it," says my associate, Peter Hiett, "but he always does so graciously and in private. Publicly, he always builds me up. As important as skills are, Ron emphasizes building character and emotional wholeness more than building skills. I try to emulate that emphasis in my own mentoring relationships with others."

Rule #7: Build an allegiance to relationships, not to issues.

I've found that people generally tend to build an allegiance to relationships or to issues. That is, people tend to become primarily concerned about other people and their feelings and quality of the relationship, or they become focused on rules, agendas, quotas, tasks, and results. The effective mentor always puts relationships ahead of issues.

My father was that kind of mentor, both in his own family and in the church he pastored for twenty-five years. Many times I heard him say, "The individual is always more important than the issue." He lived this principle daily, and he built it into my life. Today, I try to pass on this principle to others.

■ From Ron Lee Davis, *Mentoring: The Strategy of the Master* (Nashville: Thomas Nelson Publishers, 1991), pp. 50-51, 71-80. Used by permission.

A Biblical Perspective on Evaluating Performance

Myron Rush

While performance reviews are most often found in the workplace, the principle belongs to "equipping." As a teacher, your job is to equip for service, and evaluations of progress are your responsibility. Here's how!

Regardless of what many leaders and managers think, employee performance evaluation systems were not designed simply to give the personnel department something to do. It is unfortunately true, however, that many of them have degenerated to little more than that. Nevertheless, to accomplish activities and projects as planned, the manager and employee must be able to evaluate progress and take corrective action as needed. This is the major purpose and function of the performance evaluation system.

GOD'S VIEW OF PERFORMANCE

God is performance-conscious. Scripture indicates His concern about the quality and level of our work performance by saying, "Work hard and cheerfully at all you do, just as though you were working for the Lord and not merely for your masters" (Colossians 3:23, TLB). While on earth, Jesus apparently performed to the best of His ability, for those observing His actions commented, "He has done everything well" (Mark 7:37).

When Jesus told the parable of the talents (Matthew 25), He described two types of people—those with good performance and those with bad. When describing the workers with good performance the master said, "Well done, good and faithful servant!" (v. 21). But when talking to the unproductive worker, the master said, "You wicked, lazy servant!" (v. 26).

The Christian leader should be committed to a high level and quality of performance. As we read in Colossians 3:23, we are to work hard and cheerfully at all we do. The Christian's goal is high performance with a positive and cheerful attitude toward the task being performed.

This is diametrically opposed to most of the world's view of work and performance. The secular philosophy tends to be "take it easy" and "don't work too hard." Many people are committed to doing only what is required to get by in order to keep the boss off their backs. This certainly is contrary to the standard established in Colossians 3:23.

Since God desired that we perform well, the Christian community and its leaders should strive for high performance. When properly developed and maintained, the performance evaluation system can be one of the best management tools for achieving and maintaining high performance.

WHY EMPLOYEE EVALUATION SYSTEMS TEND TO FAIL

Most employee performance evaluation systems are built on the wrong objectives. Most organizational performance evaluation systems are designed to evaluate past history instead of work currently in progress. They focus on the employee's past twelve months of work. Such performance systems are usually referred to as "annual reviews." Once each year the supervisor fills out some type of performance review form that summarizes the employee's performance during the past year. Unfortunately, in most cases there is little value in recording and reviewing an employee's past year performance. It is history, and it can't be changed. Except for the minimal value such a system offers for future planning purposes, the information has little purpose.

In order to be meaningful, a performance evaluation system should allow the manager and employee to take corrective action while the project is in progress. Since it is impossible to change past actions and performance, the annual review approach becomes meaningless in terms of helping people with a given project. Therefore, instead of focusing on evaluating past history or performance, the evaluation system should evaluate current projects in progress.

Most performance evaluation systems lack clearly defined performance standards. The typical employee performance evaluation system fails not only because it evaluates past history, but it lacks clearly defined standards by which performance is evaluated.

The performance evaluation system should help both the supervisor and his employees agree on a definition of the performance standards before the employee starts working on a project in which his performance will be evaluated. If an employee is expected to do a "good" job, then he should know ahead of time what is meant by "good." Unless performance standards are clearly defined, with measurable terminology, employees have no way of knowing what is expected of them.

Most managers lack training in how to conduct meaningful performance review sessions with their employees. This is one of the major weaknesses with most employee performance review systems. It causes discomfort and anxiety for both the supervisor and his employees.

One day while I was working as a personnel director for an electronic manufacturing firm, a young lady came into my office with tears in her eyes. She said she felt like a school girl who had just come from the principal's office.

When I asked what was the matter, she said she had just come from her first performance evaluation session with her new boss and felt like quitting. "If I was doing such a bad job, she should have said something sooner," she complained. "How was I to know she wasn't happy with my work?" As she chewed on her fingernails she continued. "She treated me like I was her little girl that needed a spanking. I'm an adult and the least she can do is treat me like one."

DESIGNING AN EFFECTIVE PERFORMANCE EVALUATION SYSTEM

Follow these steps when setting up a performance evaluating system:
- Emphasize work in progress rather than evaluating past history by the use of annual reviews.
- The supervisor and subordinate should develop and agree on measurable performance standards. This should be done before the project or activity begins so that the subordinate will know by what standard his performance is being judged.
- The evaluation sessions should be done in a two-way learning environment. The supervisor's, as well as the subordinate's performance should be considered. The emphasis should be on identifying and meeting all the needs that exist in order for the project to be accomplished as planned.

SETTING PERFORMANCE STANDARDS

When setting performance standards the supervisor and employee should set both *preferred performance standards* and *minimum performance standards*. Preferred performance standards are what we are striving to achieve. However, if we would actually be willing to settle for less, the minimum performance standards tell us how far below the preferred standard we may go before repeating the activity or project becomes necessary. In other words, the minimum performance standards indicate how much tolerance exists within the standards.

IMPLEMENTING A WORK-IN-PROGRESS REVIEW SYSTEM

Following is an example of how a work-in-progress review might be done on a six-month project. The work-in-progress reviews are designed to keep the employee and supervisor informed concerning how the project is going, whether changes need to be made, and whether the project is accomplishing the original objectives. The review sessions also insure open communication between the supervisor and employee concerning the various aspects of the project.

Start: Meet with the employee to set measurable objectives and performance standards for the project.

Week 1: The employee begins work on the project.

Week 4: The supervisor and employee have the first work-in-progress review session. This session should be conducted shortly after the project begins in order to make sure there are no unexpected problems in implementing the startup phase of the work. During this session, evaluate how realistic the objectives, time tables, and performance standards are. The supervisor should place a special emphasis on trying to identify the unforeseen work needs of the employee as he pursues the project. Set the date for the next review session. The length of time between review sessions will depend on how well the project is going.

Week 12: The second work-in-progress review session should consider the remaining activities needed to complete the project on time. Is the project on schedule or not? Are new circumstances developing that weren't anticipated?

Week 22: The third work-in-progress review of this project is conducted shortly before the end to make sure no last minute changes are needed in order to complete the project as scheduled.

Week 24: The final evaluation is conducted at the end of the project. This session compares the results with the original projections.

CONDUCTING THE PERFORMANCE EVALUATION SESSIONS

Focus on developing a two-way learning environment. If the evaluation session is to be meaningful, the manager must avoid dealing only with the subordinate's performance. Instead, he must create an environment in which the employee understands that the supervisor's performance will be evaluated along with his own.

Focus on acquiring employee ideas and input. The evaluation session should be a time when the supervisor solicits ideas and input from the employee. This is not necessarily the time for lengthy lectures. The supervisor should first ask the employee for his input concerning the current status of the work, progress being made, problems that have developed since the last meeting, and recommendations for improvements or solutions to problems. This will give the employee an opportunity to use his creativity. It will also communicate that the manager trusts the employee's judgment and needs his input.

Encourage the employee to make decisions within the framework of his authority. Many employees expect the boss to solve all problems and make all decisions concerning changes and other corrective measures. The evaluation session is an excellent time to encourage the employee to solve his own problems as long as the solution falls within the employee's decision-making authority. Don't let the employee delegate problems upward to you when he is capable of developing his own solutions. The manager frequently hinders the employee from taking initiative by stepping in too quickly to rescue the employee from a problem.

Use a performance evaluation worksheet to maintain a written record of progress and actions taken. It is very important to keep written records of employee performance. Both progress and problems should be recorded, and the employee should sign the evaluation form at the end of each session. These records provide valuable information when planning similar projects in the future and when it comes time to consider employee promotions.

Always give proper recognition during the evaluation session. During the evaluation session, the manager should properly recognize the employee's performance. Proper recognition means that the manager offers praise when the job is done well, and constructive criticism when it is needed. Some managers don't mind giving praise, but they don't know how to properly handle constructive criticism.

When dealing with constructive criticism, always focus on performance. Deal with the cause of the performance problem, and never criticize unless you are prepared to offer suggestions for improvement. Stick with facts and try to avoid subjective opinions because they only lead to arguments. It is difficult for an employee to deny poor performance when you deal with facts instead of opinion.

■ From Myron Rush, *Management: A Biblical Approach* (Wheaton: Victor Books, 1983), pp. 186-199. Used by permission.

Teaching by Coming Alongside

Donald Bubna

Did you know that there are five steps to equipping anyone to do anything? Honest—it's not that complicated! And wouldn't you know it, Jesus used all five steps, over and over. That means they're guaranteed!

I f we really believe in what we are offering people, then everyone in our churches—our greeters, ushers, nursery workers, Sunday school teachers, even the parking lot attendants—won't be chosen simply because the job needs to be filled and they say they are available. We will recruit the best, always making room for good people, and we will train—disciple—them, making sure they understand what is expected of them. We will make certain that they understand their source of strength, that they are depending on the Holy Spirit to empower them for their service. They will understand the significance of their task in meeting and serving the people God brings into the fellowship. And they will render their service not out of a sense of duty, with phony smiles and handshakes, but because they want to.

Fortunately, we don't need to speculate about how this can be done. Before Jesus commanded us to go and make disciples, he showed us how to do it. When the disciples were released for ministry on Pentecost, they were prepared and empowered by the Holy Spirit. And the result was the birth and growth of the church as recorded in Acts.

STEP ONE: JESUS TOLD THEM WHAT TO DO

This is where most of our training begins and ends. We all realize training is important, and so before we give someone a job, we tell him or her what to do. Church people are told from the pulpit, or in a few minutes of instruction before they start, or in a two-hour training class, or in a written manual, or in four years of college and three years of seminary study. Nothing substitutes for knowledge, but grasping the knowledge is only step one.

Jesus told his disciples to go and preach the gospel of the kingdom. But he told them in ways that made it easy for them to remember. As a master teacher he built upon their background and interests. He talked about making them "fishers of men." He used illustrations from real life about seed sowing and soil, tares, mustard seed, and leaven, to teach them about spiritual things. These illustrations, rooted in their everyday experiences, were not easily forgotten.

I doubt that the disciples ever forgot the simple parables of the kingdom. Decades later, they would put them into writing after they had no doubt repeated them many times. We still tell those stories today.

STEP TWO: JESUS SHOWED THEM HOW TO DO IT

Jesus didn't just tell his disciples what to do. He modeled for them the kingdom mindset, knowing that training is more caught than taught. He demonstrated how to show compassion and how to handle criticism. The disciples saw Jesus minister to the down-and-outers and the up-and-outers, the blind beggars as well as the rich young rules, the tax collectors as well as the Pharisees.

Many of the lessons I have found most valuable in my ministry were learned through the influence of Dr. Richard Harvey, who was my pastor during my teen years. Because he had a boy my age, I was frequently in his home, and as often as once a week I spent the night. I had ample opportunity to watch how Dr. Harvey lived away from his public ministry. I observed how he studied, his prayer life, how he conducted himself with people who came by the house, and how he related to the elders.

One day Dr. Harvey received a call from two senior citizens in our church who had gone down to Hot Springs, Arkansas, for some health care. They needed a ride home. Dr. Harvey called me and asked if I would help him drive from St. Louis to Hot Springs and back, without an overnight stop. Without ever saying anything, this action taught me that senior citizens are important people. Four decades later, his ministry is still bearing fruit. While I do remember a few of his sermons, the example of his life in ministry and caring have had a far greater effect on my personal life and ministry as a pastor.

STEP THREE: JESUS LET THEM TRY IT

The three or more years the disciples spent together were not just spent in classroom lectures and laboratory demonstrations. Jesus had them practicing the principles and attitudes of the kingdom as he went about with them doing good. They were being trained right on the streets during Jesus' tours of Galilee and Jerusalem. While not a great deal is said about how Jesus did it, there is evidence he gave them opportunities to practice what he was teaching while he was there with them to help.

One advantage of letting people try it is that the teacher is available to help them over the hard parts. A good example is when Jesus came down from the mountain after his transfiguration. While he was away, the disciples tried and failed to cure an epileptic boy (Matthew 17:15-16). Jesus stepped in and cast a demon out of the boy, and later, in private, he explained why they had been unable to do it.

After we have been told, seen it modeled, and had a chance to try it in a controlled setting, then we are ready to go out on our own. Jesus recognized this. He knew the day would come after his crucifixion and resurrection when he would ascend into heaven. So he sent his disciples on some short missions.

STEP FOUR: JESUS SENT THEM OUT ALONE

After a time of telling, showing, and hands-on supervision, Jesus commissioned the disciples, sending them out, first two by two throughout the region and, at the end, into all the world to preach the gospel.

I well remember the initial Sundays in my first pastorate as my congregation met in a small garage, made over into a chapel. Until then, I had always assisted another pastor who had given me one or two responsibilities in a service. But that first Sunday on my own, there was no order of service to follow from the week before. There was no one to guide me in my sermon preparation. I was on my own, doing it for real.

Those first worship services and sermons were near tragedies. But it was a start, and each Sunday I noticed significant improvement. Doing it for real—experience—is an excellent teacher.

Some leaders find it hard to give others the freedom to do it on their own. It is easier for the leaders to do it themselves and make sure "it is done right." But this doesn't give the inexperienced an opportunity to grow. When we hang on to responsibilities, never delegating to others, we hinder God's call for us to make disciples.

STEP FIVE: THE EVALUATION PROCESS

After the disciples returned from their assignments, they reported to him and talked it over. We don't know all that Jesus told them, but we can be sure that there were both correction and affirmation. I owe a great deal to a network of pastors who, in my early days of ministry, gave me feedback and correction. Their encouragement kept me progressing. Unless there is some kind of evaluation with accountability, people can go on repeating their mistakes. When they do it for real, people get in situations where they are stuck. They need some way to get help.

Church ministries need some plan for giving ongoing support and critique of the workers. People need to know how they are doing. If someone is not performing well, the most loving and helpful thing that can be done is to share the insight in a way that would bring about the change without discouraging the worker. One effective way to accomplish this is through regular meetings with the workers to discuss successes and failures and ways to improve. At such meetings workers might discover they are not alone in their problems, as others didn't know how to deal with them either. As they deal with them together, with the help of able supervisors, they tend to be less discouraged by the task.

These five basic steps are the basis for training people effectively, whether it is in the restaurant business or in a Sunday school program, whether we are parents or youth workers, whether we are preparing salesmen, or visitation teams. When we encourage people in the church by thorough training, the benefits often go beyond the church walls.

The things we do well as a church inevitably are due to good training. The things we do poorly can be traced to the omission of one or more of these five basic steps. When somebody fails in carrying out an assignment, our typical reaction is, "How come? I told them what to do." Occasionally, we will add, "I specifically showed them how." In reality, we're confessing that we have only fulfilled steps one and two of the training process.

Training is more than telling. Training is equipping for service.

The Secrets of Equipping Our Students

Walter Henrichsen

Before permanent change takes place in anyone, a process occurs. Truth ultimately becomes performance when three transforming experiences take place. Learn these secrets and watch the transformation happen!

What keeps us from being "doers of the word" (James 1:22)? And how can we effectively motivate children in the direction of a deeper commitment to Christ? There are five concepts or ingredients involved in the process of permanent change. Taken together they challenge some traditional assumptions of evangelical Christianity. But these concepts must be thoroughly understood and implemented if we are going to motivate our young people to a life of Christian commitment.

1. DISCIPLINE (PERFORMANCE)

Johnny is a runningback on his school's football team. Tuesday afternoon his mother went to watch him scrimmage in preparation for Friday evening's game. Johnny is given the ball, hits the line, and is immediately demolished. She watches him pull himself up off the ground with pain written all over his face. He's again given the ball only to have the same thing happen. He is beaten and pulverized continually throughout the afternoon exercise.

At the end of football practice the coach requires the players to run two sprints around the track, and do pushups and sit-ups before heading into the locker room. As his mother watches Johnny, it is obvious he is going through a painful experience.

Now Johnny is home. His mother reminds him that before going to school he forgot to take out the garbage and make his bed. He is apologetic and promises to do better. The next day, however, he proceeds to forget again. But he does show up for football practice.

His mother is a patient, objective woman and so takes her son aside to logically work through the problem. She asks if it requires more effort to take out the garbage and make the bed than to get beat up on the football field. His obvious answer is no. She continues her inquiry by asking if there is as much pain involved, and again the answer is no. Why, then, will Johnny do one and not the other? The answer is immediately apparent—he is motivated to do one and unmotivated to do the other.

This brings us to the second of the five concepts.

2. MOTIVATION

Jane is a six year old who awakes in the morning with a headache and upset stomach. She begs her mother to let her stay home from school that day.

About ten o'clock that morning Jane's older brother comes running into the house, declaring that school for the day has been unexpectedly canceled due to some difficulties with the building. One of the neighborhood mothers has offered to take the children to the beach for a day of fun.

What happens to Jane? You guessed it. Immediately the symptoms of illness disappear. Energy surges into her body that she did not know existed. Running to her mother, she begs to be included in the beach party.

What caused the transformation, the disappearance of the headache and the eagerness to become active? In short, what motivated her? This leads us to the third concept in our sequence: hope or reward.

3. HOPE (REWARD)

There are three words which we will use interchangably for the sake of our discussion: reward, profit, and gain.

Jane eagerly sought permission from her mother to be included in the party because she was motivated by hope, that is, she hoped for a wonderful time at the beach. She hoped to enjoy herself with the other children. In her mind's eye she could see a picnic, sand castle, games, and other delightful experiences. Hope is powerful!

A person hopes in what he considers to be gain or profit. A person never hopes for the opposite of profit. If you invested some money in a business proposition, and I asked if you thought it was going to be a success, you would no doubt answer, "I hope so." You certainly would not answer, "I hope not." If I asked if you felt that the business venture would be a failure, you might answer, "I hope not." What you hope in, then, is a reflection of what you consider to be gain.

Let's go back for a moment and again take a look at Johnny. What motivates him to show up at scrimmage day after day only to be pulverized? It is hope. He hopes to make the starting lineup of the football team. He hopes to become "big man on campus." He hopes to be all-state some day and gain a football scholarship. That is what motivates him.

If hope is the thing that motivates us, then what we hope in, or what we consider to be gain or profit, is a reflection of our convictions or value system. That brings us to the fourth word in our sequence.

4. CONVICTIONS (VALUE SYSTEMS)

People hope in different things because they have differing convictions about what is valuable or important. What is gain to one person is not gain to another. Elizabeth may campaign for class president in the hope of gaining recognition from other students. She is convinced that is true gain or reward.

Bill, on the other hand, is willing to spend hours going door to door to sell Christmas cards because he can envision himself winning a free trip to Disney Land. According to his value system, he is convinced that is real gain.

Recently a wealthy senator spent several million dollars obtaining public office. He did this, I am sure, because he believed that to be a U.S. Senator would be rewarding. He hoped to obtain that office by investing his money. He was motivated to discipline himself, make campaign speeches, show up for various political functions, etc., because of his conviction. I am sure we could find a politician who views things differently—a man who would be willing to trade his political office for several million dollars. Some people are motivated by financial gain because of the value system they have chosen. Others are motivated by position.

What is the basis for one person's being convinced that one thing is gain and another that something entirely different is profitable. This leads us to our fifth and final concept in the sequence: truth.

5. TRUTH

Everyone works from the framework of a truth system. He may consider truth to be absolute or relative. For one individual, truth may be the opinion of the majority.

Whatever "they" are doing is what he considers to be important. If "they" are wearing short hair, then he wears short hair. If "they" are promiscuous and on drugs, that is what he does as well.

For another person, truth may be whatever reason says. If reason leads him to believe that a certain thing is true, he is convinced it is true, hopes for its fulfillment and is motivated in that direction. Reason may tell him that political power, accumulation of wealth or living in comfort is the most important thing. For another, social action may shape his value system and cause him to be motivated.

Some people define truth by what a charismatic leader or guru says. They are mesmerized by a Hitler or a cult leader. Whatever he says is truth.

There are also those who consider truth to be defined by the Bible. I am sure that most of those reading this article would fit this category. For us, what the Bible says is truth. The Bible is the Word of God. If God says it, it is right. We hope in the rewards which accompany God's Word and are motivated in the direction of obeying what He says as found in His Word.

The five concepts form a directional chain (see diagram below). Although we discussed it from the bottom up the fact is that motivation works in the opposite direction. What we believe to be true is the basis of our convictions and shapes our value system. This in turn is what we consider to be gain or profit and thus what we hope in. We are then motivated to discipline ourselves or to perform in a certain manner.

Process of Permanent Change

TRUTH

CONVICTION
(Value System)

HOPE
(Reward)

MOTIVATION

DISCIPLINE
(Performance)

Since we are all thus motivated, it may help to take a look at the implications.

IMPLICATIONS

1. We have noted that a person is motivated in the direction of his hope, but that hope can be negative as well as positive. That is, the person may be motivated in hoping for the absence of pain or punishment.

2. All of us, children and adults included, are motivated in the direction of our hope. What we hope in is what we consider to be gain, reward or profit. The Bible teaches that a person's desire for gain or profit is not a product of being created in the image of Adam but in the image of God.

This article is too short to thoroughly delve into a biblical justification for this position, but note a couple of things. First, all that God does is for the purpose of accruing benefit to Himself. He is a generous and gracious God, but He is also a jealous God, sharing His glory with no one. Ephesians 1:5 tells us that we are created for His, not our own, good pleasure.

Secondly, the Bible in general and the New Testament in particular never calls upon the believer to do anything of a sacrificial nature without coupling with it a promise of a reward. This desire to accrue benefit from effort forms the basis of motivation. Hope is always in the direction of gain or profit.

3. This leads us to the third and final implication. Being motivated by profit, or in the direction of our hope, is not wrong. God expects us to be so motivated. The Bible, however, clearly warns that our motivation ought to be in the direction of a proper value system, that is, a value system embraced by God rather than one embraced by the world. The world is motivated by a temporal value system, the Christian by an external value system.

For example, in Matthew 6:19-21, Jesus does not discourage us from "laying up treasures." Rather, He argues that the prudent manager of one's resources will invest in the eternal rather than the temporal. Being motivated by profit is not wrong. To be motivated by the world's definition of profit is wrong.

In influencing children toward a deeper commitment to Christ, it is imperative that we draw on their natural God-given motivation in the direction of gain. If we fail to understand this, we will ultimately use guilt and obligation as the basis for motivation. And, like a negative hope, it simply cannot sustain.

We must teach our children to hope in the promises of God rather than the promises of the world. What they hope in will motivate them.

■ From *Evangelizing Today's Child* (March–April 1987), pp. 10-12. Used by permission.

Essentials of an Equipping Ministry

Phillip W. Sell

What are the characteristics of an environment in which equipping regularly and successfully takes place? Four elements are almost always found. Evaluate your teaching/equipping setting in light of these four.

E quipping the saints for the work of service" (Ephesians 4:12) is the biblical bedrock for educational ministry in the local church. Most Christian educators wrestle with making equipping a reality in their ministries. After eight years of working in educational ministries in the church, I have concluded that there are four essential elements which are crucial for an equipping ministry, namely: *envisioning, enabling, empowering,* and *encouraging.*

1. Envisioning: the process of seeing potential in persons for ministry and inspiring those same people toward ministry. An essential truth of Scripture reminds us that all believers are given spiritual gifts to be used to build up the body of Christ (Ephesians 4:7; 1 Peter 4:10). This means that no person in the body of Christ can be excluded from serving Christ and that no Christian educator can "write off" any Christian as not having potential in ministry.

The Christian educator can do a number of things to help envision individuals in the congregation. First, teach a series on spiritual gifts. Conclude the series with a gift-inventory questionnaire which would diagnose each person's spiritual gift or gifts. Then a definite strategy should be laid for the development of spiritual gifts for ministry. Finally, ministries should be developed within the church (and identified in the community) in which those with developed spiritual gifts can serve.

Secondly, periodically run a "Ministry Interest Survey" which lists all the church's ministries and the kind of service opportunities available. Have all the people in the church fill out a survey. You should peruse the information carefully. The church I currently serve also provides examples of envisioning. Our youth pastor prepares barbeques for the football teams and cheerleaders at three of our local high school campuses where he ministers. In a low-keyed way he shares Christ and provides Bibles for those who are interested.

An equipping ministry begins by sowing vision in the lives of persons individually and in providing input for creative ministry structures corporately.

2. Enabling: the second essential element of equipping. Enabling provides the skills necessary for sustained spiritual growth and envisioned ministry. Enabling should be an intentional strategy, not an accidental process. One way to isolate necessary skills is to produce a "Profile of a Maturing Christian Adult" which lists all the crucial skills as concisely as possible. This list becomes the focus of your church's adult education program.

One item from our "Profile of a Maturing Christian Adult" will clarify how to analyze the enabling ministry in your church. The item reads, "The maturing Christian adult has identified and is developing and using his/her spiritual gift(s) in ministry in the church and community." To fulfill this item of the profile the church must do the following: 1) Provide some basic teaching on spiritual gifts consistent with the theology of the church. 2) Obtain or design a diagnostic tool to help persons in the church identify their major spiritual gifts. 3) Clump the gifts into overarching clusters for the purposes of concrete development. I use the following clusters: the caring cluster (the gifts of mercy, hospitality, and giving), the communication cluster (evangelism, teaching, and exhortation) and the kinetic cluster (helps, serving, and administration). 4) Provide practical training for the development of each of these clusters. 5) Give information concerning how these developed gifts could be used in the church, in the community, and in their daily existence.

Too often churches use the "smorgasbord approach" to adult learning and equipping. We put a diverse spread of spiritual food in front of the adult Christian and hope he picks a balanced diet appropriate for spiritual maturity. We need to be clear on how the saints need to be equipped for ministry and provide a more select and balanced diet. Years of generic Bible teaching in churches simply has not produced equipped saints. Enabling means focusing on crucial skills necessary for growth, communicating them to the church leadership and the congregation, and equipping the saints.

3. Empowering: the third essential element of an equipping ministry. Once Christians have a vision for ministry and the skills to carry out that ministry, they must be empowered for ministry. Empowering is providing ministry structures, organizational support, and legitimate decision-making opportunities for those enabled for ministry.

We must provide adequate ministry structures to accommodate those enabled for ministry. Ministry skills must be used or they will be lost. No matter how large the church, if equipping all the gifted saints is taken seriously, its ministry will never be able to accommodate all its equipped saints with "in house" ministries. Rejoice! This is exactly what God intended. He wants the body not just to meet the needs of those in the church, but also those in the community.

Empowering entails providing adequate organizational support for those doing ministry. When Christians band together for ministry purposes they need direction, supervision, and organizational structures.

4. Encouraging: the last essential element of an equipping ministry. Unfortunately most equipping pastors practice what management consultant Robert L. Lorbert calls the "Leave Alone—Zap" theory of management. They leave their ministering saints alone until they hear about some problem and then come along and zap them with advice. As equipped saints get involved in ministry their greatest motivational need is encouragement. We work at seeing the equipped saints in action and giving them as much immediate, specific and honest encouragement as we can. Make it a discipline to write as many encouraging notes as possible each Monday morning concerning what you saw on Sunday. These notes of encouragement will do wonders for the motivation and morale of those who receive them.

Envisioned, enabled, empowered, and encouraged saints will pass on the good word about the joy of ministry. They will recruit and train other saints and swell the ranks of those serving Jesus Christ. Their ministry will spill out of the church and into the community where many others will be touched.

■ Excerpted from *Christian Education Today* 40, no. 5 (Winter 1988-89), pp. 27-28. Used by permission.

Guidelines for the One-to-One Discipler

Jack Griffin

Is there one (or more) student to whom you feel personally called in a discipleship fashion? This list of guidelines by a veteran discipler will remind you of what is most fruitful and lifechanging—one-on-one.

These pointers on one-to-one discipling are from the booklet *Man to Man: How to Do Individual Disciplemaking* by Jack Griffin, who began the Navigator ministry in Australia with his wife, May, in the 1960s.

1. Make sure you are well prepared. Pray before spending one-to-one time with someone, and organize yourself.

2. Remember that you can't lead anyone further than you have gone. You cannot lay solid foundations in someone else's life with only sketchy outlines in your own.

3. You teach by the example of your life. The person who is ministering one to one must be what he is trying to teach.

4. Tailor your help to meet the need of the individual. Every person is different. Don't try to pour them all in the same mold.

5. Repeat everything. "He tells us everything over and over again, a line at a time and in such simple words!" (Isaiah 28:10, TLB). Make no apologies for repeating things.

6. In everything, show him how. We are generally too long in telling people what to do, and too short in showing them how.

7. Give achievable assignments. Don't shovel everything you have at the person you are individually following up—use an eye-dropper or a thimble.

8. Take nothing for granted. Check and double-check his progress on past commitments. "How have you been doing in your quiet times, Joe?"

9. Keep emphasizing the lordship of Christ. Jesus said, "Anyone who does not carry his cross and follow me cannot be my disciple" and, "Any of you who does not give up everything he has cannot be my disciple" (Luke 14:27).

10. Help him establish his goals in life: to know Christ and make him known.

11. Meet his needs through the Scriptures.

12. Keep sharing with him the importance of the "basics"—God's Word, prayer, fellowship, witnessing, and keeping Christ at the center of everything.

13. Explain the 2 Timothy 2:2 principle. Teach him to give his life to a few, who in turn will multiply into many. Keep sharing the vision of disciplemaking (Matthew 28:19-20).

14. Thank him for his fellowship. "Thanks, Joe, for the time with you tonight. It's been a real blessing for me." Thank God for this time as well.

15. Remember Psalm 127:1—"Unless the Lord builds the house, its builders labor in vain." It is God who builds disciples. He is the Master Trainer.

Taken from *Discipleship Journal* 3, no. 3 (May 1983), p. 30. Used by permission.

What's My Calling?

Ralph T. Mattson

In this age of performance expectations, do your students sometimes devalue their worth and contribution? Do they fail to see their value in God's economy? You can impart appreciation for their unique calling.

We've all known people like Janet: serious about her walk with God and genuinely wanting to please him. But she's confused. Her Christian family expects her eventually to be a devoted homemaker. Her pastor stresses foreign missions and challenges her to enter "full-time service." School teachers urge her to pursue a business career.

She doesn't know which role to assume, and resents the expectations piled on her. She's not alone. Most Christians, unfortunately, try to be and do it all . . . but keep wondering on the inside, does joy only come when you enter "full-time ministry?" How do we know where we belong in God's scheme? Is it OK to enjoy our work if it's different from other Christians?

As a consultant helping people become more effective in the church and secular organizations, I've heard many Christians question what they're doing. Some of the saddest stories come from people in extraordinarily well-paying jobs that utterly bore them. Arthur, for example, was pastor of a large congregation but kept asking, "Is this all there is?" Margaret, a Fortune 500 executive, asked the same thing. It was as if they were bribed by position and salary to be unhappy.

On the other hand, some people with lots of options remain in low-paying, unfulfilling jobs as if they were virtuous. Others in full-time ministry grow discontent when they realize their work is mainly secular administration. Meanwhile, some in secular work long for a "call" that would take them into work with a "mission." What a sad, sad circus.

It's one thing for worldly people to be confused about their lives and careers, but shouldn't people who claim to be led of God know what they're doing?

The world believes social institutions influence people to become what they are. If children are exposed to what's good, true, and beautiful, they'll turn out that way. The world believes teachers' college business courses make managers, sales training makes salespeople, and culinary institutes make cooks. In other words, man makes man what he wants him to be.

The Christian imitation is seen in seminars designed to create super-Christians, in colleges proclaiming they produce Christian leaders, and seminaries trying to make preachers of non-preachers. But we've all known leaders who couldn't lead because they didn't have the appropriate gifts. We've listened to trained preachers who had no gift to make the Word come alive. We can number on one hand the teachers who've really made a difference.

Neither training nor credentials make people into anything they weren't designed for by God. God, after all, gives us natural and spiritual gifts. Skills and gifts are not the same thing. We can acquire skills, how to knit, multiply, or use a computer—but we can't acquire creative, conceptualizing, persuasive, organizing, inventive, designing, entrepreneurial, or administrative gifts. They're God-given.

For the Christian, there's little difference between what's natural and spiritual, because God is in it all. We can't do anything independently of the capabilities God has given. No wonder Paul exhorted the Corinthians to think differently than the world about their gifts. Whatever you're doing, he said, "do . . . for the glory of God" (1 Corinthians 10:31). Everything we do—pray, eat, rest, minister—is for God's honor.

We don't please God any more in church than in the shop or lab or classroom or office. We're to honor him wherever we are, in whatever we're doing.

Paul told the Corinthians that God created the Body of Christ with many parts, each of which has a role to play (1 Corinthians 12:14,18). He appoints people to different roles—in the church and in the world—and provides accompanying gifts. Nobody is put into a position for which he hasn't the appropriate gifts.

And we don't have to worry that God might change his mind overnight and arbitrarily change those gifts. God sovereignly declared what and where and who we are to be when he created each of us. When he shaped us physically, he also designed gifts into us—natural capabilities we sometimes scarcely notice because we execute them so easily.

But these gifts are what make us unique. Remember pastor Arthur, who looked bleakly at his large congregation? He discovered his gift was building churches, not running them. And Margaret discovered that highly innovative marketing concepts were part of what God had given her. She needed to leave management—which drained her—and look for a position in marketing. Both had to face the insecurity of job transition, but both discovered the temper of their faith.

Each of us has specific strengths, and testing them helps us understand what we should do with our lives. This is why one person is interested in working with people, another working with ideas, another with combining the two. You may be interested in team sports, your daughter in solo athletic performances, your son in computers.

We can't identify our gifts by taking tests. Tests only measure skills, such as how fast we type, how much Spanish we know. Tests don't help us understand our giftedness. Why? Because each person is unique, and human giftedness is a complex of details that add up to an intricate but unified structure. You can look at your own history, detailing what you like to do. You'll find clues to the role for which you were made.

This doesn't eliminate prayer or decision making, but it cuts down options to a manageable degree. God's will isn't a hidden chalice for which you must go on a prolonged search. It begins with your own design, awaits discovery and then opportunities for you to become a good steward of what God has given. It's an adventure of major consequence no matter your age or sex, becoming what God—not parents, teachers, or friends—made you to be.

■ Reprinted from *The Christian Herald* magazine (March-April, 1990). Used by permission. Ralph T. Mattson is president of the DOMA GROUP, Canton Center, Connecticut.

Discipling through Teaching

Norman E. Harper

While the Great Commission of Christ is usually thought of as a missionary command, at the heart of it is lifechanging teaching. Until the church learns to teach, it can not evangelize effectively!

Our Lord's mandate to the church is to make disciples (Matthew 28:19-20). But what is a disciple? Is making a disciple the same as making a convert? It is clear from the Great Commission that true discipling involves more than bringing a person to a saving knowledge of Christ.

The convert is to be brought into the fellowship of the church and then he is to be taught. This latter means of making disciples—so often overlooked or at least underemphasized—forms the subject of this article.

THE NATURE OF TEACHING

"Teaching," as that concept appears in Matthew 28:20, is not simply a synonym for preaching. The word is an educational term. "Teaching" in the true sense occurs in the context of a personal relationship between teacher and student. It involves imparting knowledge through whatever means (lecture, discussion, storytelling, projects) in such a manner that the student is encouraged to embody the truth in his own life.

Teaching is God's means of multiplication. When a person has been rightly taught, he is equipped to teach others, who in turn are equipped to teach others. The primary teacher in the Sunday school, for example, with a class of ten students teaches more than ten people. In a very real sense, this teacher serves generations of people yet unborn. Remember the words of the Apostle Paul when he wrote to Timothy: "And the things which you have heard from me in the presence of many witnesses, these entrust to faithful men, who will be able to teach others also" (2 Timothy 2:2).

Through teaching we come to know the content of our faith. And not usually as a singular event but a continuous process. Each occasion for teaching is relating to earlier occasions in such a way that there is an increase of knowledge and a greater depth of understanding. In what other way could the church lay open to the pupil the unfolding of God's plan from Genesis 1:1 to Revelation 22:21 or confront him with the breadth and depth of the Christian life?

Teaching addresses the whole person. All too often we perceive teaching as one dimensional in its approach to life, addressing only the intellect. Teaching stretches far beyond that limited understanding. Consider the genuine joy as students discover meaning in some new dimension of God's truth. How exciting for both teacher and student when, after a period of instruction, the student in a particular moment understands what the passage means and grasps the particular application it has to his life.

THE SCOPE OF TEACHING

What should be taught when making disciples? Should the content of teaching include only the foundational truths of the Christian faith, along with some of the basic skills for spiritual growth and ministry or should there be something more?

In Matthew 28:20, Jesus said that teaching should include "all that I have commanded you." This sets the parameters for the teaching ministry of the church. "All that I have commanded you" includes all the training that Jesus gave His disciples during His public ministry: the good news of salvation, personal and social ethics, the nature and purpose of the church's ministry. But more than that, "all that I have commanded you" may be understood to be the whole of God's Word. If Jesus Christ is not only truly man but also truly God (and He is), He is also the author of all Scripture. Every "jot and tittle" is for our instruction and edification.

The church responds by applying the whole of God's Word to the whole of life— not only to our private and personal lives but to our social and cultural lives as well. Under this mandate, curriculum boundaries would allow for: the study of the unfolding plan of God's redemption both extensively (surveys) and intensively (individual book studies); the study of the church—its mission, doctrine, history, and government; and a study of the Christian life.

In such a world as ours, it is imperative that the Christian be taught to think Christianly. The whole of God's truth is involved in the making of disciples and the whole of God's truth is the direct object of teaching.

THE END OF TEACHING

The infinitive "to keep" in verse 20a comes from a Greek word which occurs sixty times in the New Testament. The characteristic use of the term conveys the idea of observing, fulfilling, or keeping. The KJV translates this term as "observe to do;" the ASV, "to observe;" the NIV, "to obey." Clearly, the intent of our Lord's command is that the content of His teaching is to be more than head knowledge. What Jesus had commanded was to be carried out in each disciple's life.

The teacher has an awesome responsibility. If his task were only one of presenting information, teaching would be comparatively easy. But such is not the case. The teacher's work is not complete until he has done all that he in good conscience can do to encourage the student to commit himself to the truth.

To accomplish this objective, the teacher must pay the price of which thorough study is only a part. An effective teacher asks himself several key questions: How can I direct the student's attention to the lesson? How can I help the student understand truth and apply it to his life? How can I alert the student to his need to respond to the Word of God? Even more important to the teacher's task is spiritual preparation. Without prayer, very little of worth can be accomplished. With prayer, and a heart and mind yielded to God, marvelous things can be done.

Our Lord was quite clear when He said to a small band of disciples, "Go ye therefore, and make disciples of all nations" (Matthew 28:19). He was equally clear when He set forth teaching as one of the primary means by which this is to be done.

■ Adapted from Norman E. Harper, *Making Disciples: Christian Education at the End of the Twentieth Century* (Christian Studies Center, 1981). Used by permission.

Revival

LAW SEVEN

TOPICAL SURVEY

How to Have a Personal Revival

A. W. Tozer

While revivals are usually talked about at the corporate or societal level, they all begin with individuals. One of the spiritual giants in the history of the church addresses the bottom line of individual responsibility.

Get thoroughly dissatisfied with yourself. Complacency is the enemy of spiritual progress. A contented soul is a stagnant soul.

2. Set your face like a flint toward a sweeping transformation of your life. Timid experimenters are tagged for failure before they start. We must throw our whole soul into our desire for God.

3. Put yourself in the way of the blessing. It is a mistake to expect God's help to come as a windfall apart from conditions known and met. There are plainly marked paths which lead straight to the green pastures; let us walk in them. To desire revival, for instance, and at the same time neglect prayer and devotion is to wish one way and walk another.

4. Do a thorough job of repenting. Do not hurry to get it over with. Hasty repentance means shallow spiritual experience and lack of certainty in the whole life. Let godly sorrow do her healing work. Until we allow the consciousness of sin to wound us we will never develop a fear of evil.

5. Make restitution wherever possible. If you owe a debt, pay it, or at least have a frank understanding with your creditor about your intention to pay, so your honesty will be above question. If you have quarreled with anyone, go as far as you can in an effort to achieve reconciliation.

6. Bring your life into accord with such Scriptures as are designed to instruct us in the way of righteousness. An honest man with an open Bible and a pad and pencil is sure to find out what is wrong with him very quickly. I recommend that self-examination be made on our knees, rising to obey God's commandments as they are revealed to us from the Word.

7. Be serious-minded. You can well afford to see fewer comedy shows on TV. Unless you break away from the funny boys, every spiritual impression will continue to be lost to your heart, and that right in your own living room. The people of the world used to go to the movies to escape serious thinking about God. You would not join them there, but you now enjoy spiritual communion with them in your own home. The devil's ideals, moral standards, and mental attitudes are being accepted by you without your knowledge.

8. Deliberately narrow your interests. Too many projects use up time and energy without bringing us near to God.

9. Have faith in God. Begin to expect. Look up toward the throne where your Advocate sits at the right hand of God. All heaven is on your side. God will not disappoint you.

Excerpted from A. W. Tozer, *How To Have a Personal Revival* (Camp Hill, Pennsylvania: Christian Publications, 1983). Used by permission.

When a Brother Stumbles

Charles Stanley

What is our responsibility when a fellow Christian stumbles in sin?
Teachers should be willing and prepared to institute those biblical
mandates concerning restoring a student who has fallen and needs help.

The apostle Paul writes the biblical prescription for forgiving a fallen brother. "Brethren, even if a man is caught in any trespass, you who are spiritual, restore such a one in a spirit of gentleness; each one looking to yourself, lest you too be tempted" (Galatians 6:1, NASB).

Notice Paul's use of the phrase "caught in any trespass." The idea expressed in the original language is one of a surprise, blunder, or fault. In other words, when Christians sin, we do not go out deliberately seeking to transgress. In a moment of weakness or indifference, we yield to or are ensnared by evil. Once the believer has blundered into transgression, the body of Christ has a God-given responsibility to restore the offender. It is a command, not a suggestion. It does not say we are to forgive someone who sins after we have examined the situation to discover guilt or innocence or if the person has suffered long enough for the indiscretion. It says we are to be involved in the restoration process, regardless of the nature of the sin.

The Greek word translated "restore" has medical overtones. The word picture is one of a physician who resets the bones of a broken limb. It portrays the setting straight of what was once crooked.

I believe if we implement the six principles listed below we will be scripturally equipped to assist in the restoration of a brother who has been ambushed or captured by sin.

1. Our first priority is to help the person recognize the failure and the consequences of the decision. The problem is not one of a slight miscue or a momentary lapse; it is a sin in the sight of the Lord. No one can deal with sin unless it is first identified as such. More often than not, the individual knows he has sinned, but he still lives in the tentacles of sin because he has not admitted that his behavior was sinful. Like David, the person must be able to confess, "I have sinned, and done what is evil in Thy sight" (Psalm 51:4).

2. Second, we must help the person acknowledge responsibility for the sin. It is easy to blame sin on somebody else. But even if someone else has been a contributing factor, the individual is still accountable. Helping a brother assume personal culpability for sinful actions is sometimes a difficult but necessary step.

3. Third, we need to lead the person to confess and repent of the sin. By repentance, I mean a change of mind that will result in a true sense of regret and remorse over the sin as well as a deliberate change of behavior. The inner person will realize the grief of disobedience before God and conduct will be positively affected.

4. The fourth principle is one of restitution. Someone who steals something needs to pay it back. Someone who criticizes others in public needs to go to them and ask for forgiveness. Restitution cannot be made for some sins, however. Genuine repentance and confession will have to suffice in those instances. For example, there is no restitution for destroying a person's moral purity. Asking for forgiveness can restore

Christlike fellowship, but it can never fully restore what was lost.

5. A fifth concern in reaching out with forgiveness to the fallen brother is helping him receive God's message through his failure. Although God does not cause us to fail, He can teach us lessons that will keep us from wandering into similar harmful situations.

6. Finally, we need to guide the person who has fallen to respond to God's chastisement with gratitude. Granted, this is not easy, but when the person comprehends God's purpose in such discipline—that he might "share His holiness" (Hebrews 12:10)—he can by an act of his will thank the heavenly Father for His loving correction. Bringing the person to this point protects against the insidious root of bitterness that can spring up in the aftermath of sin.

Our success in attempting to restore a fallen brother or sister will be determined to a great degree by the spirit in which we go about it. And what is the spirit in which we are to restore a fellow Christian? The answer is found in Galatians 6:1.

1. First of all, Paul says we are to approach the guilty one in the spirit of gentleness. More than likely the person is already hurting and as fragile as glass. Human chastisement, judgment, and condemnation would only worsen the individual's plight. Understanding and acceptance—not agreement, but acceptance—are needed instead.

2. Second, we are to forgive and restore with the spirit of humility, recognizing that what happened to the other person could also happen to us. As fellow believers, we must help the individual recognize the sin, assume responsibility for sinful actions, repent of the sin, make restitution when possible, receive gladly the message God is sending through the failure, and thank Him for His loving chastisement. But if we do it with harshness and arrogance, we will only further damage, rather than restore, the brother or sister. We must be careful about our own lives, examining ourselves, knowing that we, too, are vulnerable to all types of temptation and sin.

3. When Paul writes to the Galatians, "Bear one another's burdens, and thus fulfill the law of Christ" (6:2), he adds a third dimension to the restoration process—the spirit of love. Jesus said, "By this all men will know that you are My disciples, if you have love for one another" (John 13:35). Again He said, "This is My commandment, that you love one another, just as I have loved you" (John 15:12). In the passage in Galatians, the word burden means a "heavy load." To bear someone's burden means we are willing to get under the load with him. We are willing to vicariously suffer what he is suffering, to some degree feel what he is feeling. And we are to do this with love.

It should be clear from the Scriptures that we have a Christian responsibility to restore a fallen brother or sister. It should also be clear that this sensitive, delicate issue must be handled with great care, lest we greatly damage our witness to the unbelieving world.

Excerpted from Charles Stanley, *Forgiveness* (Nashville: Oliver-Nelson Books, 1987). Used by permission.

Confronting Sin

Mark R. Littleton

When was the last time you were the only person knowledgeable about, and in a position to address, another Christian's sin? Did you follow through in obedience? You might identify with this author's experience.

As I walked up the sidewalk to my friend's house, my pounding heart seemed nearly deafening. My mouth was dry. My mind raced. My legs quivered, ready to buckle. Something inside me kept saying, "Let it go. Just forget about it. It's nothing. You'll only make him angry."

Three times I stopped and stared at the square panel of light in his window. He knew I was coming over. But he didn't know why. I was coming to talk to him about sin. His sin, which was drinking to excess and trying to hide it from our congregation, was something I'd hoped for months he would overcome. But his wife had told me, "He's getting drunk nearly every day now." He was a good friend. Nearly a year before I'd shared the gospel with him, meeting several mornings a week with him and his wife to have a "quiet time." But that had stopped. And the drinking had started all over again. When I'd spoken with him on several occasions, he'd been resistant, saying, "It's no problem." Or, "I have a hold on it." But it had a hold on him.

Finally, I knocked on his door.

WITH A SIGN OF PEACE

Talking to a Christian about personal sin is not easy. Words like confrontation and altercation zip into our minds, perhaps from previous encounters. But the Scriptures call it restoration (Galatians 6:1). It means speaking to someone about behavior that the Scriptures clearly teach is wrong. Biblical restoration always involves tact, love, compassion, and understanding. It's not coming with a hammer or a sword, but with a handshake and a sign of peace.

Such attempts at restoration never need to be heated or even unfriendly, though they can become that way. I've participated in many that were received with joy. Paul, the great restorer, wrote most of his letters to head off or clear up problems in his churches. Jesus repeatedly told His disciples and others about the need to repent of sin.

Yet, we can almost see Jesus delivering rebuke with tears in His eyes; and as Paul writes, we can almost hear his choking breath as he penned words of fire and life. For them, such restoration was not fun. But it was necessary.

REASONS TO RESTORE

Why is restoration necessary? There are at least three reasons.

First, to preserve a saint's life. James wrote, "Whoever turns a sinner from the error of his way will save him from death and cover a multitude of sins" (5:20). When a brother or sister is committing a sin, he is literally killing himself. He destroys his effectiveness for Christ, his joy, and his fellowship with Him.

In anger, I once said some nasty things to a friend. I went home and sulked, telling myself, *There's no way I'm going to her to apologize!* But the guilt and conflict churned my stomach in hot swirls of emotion. Then my friend graciously came to me

229

and pointed out my sin. I confessed my guilt and reconciliation was effected instantly—between us, and even more importantly, between me and the Lord.

Second, the reason we must restore sinners is to preserve the church. Paul wrote, "Admonish the unruly" (1 Thessalonians 5:14, NASB). Why? Because unruly (sinning) saints can crack a church's foundations. Members become angry and leave because certain behavior is tolerated by the leaders. Others are wounded by the sinner's darts.

In one situation I know of, a teenager's disrespect for a pastor led to all kinds of gossip, anger, backbiting, and confusion in a church. The leaders' unwillingness to confront him and his parents about his behavior caused sin to spread like a stench. A church's external reputation and internal climate are wrecked by saints who sin and don't make amends.

Third, and most important, restoration is necessary to protect God's reputation. When Nathan spoke with David about his sin with Bathsheba, he said, "You have made the enemies of the Lord show utter contempt" (2 Samuel 12:14). When non-Christians observe the repeated sinful behavior of known Christians, they cry, "The church is full of hypocrites." "Christianity is for creeps." "If your Jesus allows this, I don't want your Jesus."

STEPS TO RESTORATION

Scripture contains two important passages that show us how to effect restoration. Let's consider them.

In Matthew 18:15-17, Jesus instructed His disciples, "If your brother sins against you, go and show him his fault, just between the two of you. If he listens to you, you have won your brother over." A whole process is spelled out. But note several points.

One, it's to be done in private. That's critical. Don't air your feelings in the foyer after the morning worship service. Speak with the sinner on his turf in an utterly private place. There's no need to complicate the situation by embarrassing him before his peers.

Next, try to win him. That calls for persuasion, compassion, a pledge of love, and understanding. You're pleading for his soul.

One couple I knew was continually on the brink of divorce. I began meeting with them each morning for Bible study and prayer. Slowly we began to see daylight in their journey through the darkness. Often as they argued and accused, I would begin pleading with them, even with tears, to work it out, to seek Christ, to look to His Word for insight. On one occasion, the husband was so struck by my fervor that he remarked, "Mark cares more about our marriage than we do!"

That hit me. I realized that often it's our caring, our pleading, our fervency, that finally convinces a Christian there is hope. Don't be afraid to pour out your heart. This is no place for a blasé attitude. This is a spiritual battle, and it may take some wrestling to gain a victory. But what if your brother or sister has no desire to repent or apologize? That's why Jesus spelled out a whole process. In that case, we're to find a second impartial observer and take him or her with us as we speak with the person a second time. The observer is not here to agree with us or defend us, but only to hear what's presented and to get all the facts in order.

If the sinning party still won't listen, take it to the church. Can you imagine what happens to a sinning Christian when his whole church is coming to him and saying, "Bill, you can't go on like this. Repent. Jesus loves you. We love you. Don't continue like this and destroy yourself." It has a way of turning people back before it's too late.

Ultimately, though, if a sinning brother or sister refuses to repent, the church is to regard him as a "pagan or a tax collector"; that is, to regard him as an unbeliever. Refuse to accept him as a Christian. This does not mean, however, that we regard him as an enemy, hate him, or try to destroy him. It simply means we cannot recognize him as a Christian or grant to him Christian privileges—such as communion, positions of leadership, or church membership. He may still come to church, though, if he wants to.

GUIDELINES FROM PAUL

Paul gives some further commands in Galatians 6:1: "Brothers, if someone is caught in a sin, you who are spiritual should restore him gently. But watch yourself, or you also may be tempted." Again, note several ideas.

First, approach the sinner gently.

Second, take a long look at yourself. "You who are spiritual" are the confronters. Don't go to confront someone about sin when you have the same problem yourself.

Third, go with the purpose and expectation of restoring. Be clear about that. This isn't a witch hunt. It's a lamb search. You want to bring the sinner back into fellowship.

Fourth, recognize that you're just as susceptible to the sin as he or she is. That is, get rid of the "holier than thou" attitude. You know it's only by the grace of God that you're not caught in the same trespass. Tell the one you're confronting that you recognize this.

Fifth, offer assurance that whatever the sin, it's not unforgivable. There's a way back to spiritual health.

One thing I've discovered with the restoration process is that most Christians who sin are acutely aware they've done wrong. They don't need to be clubbed. They need to be sought with compassion.

BECOMING A LIFESAVER

My friend with the drinking problem resisted me at first. But that evening, as I presented the truths of Scripture and tried to show him how he could be free, his heart melted. He admitted his sin and said, "Help me. I can't beat this thing." A short time later he went to his employer and was enrolled in a hospital program for alcoholics. In a few weeks he was dried out, and he has continued in the faith. Even now I weep as I recall him earnestly telling me that his family's support and my concern restored him to faith and hope.

From *Discipleship Journal* 8, no. 44 (March 1988), pp. 37-39. Used by permission.

God's Plan for Preserving Purity

Luis Palau

God has instituted discipline in the church for the purpose of preserving purity and holiness. If discipline is exercised against one of your students, can you support the process? It could happen!

Church discipline is not a pleasant subject. It is one of the least talked about subjects within the church. Many are afraid to discuss it. We would much rather talk about the "victorious Christian life." But we cannot lead victorious Christian lives until we understand Christian discipline. The more we learn about what God teaches on this subject, the better equipped we will be to handle crises in our personal lives, our families, and our churches.

A PROBLEM AT CORINTH

The New Testament church in Corinth lacked discipline. Paul discovered that the church hadn't properly dealt with sin in its midst. Specifically, we read in 1 Corinthians 5:1 that "there is sexual immorality among you, and of a kind that does not occur even among pagans: A man has his father's wife."

Here was a clear case of disobedience within the church, explicitly forbidden by Old Testament law (Leviticus 18:8), and a case that Paul says would disturb even the heathen. As shocking as this act of immorality was, Paul was even more shocked by the church's complacent attitude toward the sinner. Rather than being grieved by the sin, they were proud and arrogant (1 Corinthians 4:18; 5:2).

Paul was angry! These people were his converts and disciples, and therefore he proceeded to rebuke them. "Now gather the entire church and put this man out of your fellowship," he told them. "Send this man back to Satan's world. Don't allow him to pervert the purity of the church."

But that's cruel, you say. No, it was not cruel. It was done to humiliate the man and to point out his immorality, so that he could repent and be restored to the fellowship. Discipline is not carried out merely to punish, but to awaken people to their sin. It is not carried out in cruelty to destroy, but rather in love to produce conviction, sorrow, repentance, and restoration.

God does not enjoy having to exercise discipline any more than you or I do. We worship a God who wants us to live in victory, and who desires that we be content even in the midst of mounting pressures and problems. Love, joy, and peace are the fruit of his Spirit.

Why, then, aren't his people filled with love, joy, and peace? Because of sin! Sin kills joy. Satan is the murderer of love, joy, and peace (John 8:44). And we are his slaves as long as we persist in making excuses for our sin, and in refusing to seek cleansing and restoration.

Disobedience leads to unhappiness! When a church steps away from the truth, when it compromises God's holy Scriptures, a wall of darkness surrounds the congregation. When a church is obedient, there is love among the members, praises to God our Father, and a sense of happiness in the worship.

DISCIPLINE LEADS TO BROKENNESS

Discipline is a tough issue for a church to deal with correctly. It's unpleasant. Nonetheless, the Bible clearly teaches that the church is to discipline.

What is the purpose of such discipline? Discipline for sin should be done to restore a person's joy. One who commits sin and dishonors the name of the Lord loses his joy and his fullness in Christ, and this cannot be restored to the sinner until there is a period of discipline, brokenness, and repentance.

Again you say, But that's cruel!

Which is more cruel: to permit the situation to deteriorate to gossip, or to take action and attempt to restore the man to the fellowship through biblical discipline, leading to brokenness, repentance, and forgiveness—forgiveness from God, the spouse, the children, and the congregation of Jesus Christ?

FORGIVENESS FOLLOWS BROKENNESS

In Galatians 6:1 we are told to restore our fallen brother in a spirit of gentleness, because we also could be tempted and fall. Just remind yourself that it could happen to you. We are all vulnerable.

If the sinner is prideful and resists the discipline, then obviously there is no forgiveness. As Corrie ten Boom said, "The blood of Jesus never cleansed an excuse." But it does cleanse a confessed sin (1 John 1:7-9). Therefore, a person who is broken and confesses his sin must be forgiven by the church, and the church must reaffirm its love for him. Paul sets the example for the church in Corinth by saying, "If you forgive anyone, I also forgive him" (2 Corinthians 2:10).

SATANIC DESPAIR

Paul goes on in 2 Corinthians to say that forgiveness keeps Satan from gaining an advantage over us (2:10-11). Forgiveness delivers us from what I call "satanic despair." Precisely when someone is repentant and broken, Satan schemes to completely destroy that person, should the church fail to forgive him and quickly restore him to fellowship.

When someone is obviously broken and repentant, the church must stand up and say, "In the name of the Lord Jesus, rejoice! He has forgiven you and we forgive you too." The assurance from such corporate forgiveness brings healing and joy to the entire congregation.

Without this forgiveness, Satan whispers to the repentant person, "You're nothing to that church. They don't love you. Look how broken and miserable you are because of their discipline. You've confessed and asked to be forgiven, but they just want to crush you." Believe me, Satan does a fantastic job of coloring the story, for he is "the father of lies" (John 8:44).

Paul spoke of sorrow that is "godly," (2 Corinthians 7:10) but excessive despair is an opportunity for Satan to bury a person in guilt. Rather than see a man or woman destroyed by Satan, the body of Christ should realize its unique opportunity to build the person up and restore him! Love demands that we allow this person to be free from his haunting past. A free, disciplined, and forgiven person can raise his head and confidently move on, knowing that God does not remember a sin confessed—"Their sins and lawless acts I will remember no more" (Hebrews 10:17). This is the most exciting element of church discipline.

SO WHAT?

Is there anything you need to confess to the Lord Jesus? Do you need to seek his forgiveness? Is there anything you need to confess to someone else (James 5:16)?

Finally, is there anything you need to confess publicly to the elders of your church, to seek their forgiveness for? Our confession of sin should be as public and well-known as the sin we committed.

Elders, is there public sin you are aware of within the church that you have not dealt with biblically? Don't try to justify anyone's disobedience. Don't cover it up. Apply the principles of Matthew 18:15-20:

> If your brother sins against you, go and show him his fault, just between the two of you. If he listens to you, you have won your brother over. But if he will not listen, take one or two others along, so that "every matter may be established by the testimony of two or three witnesses." If he refuses to listen to them, tell it to the church; and if he refuses to listen even to the church, treat him as you would a pagan or a tax collector. I tell you the truth, whatever you bind on earth will be bound in heaven, and whatever you loose on earth will be loosed in heaven. Again, I tell you that if two of you on earth agree about anything you ask for, it will be done for you by my Father in heaven. For where two or three come together in my name, there am I with them.

If the person doesn't repent once these principles are applied, public discipline by the church is in order.

As Jesus said in this passage, "Whatever you bind on earth will be bound in heaven, and whatever you loose on earth will be loosed in heaven." There is authority in the body of Christ, and when we obey the Scriptures concerning church discipline, we are acting with and under authority. We have the sanction of heaven, according to Scripture, and we, through our obedience, allow the Holy Spirit to work with great power.

■ From *Discipleship Journal* 3, no. 4 (July 1983), pp. 17-20. Used by permission.

Revival—Where Does It Begin?

Leonard Ravenhill

Incorrectly, in modern times, revivals often address the unsaved more than the saved. The correctives of a veteran revivalist will help us refocus our attention on the true subjects—and objects— of revival.

Many people express an interest in revival. There are not so many deeply concerned about it, fewer still burdened for it, and even fewer heartbroken for it. Yet, spiritual revival is not an alternative for the nations right now. It is imperative. We misuse the term revival to announce the yearly "revival meeting"—a week's meeting with an evangelist and perhaps a singer. Such a meeting is usually geared to the unsaved. But we cannot revive what has never had life.

Walter Nigg wrote a book entitled *The Heretics,* with this challenging statement: "The history of heresy shows that Christianity is richer in content than its ecclesiastical embodiment. The gospel holds potentialities which have not yet come to the surface."

European believers correctly thought of revival as an awakening, such as the nation-transforming visitation from God through George Whitefield and the Wesleys in England. Or the earthshaking move of the Spirit in New England through Jonathan Edwards, later joined by Whitefield.

True revival is God's coming to the aid of His sick church. Evangelism is that revived church's going to a world dead in sin and, under divine power, pulling down the strongholds of Satan. Any true revival can be proven by the fact that it changed the moral climate of an area or a nation. Perhaps the offense of true revival is that:

- It cannot be organized.
  (The wind bloweth where it listeth.)
- It cannot be subsidized.
  (It does not need financial backing.)
- It cannot be advertised.
  (There is nothing more self-advertising than a fire, and revival is fire from heaven.)
- It cannot be computerized.
  (God alone knows the extent of His power.)
- It cannot be regularized.
  (We cannot lay a theological track on which it can operate.)
- It cannot be rationalized.
  (It is divine mystery beyond finite minds.)
- It cannot be denominationalized.
  (It leaps over doctrinal barriers.)
- It cannot be nationalized.
  (Preachers by the hundreds have been flying to Korea to see what God has done in that country. Most have gasped at the packed churches and returned sad that our mechanical services are so sterile.)

A recent television newscast reported that a major denomination has recommended that homosexuals be admitted to the ministry on the condition that they act wholesomely! Here is an attempt to sanctify iniquity. It reminds me of a scripture—"the iniquity of holy things" (Exodus 28:38). Will the men who want this monstrous and outrageous sin covered up allow prostitution in the churches—as long as the prostitutes tithe? We need a revival among the preachers that will purge the conscience from dead works and cause us to serve the living God.

Alas, many professing His name are walking in theological leg irons. Like Lazarus, we are raised from the dead but bound and gagged with graveclothes—the graveclothes of tradition and the bondage of man-made creeds. We are selling our birthright—our access to the throne of God—for a mess of pottage called "submission," or the fear of men. I am not trying to incite rebellion in the flock. No, I am trying to stir up the gift that is within us to reach out to the One who "ever liveth to make intercession for us."

On that blazing throne sits One who is the Light of the World. When we stand in splendid isolation before Him whose eyes are as a flame of fire, who will dare to "look full in His wonderful face"? Most of us will turn away from His flaming holiness, embarrassed that we were so accepted in a world that could not accept Him. Looking back from the throne over the path of our earthly pilgrimage, "the things of earth will look strangely dim in the light of His glory and grace."

At that awesome time of judgment, we will find that "the harvest is past, the summer is ended, and we are not saved" from burning humiliation, as untold billions of souls watch while our life's work is judged and a verdict given by the infallible Judge. Will this crisis find us with swords unbloodied in spiritual warfare? Will it find us guilty of violating His commandments, not by intentional opposition, but by sheer neglect or habitual sloth? The writer to the Hebrews repeatedly speaks of "today." Well, this is our "today." How long will it last? Now is the time to correct the slack in our faulty obedience and slim sacrifice.

I am convinced that the church (the body of truly regenerated believers) has never faced a greater challenge from the powers of darkness than she does today. We need a baptism of honesty in the courts of the Lord. Honesty means truth, and truth can be painful.

Let the fires go out in the boiler room of the church, and the place will still look smart and clean, but it will be cold. The prayer room in the church is the boiler room for its spiritual life. When holy passion has ceased to move the intercessors in the prayer room, coldness ensues, power is lost, and mortification sets in. The place still looks viable, but it is no longer a birthplace of souls.

I am often asked to pray for the healing of the nation. I am praying for the healing of the church. Then the healing of America, Britain, and other nations will follow. As the church goes, so goes the world!

■ Excerpted from Leonard Ravenhill, *Revival God's Way* (Minneapolis: Bethany House Publishers, 1983). Used by permission.

Whatever Became of Sin?

Charles W. Colson

Living in a culture that winks at sin has caused the church to adopt some non-biblical attitudes—and practices. One who has seen sin at the highest levels of government calls us back to a biblical perspective.

For most of us, the word "repentance" conjures up images of medieval monks in sackcloth and ashes or Old Testament prophets rending their garments in anguish. Or we see repentance as something someone does who is "really wicked."

But repentance is much more than self-flagellation, more than regret, more than deep sorrow for past sins; and it applies to everyone. The biblical word for repentance is *metanoia* in the original Greek. *Meta* means "change" and *noia* means "mind," so literally it means "a change of mind." One church scholar describes it as "that mighty change in mind, heart, and life, wrought by the spirit of God."

Thus, repentance is replete with radical implications, for a fundamental change of mind not only turns us from the sinful past, but transforms our life plan, values, ethics, and actions as we begin to see the world through God's eyes rather than ours. That kind of transformation requires the ultimate surrender of self.

The call to repentance—individual and corporate—is one of the most consistent themes of Scripture. The Old Testament contains vivid accounts of kings and prophets, priests and people falling before God to plead for mercy and promising to change. The demand for repentance is clear in God's commands to Moses, and its brokenhearted reality and passion flow through David's eloquent prayer of contrition. It is the consistent refrain of the prophets.

Repentance is the keynote of the New Testament as well. It is John the Baptist's single message: "Repent, for the kingdom of heaven is near." And according to Mark's Gospel, "Repent and believe the good news" was among Jesus' first public words. And His last instructions to His disciples before the Ascension included the directive that "repentance and forgiveness of sins will be preached in His name to all nations." All told, the words "repent" or "repentance" appear more than fifty times in the New Testament.

Repentance is an inescapable consequence of regeneration, an indispensable part of the conversion process that takes place under the convicting power of the Holy Spirit. But repentance is also a continuing state of mind. We are warned, for example, to repent before partaking of communion. Also, believers "prove their repentance by their deeds." Without a continuing repentant attitude—a persistent desire to turn away from our own nature and seek God's nature—Christian growth is impossible. Loving God is impossible.

If all this is true, then, some may ask, "Why is repentance so seldom preached and so little understood?" I believe there are three reasons.

THE APPEAL OF MODERN EVANGELISM

Noted church historian J. Edwin Orr sums up the first: The appeal of modern evangelism is "not for repentance but for enlistment."

Repentance can be a threatening message—and rightly so. The gospel must be the bad news of the conviction of sin before it can be the good news of redemption. Because the message is unpalatable for many middle-class congregations preoccupied with protecting their affluent lifestyles, many pastors endowed with a normal sense of self-preservation tiptoe warily round the subject.

The result of all this is a watered-down message that, in large part, accounts for today's epidemic spread of easy believism, Christianity without cost, or "cheap grace" as German martyr Dietrich Bonhoeffer so aptly labeled it a generation ago—grace in which "no contrition is required, still less any real desire to be delivered from sin . . . a denial of the living Word of God, in fact, a denial of the incarnation."

UNWILLINGNESS TO FACE PERSONAL SIN

The second reason repentance is so ignored or misunderstood comes much closer to home, as I have discovered: Often we are simply unwilling or unable to accept the reality of personal sin and therefore to accept our need for repentance.

Why is it so hard for us to see our own sin? That this has always been this way is eloquently illustrated by King David.

Soon after he was enthroned, David committed not only the sin of adultery with Bathsheba, but also the sin of murder by having her husband sent to certain death in battle. Though he was described as a man after God's own heart and administered justice and righteousness, David was blind to his own sin. He could not see what he had done until the prophet Nathan, sent by God, described the sin in parable form, attributing it to someone else. Nathan asked David to judge the man, which David did: death. Only then did Nathan tell David that it was his own sin. What he was quick to judge in others, David was unable to see in himself.

"ABSENCE" OF SIN IN CULTURE

This leads us to the third reason for our shallow understanding of repentance: Our culture has written sin out of existence. Even Christians who should understand the basic truth that all are heirs of Adam's fall and thus all are sinners are influenced, often blinded, by humanist values.

Humanism began in the Garden when the tempter invited Eve to be "like God." Ever since it has encouraged us to believe what our sinful nature wants us to believe— that we are good, getting better through science and education, and can through our own efforts become perfect, masters of our own fate. We can be our own god.

In recent decades popular political and social beliefs have all but erased the reality of personal sin from our national consciousness. Take, for example, the passionately advanced argument that society, not the individual, is responsible for the evil in our midst: individuals commit crimes because they are forced to, not because they choose to. Poverty, racial oppression, slums, hunger—these are the real culprits; the wrongdoer is in reality the victim.

No one political camp has a monopoly on perpetuating this myth. Politicians tell people what they want to hear, and people like to be told they are really "good." So speech lines like these are sure-fire applause-getters. But good politics can make bad theology; and when we begin to believe our own press releases, we become victims of our own delusions.

Whatever became of sin? Karl Menninger's startling book title and theme is the most timely question anyone could ask of the church today. The answer lies within each of us, but to find it we must come face to face with who we really are. This is a difficult process. That hidden self is buried deep inside our hearts, and, as Jeremiah warned, the human heart is deceitful above all things. Confronting that true self is an excruciating discovery.

Having been at the center of the biggest political upheaval of this century, I've had my sins—real and imagined—spread mercilessly across the front pages around the world, re-enacted in living color on movie and TV screens, and dissected in hundreds of books. As a result, I am often asked which of my Watergate perfidies causes me the greatest remorse.

My invariable reply, "None. My deepest remorse is for the hidden sins of my heart which are far worse," either puzzles or infuriates the media.

But it is an honest answer. My Watergate wrongs could be explained (though not justified) as political zealotry or expedience, misplaced idealism, blind obedience to higher authority, or even capitulation to the natural temptation of the human will, which Neitzsche said seeks power over others above all else.

As I lay in prison and watched the events of my own life parade before my eyes, I became aware of this painful reality of the human heart and saw myself: I was a sinner and my sin manifested itself in individual acts of my own making. And worst of all, I had delighted in it.

Indeed, that is where the real battle is being fought. It is not between "good" people and "bad" people, like a game of cops and robbers; it is not between "good" governments and "bad," like the U.S. and the Soviet Union. It is not being fought for mere national or international stakes. The war to end all wars is a battle for eternal stakes between spiritual forces—and it is being waged in you and in me.

When we truly smell the stench of sin within us, it drives us helplessly and irresistibly to despair. But God has provided a way for us to be freed from the evil within: it is through the door of repentance. When we truly comprehend our own nature, repentance is no dry doctrine, no frightening message, no morbid form of self-flagellation. It is, as the early church fathers said, a gift God grants which leads to life. It is the key to the door of liberation, to the only real freedom we can ever know.

■ From *Loving God* by Charles Colson (Grand Rapids: Zondervan Publishing House, 1987). © 1983, 1987 by Charles W. Colson. Used by permission of Zondervan Publishing House.

Sin

Philip Yancey

Rarely does a well-known author bare his own soul and discuss his own personal temptations and struggles to remain pure. With discretion, teachers can help students by being transparent and vulnerable about sin.

We find ourselves in the schizophrenic position of ignoring the most obvious fact about human behavior, the fact of sin. As I reflect on my own pilgrimage of faith, I find that it has mirrored the schizophrenia of the larger culture. Sometimes I am dominated by sin consciousness, sometimes I rebel vigorously against it, but most often I avoid it completely. Yet always I have been plagued by a nagging, underlying sense that I must somehow come to terms with this word that shows up on so often in Scripture.

Sin as an abstract idea teaches very little. Sinners themselves teach much, and perhaps for that reason the Bible expresses in story form most of what it says about sin. And to learn about my own sin, I had to begin by tracing its progress in my life. I had to identify my sin—not just a stray sin here or there, but patterns of sin that keep breaking out. Here are a few sins from my long list:

Deceit. I am ashamed to admit it, but I have struggled with a consistent pattern of deceit. Earlier, justifying my deceit as a creative way to oppose "the system," I would engage in such shenanigans as mailing all utility bill payments without postage stamps (causing the utility companies to pay postage, until the Postal Service wised up and stopped delivering such mail) and subscribing to record clubs in order to tape record the records and send them back for a refund. Over time, plagued by a guilty conscience, I cut out such practices, but I still recognize a deep temptation to rely on deceit when I feel trapped.

Permanent discontent. You may not find this one on any biblical lists of sins, but this root attitude affects me in many sinful ways. Years of working as an editor gave me an editor's personality that is never satisfied. I always want to strike out words, rearrange sentences, crumple up whole first drafts. While such dyspepsia can serve a worthwhile purpose in editing, in life it does not. I find myself editing my wife's behavior, and my friends'. I constantly yearn for what I cannot have and cannot be. Mainly, I make myself nearly impervious to that spirit the Bible calls joy.

Hypocrisy. All Christians fight this sin to some degree (there I go again, rationalizing), but writers perhaps more than most. I write about leprosy patients in India, and about the extraordinary humility and sacrifice of missionaries I have visited there—but I write from the comfort of an air-conditioned office, with strains of classical music filling the room. How do I live with that disparity? How should I?

Greed. Do you know of any ministry other than writing that has a one-to-one relationship between ministry and income? Each person I "reach" in a book means more money in my pocket. Need I detail the dangers of mixed motives that can result?

Egotism. Again, a most embarrassing admission I would much prefer to leave off my list of sins. Like every other author and speaker, I begin with the rather audacious assumption that I have a viewpoint worth listening to. If I did not believe that, I would not go through the painful process of writing. The danger of pride rides with every thought, every sentence, every word.

You will note that my list of sins excludes many overt ones such as child abuse, drunkenness, and adultery. I am not tempted toward those sins, and that fact offers my first clue into the nature of sin. Sin strikes at the point of greatest vulnerability.

I spend my days secluded in an office, away from people, susceptible to an introvert's self-absorption. The sins of discontent, egotism, and greed are internal sins. They grow like mold in dark, moist corners of the mind and psyche, nourished by slight rejections, mild paranoia, and loneliness—the precise occupational hazards of every writer.

A brash public figure such as quarterback Jim McMahon or comedian Joan Rivers will face a different set of temptations. And those who depend on the successful preening of their bodies for a living will likely fall at different points; adultery constantly tempts them, as Hollywood divorce rates easily prove. Similarly, while a poor man may struggle mostly with envy, a rich man battles greed.

We who battle "internal sins" can easily think our sins somehow more respectable than more blatant sins such as adultery and drunkenness. The moment we entertain such thoughts, we fall into an even deeper hole. I have attended meetings of Alcoholics Anonymous and have never met a recovering alcoholic who denied his or her own sinfulness; but I have met many Christians who find it difficult to confess their own sins. I know such Christians well, for I am one.

Malcolm Muggeridge expressed the danger this way: "It is precisely when you consider the best in man that you see there is in each of us a hard core of pride or self-centeredness which corrupts our best achievements and blights our best experiences. It comes out in all sorts of ways—in the jealousy which spoils our friendships, in the vanity we feel when we have done something pretty good, in the easy conversion of love into lust, in the meanness which makes us depreciate the efforts of other people, in the distortion of our own judgment by our own self-interest, in our fondness for flattery and our resentment of blame, in our self-assertive profession of fine ideals which we never begin to practice."

We can quickly work up ire against the decay of our society—witness the furor over abortion and violence and pornography and other external sins—but unless we also come to terms with our own private sins, we will have missed the message of the gospel. If you ever doubt that, simply turn to the Sermon on the Mount, in which Jesus painted with one brush lust and adultery, hatred and murder.

I once saw in a medical textbook side-by-side photographs of two sets of lungs. The lungs on the left were a brilliant glossy pink, so shiny and smoothly textured they could have been taken from a newborn. In stark contrast, the lungs next to them looked as if they had been used to clean a chimney. Black sediment coated them, clogging all the delicate membranes designed to capture oxygen molecules. The photo caption explained that the lungs on the left had been removed during the autopsy of a Wyoming farmer; those on the right came from a resident of a factory town who had chain-smoked all his life.

I cannot comprehend how any doctor who has seen such lungs, side by side, could ever smoke again. And I remind myself of that image whenever I think about sin. What those impurities do to a person's lungs, sin does to the spiritual life. It retards growth, ravages health, chokes off the supply of new life.

I think back to the sins I have mentioned. What effect to do they have on my own spiritual health?

Deceit. What would happen if I ignored warning signs and consistently yielded to promptings toward deceit? No one—not my neighbors, not my wife—could fully trust me. I would become a sad and lonely recluse, isolated by my own duplicity.

Permanent discontent. I have already said what this tendency produces: an instinctive resistance to joy. It also blocks out gratitude, the emotion doctors judge most nourishing to health.

Hypocrisy. Think of the worst hypocrite you know. Do I want to end up like that? Could anyone suggest that a person is better off for hypocrisy, that personal growth is encouraged and not stunted by this sin?

Greed. I know well what greed does to me. When I write, it changes the questions I ask from *Is this thought true? Does it have value?* to *Will it sell?*

Egotism. I battle it even at this moment. Should I really risk exposure in an article about sin? Should I write about my "spiritual disciplines" instead? Or will the strokes I get for honesty outweigh the criticism from those who question my spiritual maturity? Unchecked egotism would ultimately make me a manipulative bore.

Each of my sins, those I have mentioned and those secret ones I would not dare mention, represent a grave danger to my spiritual health. If I give in to any one of them as a consistent pattern, I will suffer grave loss. My spirit will shrivel and atrophy, like the lung tissue of the chain-smoker.

The more I see my sins in this light, the more I see beyond the harshness of God's punishments. I find myself gazing into the grieving eyes of a parent whose children are destroying themselves. He responds to our sins with punishment and forgiveness, which may seem opposites. But, paradoxically, both have exactly the same purpose: to break the stranglehold of sin and make wholeness possible. He offers healing; we choose the cancer.

I confess that it has taken me many years to learn to trust God. The kind of sins and the type of authority I encountered as a child proved untrustworthy. But through fits and starts of rebellion, apathy, and occasional obedience, I have learned that God himself can be trusted. I can trust him with my health, and I can trust him with my sins. He welcomes me. As Jesus said, applying the doctor image to himself, "It is not the healthy who need a doctor, but the sick. I have not come to call the righteous, but sinners to repentance."

At times, of course, I do not trust him. Sometime today, sometime tomorrow, I will recreate the original rebellion of Eden and act by my standards and my desires, and not God's. God cannot overlook such behavior; it must be accounted for, as it was with Adam and Eve. But in that reckoning he aims not to destroy but to heal. No surgeon who wills the health of a patient can effect it without some pain.

■ From *Christianity Today* 31, no. 4 (March 6, 1987), pp. 30-34. Used by permission.

Preparing for Personal Revival

Life Action Ministries

When you're ready for a penetrating and in-depth searching of your own heart and ways, work through this article. Use it as a stimulus for bringing a new commitment to holiness into the classroom—YOURS!

The questions on the next two pages are designed to reveal specific areas of spiritual need in our lives. These areas must be dealt with in preparation for personal and corporate revival.

STEPS OF ACTION

1. Pray the prayer of the psalmist: "Search me, O God, and know my heart: try me, and know my thoughts: and see if there be any wicked way in me, and lead me in the way everlasting" (Psalm 139:23-24).
2. Be totally honest as you answer each question.
3. Agree with God about each need He reveals in your life. Confess each sin, with the willingness to make it right and forsake it.
4. Praise God for His cleansing and forgiveness.
5. Renew your mind and rebuild your life through meditation and practical application of the Word of God.
6. Review the questions periodically to remain sensitive to your need for revival.

1. GENUINE SALVATION (2 Corinthians 5:17)
- Was there ever a time in my life that I genuinely repented of my sin?
- Have I placed all my trust in Jesus Christ alone to save me?
- Have I completely surrendered to Jesus Christ as the Lord of my life?

2. GOD'S WORD (Psalm 119:97; 119:140)
- Do I love to read and meditate on the Word of God?
- Are my personal devotions consistent and meaningful?
- Do I practically apply God's Word to my everyday life?

3. HUMILITY (Isaiah 57:15)
- Am I quick to recognize and agree with God when I have sinned?
- Am I quick to admit to others when I am wrong?
- Can I rejoice at others' successes even when mine go unnoticed?
- Do I esteem all others as better than myself?

4. OBEDIENCE (Hebrews 13:17; 1 Samuel 15:22)
- Do I consistently obey what I know God wants me to do?
- Do I consistently obey the authorities God has placed over my life?

5. PURE HEART (1 John 1:9)
- Do I confess my sin by name?
- Do I confess and forsake sin quickly as God or others reveal it?
- Am I willing to give up all sin for God?

6. CLEAR CONSCIENCE (Acts 24:16)
- Do I consistently seek forgiveness from those I wrong or offend?

•Is my conscience clear with every man?

7. PRIORITIES (Matthew 6:33)
- Does my schedule reveal that God is first in my life?
- Does my checkbook reveal that God is first in my life?
- Is serving my family second only to serving God ?

8. VALUES (Colossians 3:12)
- Do I love what God loves and hate what God hates?
- Do I value highly the things that please God?
- Are my affections and goals fixed on eternal values?

9. SACRIFICE (Philippians 3:7-8)
- Am I willing to sacrifice anything to see God move in my life and church?
- Is my life characterized by genuine sacrifice for the cause of Christ?

10. SPIRIT CONTROL (Galatians 5:22-25; Ephesians 5:18-21)
- Am I allowing Jesus to be Lord of every area of my life?
- Am I allowing the Holy Spirit to "fill" (control) my life each day?
- Is there consistent evidence of the "fruit of the Spirit" in my life?

11. "FIRST LOVE" (Philippians 1:21, 23)
- Am I as much in love with Jesus as I have ever been?
- Am I thrilled with Jesus, making Him the continual object of my love?

12. MOTIVES (Acts 5:29; Matthew 10:28)
- Am I more concerned about God's opinion than I am man's?
- Would I serve God faithfully even if nobody ever noticed?

13. MORAL PURITY (Ephesians 5:3-4)
- Do I avoid anything that could stimulate morally impure thoughts?
- Are my conversation and behavior pure and above reproach?

14. FORGIVENESS (Colossians 3:12-13)
- Do I seek to resolve conflicts in relationships as soon as possible?
- Am I quick to forgive those who wrong me or hurt me?

15. SENSITIVITY (Matthew 5:23-24)
- Am I sensitive to the conviction and promptings of God's Spirit?
- Do I respond quickly in humility to the conviction of God's Spirit?

16. EVANGELISM (Romans 9:3; Luke 24:46-48)
- Do I have a burden for lost souls?
- Do I consistently witness for Christ?

17. PRAYER (1 Timothy 2:1)
- Am I faithful in praying for the needs of others?
- Do I pray specifically for revival in my life, my church, and our nation?

From *Spirit of Revival* 18, no. 1 (Special Edition), pp. 37-39. © Life Action Ministries, Buchanan, Michigan 49107. Used by permission.

How I Prepare Myself for Worship

Jack Hayford

Do those who teach pray regularly, in creative ways, for their class? Following the examples presented here by a prayerful pastor, any teacher can radically alter the impact of time spent in the classroom.

When I regularly engage in three particular forms of prayer, I develop an attitude conducive to leading worship. When I was a boy, each Friday night my father would give me a list of chores for Saturday. He usually worked on Saturday and wouldn't arrive home until after four o'clock. But then he'd walk with me and examine the work I'd done. He was a perfectionist, although not an unkind man. He had been in the Navy where everything was shipshape. So, he'd examine my yard work carefully. If I left a couple of leaves in a flower bed, he'd just point, and I'd know to go over and pick them up. If he saw a weed I'd missed, he'd point it out.

For me this was a positive experience. I loved my dad, and I wanted to do well for him. When he looked at what I'd done, I wanted him to be happy. So when he pointed things out that I'd missed, I didn't mind. I would have done those things had I seen them, but I saw them only when he pointed them out.

King David wrote, "Search me, O Lord, and know my heart. Try my thoughts and see if there be some wicked way and lead me in the way everlasting." When it comes to preparing myself for worship, that's my desire as well. I want my Heavenly Father to walk with me through the garden of my heart and see if I've missed anything.

CLEANSING PRAYER

I do this by regularly engaging in cleansing prayer. This is different from my daily devotions; it's more intense. Sometimes I feel like I need a thorough cleaning, like a car radiator periodically needs to be flushed. It usually happens about once a month. I take a day and devote it to prayer and self-examination.

I don't have a specific agenda. I usually prostrate myself and "call on the Lord," as the psalms put it. I'm not loud, but since I'm alone in a closed room, I feel free to speak aloud. I try to let God stir within me. I don't think I'm finished just because I feel stirred or teary-eyed. I'm ultimately looking for a new perspective on myself, a revelation of pride or self-centeredness, or an insight into what God would have me do next in ministry.

During one of these cleansing prayers, for instance, I was feeling a vague hollowness. I couldn't put my finger on a glaring sin, but eventually I realized I felt empty because I had been squandering my free time. It wasn't an earth-shattering revelation, but I had to acknowledge that I had been watching an excessive amount of television.

I see nothing intrinsically wrong with TV. It's just that there are few constraints to watching it. And it doesn't demand anything of me. In short, if I watch it too much, I begin to get lazy. I also enjoy reading novels and playing basketball, and these are activities that truly refresh me. I felt like the Holy Spirit was prompting me to prune this form of sloth to allow me to nurture better activities. So, regular cleansing prayer keeps my spiritual garden in order. It helps me maintain attitudes that assist me in worship.

PRAYING THROUGH THE SANCTUARY

For me, Sunday morning starts on Saturday night, and Saturday night begins with a special form of prayer. Almost every Saturday night about 7:00 or 8:00, I go to the church, walk through the sanctuary, lay hands on each chair in the room, and pray. Sometimes I'll walk down every row, sometimes I'll go down every other, but I'll let my hand at least slide over every seat. Once in a while, I'll sing a hymn or chorus as I walk. Sometimes I'll do this alone, other times with a few church leaders. Praying through the sanctuary usually takes about fifteen to twenty minutes, but it makes a profound difference in the next day's service. Specifically, it does three things.

1. I become open to God's power. Although God is present with me at all times, when I acknowledge his presence and get in touch with his power, I become more dependent on him.

As I walk along, I might pray, "Lord, you've given me gifts as a speaker. But I also know I can't touch all those people where they need to be touched. Only your Spirit can touch their spirits. I ask you to do that tomorrow."

Sometimes I will so feel the presence of God, I'll be moved to tears. Other times I won't feel a thing. At such times, I go to the back of the sanctuary afterward, look over the room, and pray, "Lord, I'm glad you're here, even though I don't feel one thing. And I'm depending on you being here tomorrow."

2. I allow the Spirit to lead. As I pray through the sanctuary, I'm also asking the Holy Spirit, "What is the one thing you most want to do tomorrow?" By this time, we have the essential outline of the service put together, but without the final details. So, it's a time when we can still adjust and decide which element of the service we will highlight. That decision, then, flows from this prayer time.

In our tradition, a "word of prophecy" is a message from God for the present moment. So sometimes as I'm praying this prayer and walking along, I literally will feel grief for people who have been bereaved. Another time I'll feel weepy for sick people. Yet another time, I'll become angry at Satan's attacks that have divided homes, abused children, or encouraged drug abuse.

I believe these feelings are more than coincidence; they're burdens the Spirit gives me. Naturally, they arise out a complex set of factors: what I've been reading, who I've been talking with, what I've just seen on the news. But in the end, I believe the Spirit focuses these concerns and gives me a specific emphasis that should be woven into the next day's service.

Often, based on this experience, I will return home and rewrite the introduction to my sermon or the opening remarks of the service. I'm not talking about changing radically any part of worship at this point. It's more a matter of bringing an emphasis to certain parts.

People have told me I have a knack for opening sermons, for getting people's attention. If that's true, I attribute it to these times when I walk through the sanctuary, pray, and literally place my hands on the chairs where individuals will be sitting the next day, spiritually standing with them, identifying with their lives and need.

3. I impart a blessing to people. I also believe that in some personal way I impart a blessing to people by touching the seats and praying. It's not magic. I believe the Holy Spirit uses physical means (such as human touch or bread and grape juice, for instance) to communicate himself to others. I don't speculate on how God does it, and I strongly guard against the superstition such a truth can breed. But I've found God often integrates the visible and invisible realms to communicate himself.

We regularly receive letters from people who have visited our service. They say that as soon as they walked in the door, something began happening within them. They immediately sensed the presence of the Lord. What changes their life is not the smooth service or dynamic preaching, but their conviction that God was present when they were here. I believe our Saturday night prayers are part of the reason people feel that way on Sunday morning.

In the same way, the night before a baptismal service, I'll often go to the baptistery, get down on my knees to reach into it, and stir the water with my hands as I pray. I believe the Lord wants to make every baptistery like the pool of Bethesda—a place where people are delivered from the crippling effects of sin. There is, of course, no handy formula, no set prayer that will guarantee spiritual results. Praying over the chairs on Saturday night is not a third ordinance. But for me, it has been a practice that has borne spiritual fruit on Sunday morning.

PRAYING THROUGH THE SERMON

On Sunday morning, like many pastors, I pray in preparation for worship. And this prayer takes a different form still: I pray through the sermon. Sometimes I look at notes as I do it, but most of the time I simply think the thoughts of the sermon and pray about each one.

This has a homiletic aim, of course. It's one way to get the sermon firmly fixed in my mind. But for me the spiritual goal is more important. I liken the process to Elijah stacking the wood at the altar. What I'm doing in my study is stacking wood, and I'm asking for the fire of the Lord to come down upon the message and the congregation. I often pray something like, "Lord, I want to enter the service with my thoughts fresh and clear. And especially I want you to glow within me."

Often it's during this prayer that a fire for the sermon is ignited within me. One Sunday I was praying through my sermon based on the woman at the well. The subject was missions, and the main text was Jesus' statement: "Whoever drinks this water will never thirst again." I was feeling a little empty because it seemed such an obvious thing that people need Jesus to never thirst spiritually again. Ninety-eight percent of those attending the service already believed in Christ, so I didn't want this to be a sermon only to people outside of Christ.

As I was praying, suddenly I was stirred with the thought that many in the body of Christ, even though they know him, still go back and drink at the old watering holes. They find, of course, that it's no more satisfying than before. But the reason they go back is because they've become preoccupied with their own thirst. If they would seek their satisfaction by satisfying other people's thirst, they wouldn't be thirsty for the things that used to attract them.

I can't convey in print what a difference that made in the service, but it became a powerful point in the message. It helped people identify with the woman at the well and to recommit themselves to satisfying others' needs and not just their own.

Whether in preparation for preaching or teaching, I have found that the absence of prayer can make a marked difference in the spiritual and practical results of the instruction which I offer.

■ From *Leadership* 11, no. 3 (Summer 1990), pp. 80-85. Used by permission.

The Morning Watch

Andrew Murray

Some deep thoughts here on time spent alone with God—the morning watch—by one who dwelt in His presence. Has your morning watch lost its fervency? Its vitality? Its passion? You may find the reason here.

It is in the closet, in the morning watch, that our spiritual life is both tested and strengthened. There is the battlefield where it is to be decided every day whether God is to have all, whether our life is to be absolute obedience. If we truly conquer there, getting rid of ourselves into the hands of our Almighty Lord, the victory during the day is sure. It is there, in the inner chamber, where proof is to be given as to whether we really delight in God, and make it our aim to love Him with our whole heart, or not.

Let this, then, be our first lesson: The presence of God is the chief thing in our devotions. To meet God, to give ourselves to His holy will, to know that we are pleasing to Him, to have Him give us our orders, to lay His hand upon us, and say to us, "Go in this thy strength"—it is when the soul learns that this is what is to be found in the morning watch, day by day, that we shall learn to long for it and delight in it.

Let us speak of the reading of God's Word, as part of what occupies us there. With regard to this, I have more than one thing I wish to say.

1. Unless we beware, the Word, which is meant to point us to God, may actually intervene and hide Him from us.

The mind may be occupied and interested and delighted at what it finds, and yet because this is more head knowledge than anything else, it may bring little good to us. If it does not lead us to wait on God, to glorify Him, to receive His grace and power for sweetening and sanctifying our lives, it becomes a hindrance instead of help.

2. Only by the teaching of the Holy Ghost can we get at the real meaning of what God means by His Word, and that the Word will really reach into our inner life, and work in us.

The Father in heaven, who gave us His Word from heaven, with its divine mysteries and message, has given us His Holy Spirit in us, to explain and internally appropriate that Word. The Father wants us each time to ask that He teach us by His Spirit. He wants us to bow in a meek, teachable frame of mind, and believe that the Spirit will, in the hidden depth of our heart, make His Word live and work. He wants us to remember that the Spirit is given us that we should be led by Him, should walk after Him, should have our whole life under His rule, and that therefore He cannot teach us in the morning unless we honestly give up ourselves to His leading. But if we do this and patiently wait on Him, not to get new thoughts, but to get the power of the Word in our heart, we can count upon His teaching. Let your closet be the classroom, let your morning watch be the study hour in which your relation of entire dependence on and submission to the Holy Spirit's teaching is proved to God.

3. Study God's Word in the spirit of unreserved surrender to obey.

You know how often Christ, and His apostles in their Epistles, speak of hearing and not doing. If you accustom yourself to study the Bible without an earnest and very definite purpose to obey, you are getting hardened in disobedience.

Never read God's will concerning you without honestly giving up yourself to do it at once, and asking for grace to do so. God has given us His Word, to tell us what He wants us to do and what grace He has provided to enable us to do it; how sad to think it a pious thing just to read that Word without any earnest effort to obey it! May God keep us from this terrible sin!

Let us make it a sacred habit to say to God, "Lord, whatever I know to be Thy will, I will at once obey." Ever read with a heart yielded up in willing obedience.

4. Read God's Word with a deep desire to know all His will. I have here spoken of such commands as we already know, and as are easily understood. But, remember, there are a great many commands to which your attention may never have been directed, or others of which the application is so wide and unceasing that you have not taken it in. If there are things which appear difficult, commands which look too high, or for which you need a divine guidance to tell you how to carry them out—and there are many such—let them drive you to seek a divine teaching. It is not the test that is easiest and most encouraging that brings most blessing, but the text, whether easy or difficult, which throws you most upon God. God would have you "filled with the knowledge of His will in all wisdom and spiritual understanding;" it is in the closet this wonderful work is to be done. Do remember, it is only when you know that God is telling you to do a thing that you feel sure He gives the strength to do it. It is only as we are willing to know all God's will that He will from time to time reveal more of it to us and that we will be able to do it all.

What a power the morning watch may be in the life of one who makes a determined resolve to meet God there to renew the surrender to absolute obedience, humbly and patiently to wait on the Holy Spirit to be taught all God's will and to receive the assurance that every promise given him in the Word will infallibly be made true!

■ Taken from *The School of Obedience* by Andrew Murray. Moody Bible Institute of Chicago. Moody Press. Used by permission. (Public domain.)

How to Revive Your Quiet Time

Hannelore Bozeman

Teacher, can you share with your students what to do when they meet with God? Here's a discussion of numerous spiritual disciplines which can be incorporated with profit into a devotional time with God.

SEEK GOD WITH DETERMINATION

Resist the temptation to quit your devotions when they become dry. Instead, set aside extra time for the Lord, even if it means giving up some television, a meal, or some sleep.

God repeatedly commands His people to turn to Him with all our hearts. He is the Lord of the universe, waiting for us to humble ourselves. When we come near to God, He will come near to us (James 4:8).

We can express our humility outwardly by kneeling or even prostrating ourselves before Him. Such outward actions, though never a substitute for true devotion, often affect our attitudes and can help us focus on experiencing God Himself.

Putting away all excuses for spiritual slackness, we can ask Him for forgiveness and tell Him we want to seek Him with all our hearts, even if we do not feel like it.

2. ASK GOD TO SEARCH YOUR HEART

A period of dry devotions can be a warning sign that spiritual clutter has piled up. We need to open the door to the attic and pray, "Search me, O God, and know my heart; test me and know my anxious thoughts. See if there is any offensive way in me, and lead me in the way everlasting" (Psalm 139:23-24). Then we need to listen patiently for God to reveal the clutter.

Jesus warns us of three sins that choke the Word of God in our hearts: the worries of this life keep us from trusting God; the deceitfulness of wealth tempts us to think we don't need Him; and the desire for other things distracts us from our love for Jesus (cf. Mark 4:19).

3. SEEK TO KNOW GOD

In each generation those who focus on God, who hunger to know Him, stand out as spiritual giants. But God's call to know Him extends to all believers, regardless of time pressures and obligations. The apostle Paul not only traveled frequently, founded numerous churches, and wrote half of the New Testament, but also supported himself by tent-making—yet his prayer life was constant. David was a busy king, but he still sought God constantly and his prayers—recorded in the psalms—bless us today. Jesus ministered to people all day long but still found time for an extensive prayer life.

Begin where you are. Ask God to give you great hunger and thirst for Him. Tell Him you want to be changed. As you learn to focus on Him, reordering your priorities will become easier, until you can say with Paul, "I consider everything a loss compared to the surpassing greatness of knowing Christ Jesus my Lord" (Philippians 3:8).

4. THANK AND PRAISE GOD

The proper way to come before the King of the universe is with thanks-giving and praise (Psalm 100:4). God wants people to worship Him in spirit and in truth (John 4:23). Therefore worship is essential to entering His presence. Study Psalms to learn ways to worship God. Singing, shouting, clapping or raising your hands, dancing, and falling down before Him are all scriptural ways of worship. Jewish believers weren't inhibited in worship! We shouldn't be, either.

5. FEED MAINLY ON THE BIBLE

Beware the temptation to let Christian books—devotional books, works of theology, commentaries—become the main element in your spiritual diet. Useful as they are, they cannot take the place of God's written Word. It alone is "living and active and sharper than any two-edged sword, and piercing as far as the division of soul and spirit, of both joints and marrow, and able to judge the thoughts and intentions of the heart" (Hebrews 4:12; NASB).

6. ADJUST BIBLE STUDY TO YOUR NEEDS

I pick a book and read it through, often taking weeks. But whenever God speaks to me about a subject, I take a few days to do a topical study. (A good reference Bible makes topical studies easy and rewarding.) Then I can go back to my study through the book of the Bible. Experiment with you own flexible Bible reading plan until you find what works for you.

7. ASK

"You do not have, because you do not ask God" (James 4:2). Has your study of the Bible seemed fruitless lately? Perhaps it is because you haven't asked God to teach you new and exciting things, things that will change your life. Begin by asking, "Lord, what are You saying to me? What do You want me to do?" Seek insight on how to apply the Word in various areas of your life. The more questions you ask, the more answers you will receive.

8. USE A DEVOTIONAL NOTEBOOK

If you write down insights from the Word, you will remember them better. But a notebook can also help you in other aspects of your devotions. Write down what to thank and praise God for, then use your list during your worship. A record of prayers and answers will build your faith. I like to note commands the Lord gives me in my Bible reading, so that I can check on my obedience later. (For more extensive help on journal keeping, read Ronald Klug's *How to Keep a Spiritual Journal* [Nashville, Tennessee: Thomas Nelson, 1982].

9. FOUR FOUNDATIONS FOR PRAYER

If you feel as if you have been just "going through the motions" in prayer lately, you might apply four principles from Joshua 24:14: "Now, therefore, fear the Lord and serve Him in sincerity and truth . . ." (NASB).

When you pray, fear—or reverence—the Lord. The essence of man's rebellion against God is his refusal to submit to God as Lord and Ruler over everything, including self. Root your prayer in service to God in His Kingdom. Go to Him for instructions. Ask Him for the power to do as He commands. And commit yourself to obeying Him.

Pray with sincerity. Be completely honest with God. He knows all your thoughts and feelings anyway, but often won't deal with them until you open yourself to Him.

Pray according to truth. In other words, be guided in your prayers by the Word (John 17:17). For example, instead of complaining that God seems far way, tell Him, "Lord, You say in Your Word that You draw near to those who draw near to You. I seek You now, and I thank You that I will find You." God answers such reverent prayers, offered in faith. He cannot deny Himself or His Word.

10. BE SURE TO OBEY

What you do after your daily quiet time determines its quality at least as much as what you do during it.

We show our love for the Lord by obeying Him in every area of life. "Whoever has my commands and obeys them," Jesus said, "he is the one who loves me" (John 14:21). "If you obey my commands, you will remain in my love. . . . You are my friends if you do what I command" (John 15:10, 14).

What we learn from Scripture and in prayer during our quiet times must make a difference in our lives, or we'll soon forget it. And our consciences will make us increasingly uncomfortable because of the disrespect we show God by ignoring the commands He gives us. If we want to walk continually in a love relationship with Him, we must make it our goal to please Him by obeying Him.

Seek God with a sincere heart; confess and forsake your sins; make God Himself—not spiritual knowledge—your goal; worship and praise Him; feed on the Word in ways that meet your current needs; ask God for what you need; reflect on what God is doing in your life; pray with reverence, sincerity, truthfulness, and the desire to serve Him; and practice all day what you learn in communion with God in prayer and the Word, and your quiet time will become vital and exciting.

■ Excerpted from *Discipleship Journal* 6, no. 2 (March 1986), pp. 28-30. Used by permission.

How D. L. Moody Revived a Sunday School Class

George Sweeting

If you have ever seen a spiritual need in the life of one or more of your students, but felt hesitant to address it, let this account of D. L. Moody encourage you. The result: souls saved, lives changed, through boldness!

One day a Sunday school teacher fell ill and asked Moody to teach his class, a group Moody described as "without exception the most frivolous set of girls I ever met. They laughed in my face, and I felt like opening the door and telling them all to get out and never come back."[1]

Later that week the teacher stopped by the shoestore to talk to Moody. "I have had another hemorrhage of my lungs," the teacher said. "The doctor says I cannot live on Lake Michigan, so I am going to New York state. I suppose I am going to die."

Moody sensed that something else was troubling the man; he asked what it was. "Well, I have never led any of my class to Christ," the man confided. "I really believe I have done the girls more harm than good."

"Suppose you tell them how you feel," Moody suggested. Moody later wrote:

He consented, and we started out together. It was one of the best journeys I ever had on earth. We went to the house of one of the girls . . and the teacher talked to her about her soul. There was no laughing then! Tears stood in her eyes before long. After he had explained the way of life, he suggested that we have prayer. He asked me to pray. True, I had never done such a thing in my life as to pray God to convert a young lady there and then. But we prayed, and God answered my prayer.[2]

For the next ten days, Moody and the teacher visited home after home, both together and separately. It wasn't long before the teacher returned to the shoestore to tell Moody the last girl in his class had yielded herself to Christ.

Without any prior arrangement, the entire class arrived at the train depot the evening the teacher left town. "What a meeting that was!" Moody said.

We tried to sing, but we broke down. The last we saw of that dying teacher he was standing on the platform of the rear car, his finger pointing upward, telling us to meet him in heaven. . . . I had got a taste of another world, and cared no more for making money. For some days after, the greatest struggle of my life took place. Should I give up business and give myself to Christian work, or should I not? I have never regretted my choice[3]

Notes:
1. Arthur Percy Fitt, *Moody Still Lives* (Old Tappan, New Jersey: Revell, 1936), 21.
2. Ibid., 22.
3. Ibid., 22-23.

Demons—Our Invisible Enemies

C. Fred Dickason

Can demons afflict Christians? Could demons oppress one of your students, or disrupt your classroom, or even discourage you? A great need for biblical information is met with this article on demons.

Among those who hold that Satan and demons exist, few know much about them. Some even choose to stay uninformed, as if biblical information could be dangerous! I have even heard pastors discourage the study of demons because the very idea is repulsive! What an attitude for leaders of those who are "more than conquerors" in Christ.

We need to know what God's Word says about these enemies in order to guard ourselves, to instruct and warn others, and to deliver those who through fear are in bondage to Satan.

THE REALITY OF DEMONS

The Lord Jesus spoke of Satan and demons as living beings, just as real as Himself. He claimed that His binding of Satan and casting out of demons by the Spirit of God was proof that He was God and Messiah (Matthew 12:22-29). When the disciples could not cast out a demon, Jesus ordered the "deaf and dumb spirit" to come out and the boy was healed. Later Jesus privately explained the problem. "This kind can come forth by nothing, but by prayer and fasting" (Mark 9:29). He did not tell them that the problem was only psychosomatic and that they needed the power of positive thinking!

Satan and demons may be invisible, but according to Christ and the Bible, they are real, personal spirit beings who are enemies of God and mankind, especially of God's children. All the New Testament writers (though not every book) mention Satan and demons. We can be assured that the Son of God, who personally confronted Satan (Matthew 4:1-11) and demons (Luke 8:26-39), knows the truth of their reality and power. He spoke and acted in accord with truth in defeating them.

THE ORIGIN OF DEMONS

The best biblical evidence supports that demons are fallen angels. When Lucifer, the highest ranking angelic cherub, rebelled against God in his desire to be like the Most High and rule over men and angels, he carried with him an army of followers, probably a third of all angels, who became demons (Revelation 12:3-7). Lucifer (Hebrew, "the shining one") became Satan (Hebrew, "opposer"). His glorious and perfect creaturely nature became totally corrupt and his powers perverted.

In Scripture the term "spirit" is always used in reference to personal beings. Demons have intellect, emotion, and will. In other words, they have personality. Demons have supernatural intelligence and strength which are sometimes used to control men (Acts 19:16; Mark 5:3). They are not restricted by physical barriers, as men are.

WHAT DO DEMONS DO?

Basically, demons are Satan's untiring and devoted henchmen, organized to accomplish their common purpose of opposing God's program. They promote the philosophy of creature-centeredness in individuals, in governments, and in the world system (1 John 2:15-17; John 12:31). They promote rebellion against God and against human governments. They slander God's character and encourage men to blame God for restrictions and for the existence of evil and suffering (Revelation 16:9, 11; 18:8-10). They accuse men before God, as does Satan, and often cause condemning thoughts, even when Christ has already brought forgiveness (1 John 1:9; 2:1-2).

WHAT DO DEMONS DO TO BELIEVERS?

Demons may do to believers much of what they do to unbelievers. The believer is eternally secure in the grace of salvation (Romans 8:38-39). However, the battle here and now has its dangers. We do not wrestle merely with humans in opposition to the gospel and to godly living, but against the Devil, his henchmen, and their schemes (Ephesians 6:10-18).

Though much of our struggle against sin comes from our own sinful nature (Romans 7:21-24; James 1:14-15), we must recognize the possibility of demonic attacks personally or corporately as a church. We cannot as Christians true to God's Word, dismiss the possibility of demonic affliction.

Demons attack confidence in God's Word, God's love and goodness, and seek to destroy commitment to Christ. They may create divisions within the church by false doctrine, bad lifestyles, faulty leadership, and worldly philosophy of ministry (1 Timothy 4:1-3; Jude 4; Revelation 2:20-24; Colossians 2:16-22; 1 Timothy 3:5-9; 6:3-10).

Opposition to evangelizing and discipling efforts come from demons and the men they use. They may incite persecution and seek our death. Some men in following them may actually think they are serving God (John 16:1-3).

While God may overrule demonic activity by forcibly halting it (1 Samuel 19:9, 23), this may not always be the case. Indeed He may wish to use demonic activity to correct defection (1 Timothy 1:19-20; 1 Corinthians 5:5), create discernment (Job 40:1-4; 42:1-6), cultivate dependence (2 Corinthians 12:7-10), or arouse to battle (Ephesians 6:10-18).

DEMONS AND THE OCCULT

Christians ought not to be deceived by fortune-tellers. They may be demon energized and confirmed by the conspiracies of Satan and his host (Acts 16:16-19). Astrology, laying of cards, palm reading, rod and pendulum, water witching, ESP, and certain dreams and visions are used by demons to turn men from depending upon God and to seeking personal advantage by forbidden knowledge and power. When Saul sought Samuel's spirit by the medium of Endor, he was judged by God (1 Samuel 28:3, 9; 1 Chronicles 10:13-14). Occult practices may result in demonic oppression and, frequently, inhabitation. God may allow this as part of the judgment upon idolatrous practices (Exodus 20:4-6; Romans 1:18-32).

WHAT IS DEMON POSSESSION?

The term *possession* is a misleading translation, picturing someone under total control, wild and violent, or maliciously evil. The term demonized, as opposed to demon possession, better reflects the Greek *daimonizomenos* (Matthew 15:22), literally *a state of demon-caused passivity*. Practically, it refers to the condition of a person who is controlled (more or less) in various ways by inhabiting demons. Its equivalent is to have a demon (Mark 1:23; 9:17; Acts 8:7).

The Lord Jesus described this reality of spirits inhabiting and affecting a person (Matthew 12:22-28) and claiming the person's body as his residence (Matthew 12:43-45).

We cannot, as honest, thinking Christians, believe the Bible and Christ, and at the same time, deny the phenomenon of demonization.

Symptoms may seem to overlap with certain mental, emotional, or physical disorders, as they did in the Gospels. But symptoms such as unusual physical strength or intelligence, sudden changes and reverses in emotions, manifestations of another personality, continual blasphemous thoughts, and recurrent urges to harm or to commit suicide must be considered as possibly demonic in estimating a person's condition (see Mark 5:1-20). Inability to trust God, pray, read the Bible, say the name of the Lord Jesus, and resistance to spiritual truth are even more suspicious symptoms. So also are pressures or invisible attacks upon the body and appearances of dark figures. Mediumistic or clairvoyant powers, falling into trances, change of persons speaking, magical abilities, inserted or unwanted thoughts, and voices that attack God or the person all point in the direction of demonic activity.

WHAT DEFENSE IS THERE AGAINST DEMONS?

As believers we should respect Satan's cunning and power, but realize that he is sovereignly restricted by God (Job 1:12; 2:6; 1 John 4:4). He cannot touch our salvation nor separate us from the love of God (Romans 8:38-39). We should refuse to be naive, but know what the Bible says about Satan's tactics. Christ has defeated our enemies and stripped them of weapons through His death and resurrection (Hebrews. 2:14-15; Colossians 2:15). He prays for us today as He did on earth for the disciples (John 17:15; Luke 22:31-32; 1 John 2:1-2; Hebrews 7:25). We have a position of acceptance and authority "in Christ" (Romans 8:1; Ephesians 1:6). We have been crucified, raised, and seated with Christ in the heavenlies, far above all demonic authority (Ephesians 1:21-22; 2:6). The demons believe and shudder (James 2:19). God may use demonic opposition to cause us to depend more upon Him (Job 1-2; 2 Corinthians 12:7-10), and God will see us through it all (Romans 8:28-29).

James 4:7 summarizes, "Submit yourselves therefore to God. Resist the devil, and he will flee from you." We must confess and renounce all practices and attitudes contrary to God's Word (see Exodus 20:4-6). We must put on all the armor of God. Each piece has its purpose and suggests how Satan attacks and how we can resist (Ephesians 6:10-18). We must live godly lives for the glory of God. This involves making no provision for sin (Romans 13:13-14), praying for protection (Matthew 6:13; 26:41), being alert, watching in soberness (1 Thessalonians 5:6-8; 1 Peter 5:8). We must cultivate our spiritual lives with the Word of God (Matthew 4:4), using it against demonic attack (Ephesians 6:17).

■ From *Fundamentalist Journal* 3, no. 9 (October 1984), pp. 21-23. Used by author's permission.

Put on Your Armor in Prayer

Victor Matthews

Meaty and deep, these scriptural meditations can be used as a daily confession of faith or prayer for spiritual defense by the discerning teacher. A mind set upon truth is a poor target for the enemy.

DAILY AFFIRMATION OF FAITH
Today I deliberately choose to submit myself fully to God as He has made Himself known to me through the Holy Scripture which I honestly accept as the only inspired, infallible, authoritative standard for all life and practice. In this day I will not judge God, His work, myself, or others on the basis of feelings or circumstances.

1. I recognize by faith that the triune God is worthy of all honor, praise, and worship as the Creator, Sustainer, and End of all things. I confess that God, as my Creator, made me for Himself. In this day I therefore choose to live for Him (Revelation 5:9-10; Isaiah 43:1,7,21; Revelation 4:11).

2. I recognize by faith that God loved me and chose me in Jesus Christ before time began (Ephesians 1:1-7).

3. I recognize by faith that God has proven His love to me in sending His Son to die in my place, in whom every provision has already been made for my past, present, and future needs through His representative work, and that I have been quickened, raised, seated with Jesus Christ in the heavenlies, and anointed with the Holy Spirit (Romans 5:6-11; 8:28-39; Philippians 1:6; 4:6-7, 13, 19; Ephesians 1:3; 2:5-6; Acts 2:1-4, 33).

4. I recognize by faith that God has accepted me, since I have received Jesus Christ as my Lord and Saviour (John 1:12; Ephesians 1:6); that He has forgiven me (Ephesians 1:7); adopted me into His family, assuming every responsibility for me (John 17:11,17; Ephesians 1:5; Philippians 1:6); given me eternal life (John 3:36; 1 John 5:9-13); applied the perfect righteousness of Christ to me so that I am now justified (Romans 5:1; 8:3-4; 10:4); made me complete in Christ (Colossians 2:10); and offers Himself to me as my daily sufficiency through prayer and the decisions of faith (1 Corinthians 1:30; Colossians 1:27; Galatians 2:20; John 14:13-14; Matthew 21:22; Romans 6:1-19; Hebrews 4:1-3, 11).

5. I recognize by faith that the Holy Spirit has baptized me into the Body of Christ (1 Corinthians 12:13); sealed me (Ephesians 1:13-14); anointed me for life and service (Acts 1:8; John 7:37-39); seeks to lead me into a deeper walk with Jesus Christ (John 14:16-18; 15:26-27; 16:13-15; Romans 8:11-16); and to fill my life with Himself (Ephesians 5:18).

6. I recognize by faith that only God can deal with sin and only God can produce holiness of life. I confess that in my salvation my part was only to receive Him and that He dealt with my sin and saved me. Now I confess that in order to live a holy life, I can only surrender to His will and receive Him as my sanctification; trusting Him to do whatever may be necessary in my life, without and within, so I may be enabled to live today in purity, freedom, rest and power for His glory (John 1:12; 1 Corinthians 1:30; 2 Corinthians 9:8; Galatians 2:20; Hebrews 4:9; 1 John 5:4; Jude 24).

Having confessed that God is worthy of all praise, that the Scriptures are the only authoritative standard, that only God can deal with sin and produce holiness of life, I again recognize my total dependence upon Him and submission to Him. I accept the truth that praying in faith is absolutely necessary for the realization of the will and grace of God in my daily life (1 John 5:14-15; James 2:6; 4:2-3; 5:16-18; Philippians 4:6-7; Hebrews 4:1-13; 11:6, 24-28).

Recognizing that faith is a total response to God by which the daily provisions the Lord has furnished in Himself are appropriated, I therefore make the following decisions of faith:

1. For this day (Hebrews 3:6, 13, 15; 4:7) I make the decision of faith to surrender wholly to the authority of God as He has revealed Himself in the Scripture—to obey Him. I confess my sin, face the sinful reality of my old nature, and deliberately choose to walk in the light, in step with Christ, throughout the hours of this day (Romans 6:16-20; Philippians 2:12-13; 1 John 1:7, 9).

2. For this day I make the decision of faith to surrender wholly to the authority of God as revealed in the Scripture—to believe Him. I accept only His Word as final authority. I now believe that since I have confessed my sin He has forgiven and cleansed me (1 John 1:9). I accept at full value His Word of promise to be my sufficiency and rest, and will conduct myself accordingly (Exodus 33:1; 1 Corinthians 1:30; 2 Corinthians 9:8; Philippians 4:19).

3. For this day I make the decision of faith to recognize that God has made every provision so that I may fulfill His will and calling. Therefore, I will not make any excuse for my sin and failure (1 Thessalonians 5:24).

4. For this day I make the decision of faith deliberately to receive from God that provision which He has made for me. I renounce all self-effort to live the Christian life and to perform God's service; renounce all sinful praying which asks God to change circumstances and people so that I may be more spiritual; renounce all drawing back from the work of the Holy Spirit within and the call of God without; and renounce all nonbiblical motives, goals, and activities which serve my sinful pride.

a. I now sincerely receive Jesus Christ as my sanctification, particularly as my cleansing from the old nature, and ask the Holy Spirit to apply to me the work of Christ accomplished for me in the crucifixion. In cooperation with and dependence upon Him, I obey the command to "put off the old man" (Romans 6:1-14; 1 Corinthians 1:30; Galatians 6:14; Ephesians 4:22).

b. I now sincerely receive Jesus Christ as my sanctification, particularly as my enablement moment by moment to live above sin, and ask the Holy Spirit to apply to me the work of the resurrection so that I may walk in newness of life. I confess that only God can deal with my sin and only God can produce holiness and the fruit of the Spirit in my life. In cooperation with and dependence upon Him, I obey the command to "put on the new man" (Romans 6:1-4; Ephesians 4:24).

c. I now sincerely receive Jesus Christ as my deliverance from Satan and take my position with Him in the heavenlies, asking the Holy Spirit to apply to me the work of the ascension. In His Name I submit myself to God and stand against all of Satan's influence and subtlety. In cooperation with and dependence upon God, I obey the command to "resist the devil" (Ephesians 1:20-23; 2:5; 4:27; 6:10-18; Colossians 1:13; Hebrews 2:14-15; James 4:7; 1 Peter 3:22; 5:8-9).

d. I now sincerely receive the Holy Spirit as my anointing for every aspect of life and service for today. I fully open my life to Him to fill me afresh in obedience to the command to "be filled with the Holy Spirit" (Ephesians 5:18; John 7:37-39; 14:16-17; 15:26-27; 16:7-15; Acts 1:8).

Having made this confession and these decisions of faith, I now receive God's promised rest for this day (Hebrews 4:1-13). Therefore, I relax in the trust of faith, knowing that in the moment of temptation, trial, or need, the Lord Himself will be there as my strength and sufficiency (1 Corinthians 10:13).

BELIEVER'S WARFARE PRAYER

Heavenly Father, I bow in worship and praise before You. I cover myself with the blood of the Lord Jesus Christ as my protection. I surrender myself completely and unreservedly in every area of my life to You. I take a stand against all the workings of Satan that would hinder me in my prayer life. I address myself only to the True and Living God and refuse any involvement of Satan in my prayer.

(I command Satan, in the name of the Lord Jesus Christ, to leave my presence with all of his demons. I bring the blood of the Lord Jesus Christ between Satan and myself.)

Heavenly Father, I worship You and give You praise. I recognize that You are worthy to receive all glory and honor and praise. I renew my allegiance to You and pray that the Blessed Holy Spirit would enable me in this time of prayer. I am thankful, Heavenly Father, that You have loved me from past eternity and that You sent the Lord Jesus Christ into the world to die as my substitute. I am thankful that the Lord Jesus Christ came as my representative and that through Him You have completely forgiven me. You have adopted me into Your family; You have assumed all responsibility for me; You have given me eternal life; You have given me the perfect righteousness of the Lord Jesus Christ so I am now justified. I am thankful that in Him You have made me complete, and that You have offered Yourself to me to be my daily help and strength.

Heavenly Father, open my eyes that I might see how great You are and how complete Your provision is for this day. I am thankful that the victory the Lord Jesus Christ won for me on the Cross and in His Resurrection has been given to me and that I am seated with the Lord Jesus Christ in the heavenlies. I take my place with Him in the heavenlies and recognize by faith that all wicked spirits and Satan himself are under my feet. I declare, therefore, that Satan and his wicked spirits are subject to me in the Name of the Lord Jesus Christ.

I am thankful for the Armor You have provided. I put on the Girdle of Truth, the Breastplate of Righteousness, the Sandals of Peace, and the Helmet of Salvation. I lift up the Shield of Faith against all the fiery darts of the enemy; and I take in my hand the Sword of the Spirit, the Word of God. I choose to use Your Word against all the forces of evil in my life. I put on this Armor and live and pray in complete dependence upon You, Blessed Holy Spirit.

I am grateful, Heavenly Father, that the Lord Jesus Christ spoiled all principalities and powers and made a show of them openly and triumphed over them in Himself. I claim all that victory for my life today. I reject all the insinuations, and accusations, and the temptations of Satan. I affirm that the Word of God is true and I choose to live today in the light of God's Word. I choose, Heavenly Father, to live in obedience to You and in fellowship with Yourself. Open my eyes and show me the areas of my life that do not please You. Work in me to cleanse me from all ground that would give Satan a foothold against me. I do in every way stand into all that it means to be your adopted child and I welcome all the ministry of the Holy Spirit.

By faith and in dependence upon You I put off the old man and stand into all the victory of the Crucifixion where the Lord Jesus Christ provided cleansing from the old nature. I put on the new man and stand into all the victory of the Resurrection and the provision He has made for me to live above sin.

Therefore, today I put off the old nature with its selfishness and I put on the new nature with its love. I put off the old nature with its fear and I put on the new nature with its courage. I put off the old nature with its weakness and I put on the new nature with its strength. I put off the old nature with all its deceitful lusts and I put on the new nature with its righteousness, purity, and honesty.

In every way I stand into the victory of the ascension and glorification of the Lord Jesus Christ, whereby all the principalities and powers were made subject to Him. I claim my place in Christ as victorious with Him over all the enemies of my soul. Blessed Holy Spirit, I pray that You would fill me. Come into my life, break down every idol and cast out every foe.

I am thankful, Heavenly Father, for the expression of Your will for my daily life as You have shown me in Your Word. I therefore, claim all the will of God for today. I am thankful that You have blessed me with all spiritual blessings in heavenly places in Christ Jesus. I am thankful that You have begotten me unto a living hope by the resurrection of Jesus Christ from the dead. I am thankful that You have made a provision so that today I can live filled with the Spirit of God with love and joy and peace, with longsuffering, gentleness and goodness, with meekness, faithfulness, and self-control in my life. I recognize that this is Your will for me and I therefore reject and resist all the endeavors of Satan and his wicked spirits to rob me of the will of God. I refuse in this day to believe my feelings and I hold up the shield of faith against all the accusations and distortion and insinuations that Satan would put into my mind. I claim the fullness of the will of God for my life today.

In the Name of the Lord Jesus Christ I completely surrender myself to You Heavenly Father, as a living sacrifice. I choose not to be conformed to this world. I choose to be transformed by the renewing of my mind, and I pray that You would show me Your will and enable me to walk in all the fullness of Your will today.

I am thankful, Heavenly Father, that the weapons of our warfare are not carnal but mighty through God to the pulling down of strongholds, to the casting down of imaginations and every high thing that exalteth itself against the knowledge of God, and to bring every thought into obedience to the Lord Jesus Christ. Therefore, in my own life today I tear down the strongholds of Satan and smash the plans of Satan that have been formed against me. I tear down the strongholds of Satan against my mind, and I surrender my mind to You, Blessed Holy Spirit. I affirm, Heavenly Father, that You have not given me the spirit of fear but of power and of love and of a sound mind. I break and smash the strongholds of Satan formed against my emotions today and I give my emotions to You. I smash the strongholds of Satan formed against my will today, I give my will to You, and choose to make the right decisions of faith. I smash the strongholds of Satan formed against my body today, I give my body to You recognizing that I am Your temple. I rejoice in Your mercy and goodness.

Heavenly Father, I pray that now and through this day You would strengthen and enlighten me, show me the way Satan is hindering and tempting and lying and distorting the truth in my life. Enable me to be the kind of person that would please You. Enable me to be aggressive in prayer and faith. Enable me to be aggressive mentally, to think about and practice Your Word, and to give You Your rightful place in my life.

Again I cover myself with the blood of the Lord Jesus Christ and pray that You, Blessed Holy Spirit, would bring all the work of the Crucifixion, all the work of the Resurrection, all the work of the Glorification, and all the work of Pentecost into my life today. I surrender myself to You. I refuse to be discouraged. You are the God of all hope. You have proven Your power by resurrecting Jesus Christ from the dead, and I claim in every way this victory over all Satanic forces in my life. I pray in the Name of the Lord Jesus Christ with thanksgiving. Amen.

Why Can't There Be an Easier Way?

Joni Eareckson Tada

From the heart and life of one who has persevered in a difficult way come words to encourage any teacher. The hard way accomplishes much in the sight of God. Read and discover why He has ordained it so.

Every day, you and I go into battle against the world, the flesh, and the devil. The fight is perpetual; there is no truce. One day we feel like we're in a mild skirmish—playing mind games, reaching for the arms of strangers in our daydreams. Another day we know we're in the thick of a devastating battle—stepping out of our daydreams and grappling with a very real someone. In the thick of the battle, our enemies can slice through a heart swollen with pride, a heart that runs mental movies of past successes. Or we might feel miles from the front lines, indifferent and uncaring because our hearts are dulled and deflated by dryness. No doubt about it—life for a believer is a battle.

Wouldn't it be easier if, right now, God yanked our one foot out of the mud and firmly planted it alongside our other foot in heaven? The justification-sanctification-glorification scenario would be less messy if the middle part could be dropped, wouldn't it? Why does God leave us on earth to face the battleground of practical holiness? What does God have in mind?

PLEASING GOD

The Sign of Life. When we struggle with trials and temptations, God is pleased first of all on our own behalf. Good things are in store for those who strive to be holy. If you're battling pride, lust, or temptation, you're in a better state than many who have grown numb to the struggle, stagnated in apathy or indifference. The very fact that the devil assaults you, targeting you as a threat, should fill your mind with hope. If being at peace with the world, the flesh, and the devil means being at enmity with God, then being at war with them must mean being at peace with God. As Paul wrote in Romans 2:10, there will be "glory, honor, and peace for everyone who does good."

The Prelude to Glory. God also has in mind that day when He pins on our war medals. Take a look at Romans 8:17: "Now if we are children, then we are heirs of God and co-heirs with Christ, if indeed we share in his sufferings in order that we may also share in his glory." Those soldiers who face the greatest conflict, yet remain faithful, have the greatest confidence of sharing in Christ's glory. Our glory in Him will be so glorious as to more than abundantly outweigh anyone's struggles. I may not know how this can be, but I know it's true.

THE GLORY OF SACRIFICE

Imagine standing with Jesus and His disciples in the Temple. Catch a glimpse of the joy on your Lord's face as He delights in the sacrificial act of one poor striving widow (Mark 12:41-34). Her example reminds us that it is voluntary, yet costly, to remain faithful in battle. And that is what pleases God.

If someone with severe cerebral palsy baked you a birthday cake, it would mean more to you than ten birthday cakes baked by an able-bodied person. Why? Because it

261

would involve greater cost and sacrifice. Holiness costs us something; paying the price expresses our willingness to make sacrifices for Him. If He made us instantly holy, bypassing the struggle, what would our faithfulness mean to Him? Little, I suspect.

WE BATTLE FOR OTHERS

What a sight we believers make with all our stumbling and bumbling! Yet through our weak, lowly, and despised striving, unbelievers are shamed and their boasting is nullified. Yes, unbelievers benefit from our struggles: they are driven, ashamed of their boasting, to God, who delights in unlikely, unlovely people. If God instantly made us holy, would not that emasculate the ongoing preaching of the gospel? We are supposed to "have this treasure in jars of clay to show that this all-surpassing power is from God and from us" (2 Corinthians 4:7).

ENCOURAGING FELLOW BELIEVERS

Not only unbelievers, but believers also are helped by our striving. My conversation with a suffering friend named Lori touched on that.

"Don't forget, my friend," I said to her, "if you remain faithful, despite the odds, it helps people like me more than you'll ever know."

"But it's hard . . . to think of others . . . when you're hurting."

"I know," I said, my voice a mere whisper. I had been where she was.

"Listen to this," I said. "Another guy with a disability once said, 'For just as the sufferings of Christ flow over into our lives, so also through Christ our comfort overflows. If we are distressed, it is for your comfort and salvation; if we are comforted, it is for your comfort, which produces in you patient endurance of the same sufferings we suffer'" (2 Corinthians 1:5-6).

LEARNING THROUGH SUFFERING

Look at Jesus Himself. Although He was perfectly holy, "he learned obedience from what he suffered" (Hebrews 5:8). How Jesus was perfectly holy and yet "learned obedience" is a mystery to me. But this much is clear: If Christ submitted Himself to such a process, can I, His servant, expect to do less?

Suffering is the path to obedience for us just as it was, in some mysterious way, for Jesus Himself (1 Peter 3:14-15; 4:1-2).

NO SHORTCUTS

While I was in the hospital, nurses did their duty properly and well. But there is a vast difference between those nurses and my husband, who now helps me with my daily needs. They acted out of duty; he acts out of affection and love. We gain no holy ground if we fight merely from a sense of duty or from knowledge of what is right and proper. Love for Christ must energize our warfare. I, for one, don't wish for a shortcut to bypass the battlefield. I am glad that God gives me the chance to fight in the trenches. For when the final battle is over, soldiers like Lori will experience the most joy, the most satisfaction. They will shine most brightly for God's glory. I want to be one of them.

Excerpted from *Discipleship Journal* (Issue 49, 1989), pp. 23-26. Used by permission.

The Top Ten Devotional Books

Leadership Journal

While Scripture is at the heart of a pure walk with God, the insights and meditations revealed by God to others—and recorded in their writings—make valuable the collecting and reading of classic devotional works.

One of the questions we asked on our survey of readers' devotional habits was: "What is the single most helpful book, other than the Bible, you've used as a devotional aid?" Almost two hundred different books were mentioned. Naturally, some were mentioned more frequently than others, and we've compiled in order a list of the top ten.

There's a danger in recommending a list of books for devotional reading. Some will buy the books on the list and slavishly read them without ever fully entering into the spiritual purpose of the enterprise—the worship of God.

Perhaps a way of guarding against that danger would be to buy only one book at a time and make sure you fully digest it before purchasing another. You may never get through the list, but you'll probably be the better off for it.

1. Chambers, Oswald. *My Utmost For His Highest.* New York: Dodd, Mead, and Company, 1935. Other Chambers books can be obtained from Christian Literature Crusade, Fort Washington, Pennsylvania.
2. Lewis, C. S. *Mere Christianity.* Riverside, New Jersey. Macmillan Publishing Company, 1964.
3. Barclay, William. *Daily Celebration.* Waco, Texas. Word Books, 1971.
4. Tozer, A. W. *The Pursuit of God.* Harrisburg, Pennsylvania. Christian Publications.
5. Packer, J. I. *Knowing God.* Downers Grove, Illinois. InterVarsity Press, 1973.
6. DeHaan, Martin. *Our Daily Bread.* Edited with Henry Bosch. Grand Rapids, Michigan. Zondervan Publishing House. Several annual volumes.
7. Foster, Richard. *Celebration of Discipline.* New York, New York. Harper & Row, 1978.
8. Nee, Watchman. *Release of the Spirit.* Cloverdale, Indiana. Ministry of Life Publications.
9. Spurgeon, Charles H. *Morning and Evening.* Grand Rapids, Michigan. Zondervan Publishing House, 1980.
10. Nouwen, Henri. *The Wounded Healer.* New York, New York. Doubleday and Company, 1972.

■ From *Leadership* 3, no. 1 (Winter 1982), p. 34. Used by permission.

Praying Boldly

David R. Mains

This prayerful leader believes that our lives—and the church—would be sooner revived if we would learn to pray boldly, as if Jesus were in our very presence! Of course, He is among us, and we should pray accordingly.

Boldness regarding prayer is mentioned frequently in the New Testament, and I'm convinced that boldness for the most part is lacking in the prayers of the Church and desperately needs to be rediscovered. Never has there been awakening without God's people learning the efficacy of prayer.

The Church knows boldness when all its people pray exactly as though they were talking to Jesus face to face. How would the life of the Church be transformed if we were all actually to hear Jesus say, "My subjects, I'm attentive and receptive right now to what you as a people have to say to me."

I often get a feeling, when people share their prayer requests, that the requests relate more to surface issues than to substantive ones. Seldom do the manners at hand touch in any way the deep concerns of the King who is being addressed. Instead, most of the requests expressed seem to center on the comfort of the subject voicing it. I believe that the church must learn to refrain from voicing requests that would sound silly were the King bodily present to hear and to respond.

If our prayers in church were actually spoken as though we were talking to Christ face to face, sooner or later a spiritual reality would begin to make itself known. This authenticity would then be caught by Sunday morning attendees, and eventually would make its way into the small prayer groups in the church, as well as into individual prayer closets and private groanings before the Lord. God's people would rapidly begin to know a new and mighty confidence and boldness. When we realize that this is the King of the universe and that he has truly given us his attention, that realization results in boldness. And before we know it, we see early signs of awakening. Revival and prayer always go together. They are inseparably linked.

Some might think boldness in prayer means storming into heaven's courts demanding attention. This is not boldness in the way Christ taught it or modeled it. Instead, boldness is the picture of a confident servant coming to his master in an attitude of praise. The mindset is one of wanting most of all to serve the Lord well. Knowing God's will and doing it is the primary desire.

How the Church today languishes for this kind of praying. And in order for us to know success in this area, I believe huge adjustments must be made. I challenge all concerned Christians to examine their personal and corporate prayer lives in this light.

I suspect that the way to begin correcting this problem is in the privacy of our own times alone with Christ. And whether it's a short session or a long season of prayer—the question of importance is this: Are you conscious that Christ is there in the room with you, or are you just talking to the walls? Are you *bold* in prayer?

▮Excerpted from *Christian History* 9, no. 2 (Issue 26), p. 35. Used by permission of author.

Patterns of Spiritual Renewal

Keith Hardman

The lessons of history are there to serve us if we will observe and learn. Revivals and renewals bear striking similarities from the Old Testament to the present day. We should pursue revival consistent with precedent.

Scripture shows us that God's people go through periods of spiritual renewal, and periods of spiritual decline. We might think of these times like waves and troughs, or like mountains and valleys.

During a renewal, or awakening, there will be not only a *great reviving of Christians*, but also a *large impact on the problems of society*. The renewal may last for many years, as did the Second Great Awakening in America, or be rather brief, as was the Third Awakening of the late 1850s.

When the winds of a renewal have passed, the Church may enter a period of lethargy, possibly for many years. Such cycles have already been repeated many times during the 2,000 years of Church history. It is not that the Spirit of God *cannot* sustain the higher life for Christians; rather, the Spirit allows times of decline to cause His people to pray for growth and for power.

In Old Testament times, renewal came to the Israelites under King Jehoash (2 Kings 11-12), King Hezekiah (2 Kings 18), King Asa (2 Chronicles 15), and especially under King Josiah (2 Kings 22-23). Awakening also came at the time of Zerubbabel (Ezra 5-6), and under Nehemiah (Nehemiah 8-9,13).

In New Testament times, awakening came upon God's people at Pentecost (Acts 2). This pouring out of the Spirit set a pattern that we see in later awakenings. Again, in Acts 4:23-37 we read of a renewal that prepared the infant Church for the fierce persecutions to come.

Spiritual awakenings, whether in biblical or Church history, manifest patterns that are similar, often strikingly so. While all of the following elements may not be present in each instance, for the most part awakenings progress through a cycle whose phases include these various aspects of God's working.

1. Awakenings are usually preceded by a time of spiritual depression, apathy and gross sin, in which a majority of nominal Christians are hardly different from the members of secular society, and the churches seem to be asleep.

The causes of each decline differ widely, but when the prophetic voice and moral leadership of the Church has been stilled for some time, social evils are usually rampant. Eighteenth-century England is an excellent example. Alcoholism was at an all-time high, capital punishment was used routinely for trivial crimes, slavery was practiced throughout the British Empire, the churches were out of touch. The Evangelical Awakening led by John Wesley and George Whitefield aroused the English conscience and by direct political pressure and action, cured these and many other ills.

2. An individual or small group of God's people becomes conscious of their sins and backslidden condition, and vows to forsake all that is displeasing to God.

Christians recall past outpourings of God's grace and power, and long to see them again. When histories of awakenings have been written in later years, it has been occasionally discovered that individuals at great distances and completely unknown to each other had, prior to the awakening, been praying simultaneously to the same end!

3. As some Christians begin to yearn for a manifestation of God's power, a leader or leaders arise with prophetic insights into the causes and remedies of the problems, and a new awareness of the holy and pure character of the Lord is present.

This standard of holiness exposes the degeneracy of the age and stimulates a striving after holiness by God's people. The leaders find that their eagerness for God's moving is shared by many who have been waiting for God to act, and who will rise to follow.

4. The awakening of Christians occurs: many understand and take part in a higher spiritual life.

The evangelism of the unsaved may or may not accompany this renewal of Christians. (In the great revival of the Reformation, the bringing of salvation to those outside the Church was not a primary issue, whereas the spreading of scriptural doctrine was.) This is a good reason why it is wrong to make the term "revivalism" synonymous with "evangelism." Revival and mass evangelism are *not* the same thing.

Certainly in all genuine movements of God's Spirit, people are converted. But if a society has been bathed in the teachings of the gospel for a long period, evangelism may not be the central thrust. This was the case in the Welsh revival of 1905.

In examining the example of Pentecost in Acts 2, we see that the awakening of Christ's redeemed people and the bestowal of the Holy Spirit at the "birthday" of the Church (2:1-4) was followed by evangelism of the unsaved (2:5-12, 37-41). This illustrates the two aspects of the Holy Spirit's work in the awakening of the Church, but keeps them separate. We could say that an awakening is a widespread renewal that includes the simultaneous conversion of many people to Christ.

5. An awakening may be God's means of preparing and strengthening His people for future challenges or trials.

Throughout history, renewal has often come before persecutions and severe trials that God sent to test and teach His people.

■ This article adapted from *Christian History* 8, no. 3 (Issue 23), pp. 6-7. Used by permission of author.

Indexes

Scripture Index